# Learn Electronics
# with Arduino

Donald Wilcher

Apress·

**Learn Electronics with Arduino**

Copyright © 2012 by Donald Wilcher

This work is subject to copyright. All rights are reserved by the Publisher, whether the whole or part of the material is concerned, specifically the rights of translation, reprinting, reuse of illustrations, recitation, broadcasting, reproduction on microfilms or in any other physical way, and transmission or information storage and retrieval, electronic adaptation, computer software, or by similar or dissimilar methodology now known or hereafter developed. Exempted from this legal reservation are brief excerpts in connection with reviews or scholarly analysis or material supplied specifically for the purpose of being entered and executed on a computer system, for exclusive use by the purchaser of the work. Duplication of this publication or parts thereof is permitted only under the provisions of the Copyright Law of the Publisher's location, in its current version, and permission for use must always be obtained from Springer. Permissions for use may be obtained through RightsLink at the Copyright Clearance Center. Violations are liable to prosecution under the respective Copyright Law.

ISBN-13 (pbk): 978-1-4302-4266-6

ISBN-13 (electronic): 978-1-4302-4267-3

Trademarked names, logos, and images may appear in this book. Rather than use a trademark symbol with every occurrence of a trademarked name, logo, or image we use the names, logos, and images only in an editorial fashion and to the benefit of the trademark owner, with no intention of infringement of the trademark.

The use in this publication of trade names, trademarks, service marks, and similar terms, even if they are not identified as such, is not to be taken as an expression of opinion as to whether or not they are subject to proprietary rights.

While the advice and information in this book are believed to be true and accurate at the date of publication, neither the authors nor the editors nor the publisher can accept any legal responsibility for any errors or omissions that may be made. The publisher makes no warranty, express or implied, with respect to the material contained herein.

President and Publisher: Paul Manning
Lead Editor: Tom Welsh
Technical Reviewer: Razvan Chiriac
Editorial Board: Steve Anglin, Ewan Buckingham, Gary Cornell, Louise Corrigan, Morgan Ertel, Jonathan Gennick, Jonathan Hassell, Robert Hutchinson, Michelle Lowman, James Markham, Matthew Moodie, Jeff Olson, Jeffrey Pepper, Douglas Pundick, Ben Renow-Clarke, Dominic Shakeshaft, Gwenan Spearing, Matt Wade, Tom Welsh
Coordinating Editor: Corbin Collins
Copy Editors: Damon Larson and Mary Behr
Compositor: SPi Global
Indexer: SPi Global
Artist: SPi Global
Cover Designer: Anna Ishchenko

Distributed to the book trade worldwide by Springer Science+Business Media New York., 233 Spring Street, 6th Floor, New York, NY 10013. Phone 1-800-SPRINGER, fax (201) 348-4505, e-mail orders-ny@springer-sbm.com, or visit www.springeronline.com.

For information on translations, please e-mail rights@apress.com, or visit www.apress.com.

Apress and friends of ED books may be purchased in bulk for academic, corporate, or promotional use. eBook versions and licenses are also available for most titles. For more information, reference our Special Bulk Sales–eBook Licensing web page at www.apress.com/bulk-sales.

Any source code or other supplementary materials referenced by the author in this text is available to readers at www.apress.com. For detailed information about how to locate your book's source code, go to www.apress.com/source-code.

*To Mattalene, Tiana, D'Vonn, and D'Mar. Thanks for being supportive and understanding. I love you all.*

*–Donald Wilcher*

# Contents at a Glance

# Contents

# Foreword

Don Wilcher is a gifted experimenter and circuit designer who has applied his creativity and engineering abilities to producing a series of electronics books and articles. In this latest book, Don presents an array of Arduino projects, each in a standalone chapter that zeroes in on a specific aspect of electronics. He includes various experiments, describes how to use electronic test instruments, and introduces the reader to the world of Arduino microcontroller software development.

Projects in this book include an LED sequencer, a DC motor controller, a music box, a sound effects generator, an interactive LCD display, and more. Like Don's other books, this new volume is packed with details and diagrams. For example, when Don describes how to control a relay using an Arduino, he includes a helpful explanation of why a diode is connected across the relay coil to bypass the voltage spike generated when current suddenly stops flowing through the coil. He also provides detailed explanations for transistor driver circuits, LEDs, sensors, circuit testing, and other topics, using Multisim circuit simulation when appropriate. Don is no novice, for he has worked as an electrical engineer and as a columnist and feature writer for *Nuts and Volts* magazine. He has considerable experience with LEGO Mindstorms as well as the Basic Stamp, the PICAXE, and the Arduino microcontrollers.

In between tinkering with the projects in this book, you can learn much more about Don, his many interests and activities, and his advocacy of engineering education at `www.family-science.net`.

—Forrest Mims III

# About the Author

**Donald Wilcher** has 26 years of electrical engineering experience. He's worked on industrial robotic systems, automotive electronic modules and systems, and embedded wireless controls for small consumer appliances. While working at Chrysler Corporation, he developed a weekend enrichment pre-engineering program for inner-city kids. In addition, he's the author of *LEGO Mindstorms Interfacing* and *LEGO Mindstorms Mechatronics* (McGraw-Hill) and one self-published book on sci-tech and robotic gadgets. He writes for inventors, students, and engineering educators. He's taught computer and electronics engineering technology classes at universities, community colleges, and technical institutes.

# About the Technical Reviewer

**Razvan Chiriac** was born in Bucharest, Romania and went to school there until tenth grade, when he and his family moved to the United States. He was fascinated by electronics and physics at a young age. Electronics was a mystery and physics had the answers to everything around him. Once in the States, he started making robots and programming microchips such as Arduino and Teensy. He likes programming in C for the microchips and Java for computer programming. He has worked on many projects with the Arduino, which is his favorite microcontroller.

# Acknowledgments

Many thanks to the Arduino Team, who created a wonderful tool to teach electronics. I would like to thank Technical Reviewer Razvan Chiriac for reviewing the circuits, sketches, and Fritzing models with a critical eye. Thanks also to Development Editor and writing coach Tom Welsh of Apress for challenging me to let my voice be heard in the pages of this book and to Michelle Lowman, Apress Acquisitions Editor, who saw the real subject matter of this book from my sketchy proposal. I would also like to thank Limor Fried of Adafruit for providing a wealth of technical Arduino resources on her web site.

Thanks to Forrest Mims III for writing a wonderful foreword. Also, I thank my kids, D'Vonn, D'Mar, and Tiana, for being understanding while I spent most of my time in the lab building circuits, drawing schematic diagrams and illustrations, and writing this book. Finally, I thank my wonderful wife, Mattalene, for encouraging to me write and for providing a fresh perspective to editing the manuscript.

# Introduction

Have you ever wondered how electronic products are created? Do you have an idea for a new electronic gadget but no way of testing the feasibility of the device? Have you accumulated a junk box of electronic parts and now wonder what to build with them? Well, this book will answer all your questions about discovering cool and innovative applications for electronic gadgets using the Arduino. The book makes use of the Arduino plus discrete, integrated circuit components and solderless breadboards. Multisim software is used for circuit simulation and design equations.

## Who Should Read This Book?

This book is for anyone interested in building cool Arduino electronic gadgets using simple prototyping techniques.

## How This Book Is Structured

The chapters in this book are organized in such a way that the reader can choose to jump around the projects and discovery labs. Each chapter gives an introduction to the relevant key electronics components and supporting technologies. Also, each chapter explains the basic theory of operation of the electronic circuits with detailed circuit schematic diagrams. Build instructions with troubleshooting tips are included to help you detect and fix hardware/software bugs for each project. Last but not least, each chapter zooms in on a specific aspect of electronics technology followed by several semiconductor device-specific experiments. The experiments will help you understand the semiconductor device's electrical behavior as well as the setup of basic electronic test equipment and the Arduino software IDE tool via sketches.

You'll be introduced to circuit analysis techniques and the Discovery Method, which offers suggestions for further fun ways of learning about electronics technology. The goal of these hands-on activities is to encourage readers (whether inventors, engineers, educators, or students) to develop skills in engineering their own cool gadgets using simple prototyping techniques.

## Downloading the Code

The code for the examples shown in this book is available on the Apress web site, www.apress.com. A link can be found on the book's information page under the Source Code/Downloads tab. This tab is located underneath the Related Titles section of the page.

## Contacting the Author

Should you have any questions or comments—or if you spot a mistake—please contact the author at author@writing.com.

■ ■ ■

# CHAPTER 1

# Electronic Singing Bird

The Arduino is a small yet powerful computer board that uses physical computing techniques with an Atmel microcontroller (processing development environment) and the C programming language. To illustrate the versatility of the Arduino in turning ordinary electronic circuits into cool smart devices, I will show how to make an interactive electronic singing bird in this chapter. The required parts are pictured in Figure 1-1.

## Parts List

Arduino Duemilanove or equivalent

0.047uF capacitor

0.1uF capacitor

470uF electrolytic capacitor

1 K resistor

50 K trimmer potentiometer

Audio transformer

2N3906 PNP transistor

2N3904 NPN transistor

5VDC relay

1 N4001 silicon diode

100Ω resistor

8Ω speaker

Cadmium sulfide (CdS) photocell

1 small solderless breadboard

22 AWG solid wire

Digital multimeter

Oscilloscope (optional)

Electronic tools

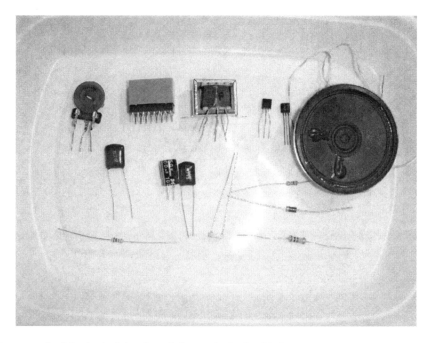

*Figure 1-1. Parts required for the Arduino-based electronic singing bird*

# What Is Physical Computing?

The interaction between a human, an electronic circuit, and a sensor is *physical computing*. In this project I will demonstrate physical computing with an electronic singing bird. Placing a hand over the sensor allows the electronic circuit to produce a sound similar to a singing bird. Figure 1-2 shows a system block diagram of the mixed-signal circuit connected to an Arduino.

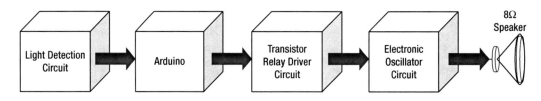

*Figure 1-2. System block diagram for the electronic singing bird*

---

▦ **Note** An electronic oscillator is a circuit that produces a repetitive sine wave or square wave signal.

---

# How It Works

The operation of the electronic singing bird starts with a cadmium sulfide (CdS) cell (photocell) detecting the absence of light. If no light is present, a voltage drop appears across the light-dependent resistor. The voltage across the CdS cell is approximately +2.5VDC, allowing the D2 pin of the Arduino to respond to the binary 1 logic signal. The software that is programmed into the Atmega328 microcontroller will turn on the D13 pin, making it switch from a binary 0 (0 V) to a binary 1 (+5VDC). With an output voltage of +5VDC, the transistor Q2 is able to turn on, allowing it to switch or energize the K1 relay coil. The iron core that is inside of the relay coil establishes a magnetic field attracting the electrical contact to the armature or common (COM) contact. The closing of the relay contacts will supply +5VDC to the electronic oscillator circuit. The chirping sound can be heard through the 8Ω speaker.

---

▨ **Note**   The ability to apply the appropriate voltage and current to the base of a transistor to turn it on is known as *biasing.*

---

Conducting a deep dive into the system block diagram reveals the circuit schematic diagram of the electronic singing bird shown in Figure 1-3.

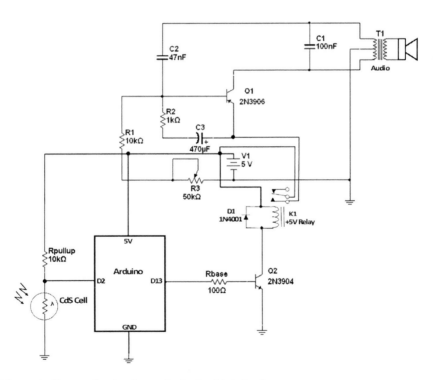

***Figure 1-3.*** *Schematic diagram for the electronic singing bird circuit*

If you change the capacitance value of C3 (470uF), the electronic singing bird's tone duration will be affected. The smaller the capacitance value, the faster the time between bird chips heard through the 8Ω speaker. The rheostat (50 K trimmer potentiometer) affects the switching time of the chirps. This control provides flexibility in terms of the type of chirp that can be heard through the 8Ω speaker. The shape of the waveform is based on the 470uF capacitor charging from the +5VDC power supply and discharging through the 1 K resistor. This charging-and-discharging electrical behavior biases the 2N3906 PNP transistor, thereby allowing it to switch on and off at a repetitive rate. The series combination of resistors, consisting of a 10K fixed resistor and 50 K trimmer potentiometer, helps manage the switching time of the charging-and-discharging capacitor mentioned before. Capacitors C2 (47 nF) and C1 (100 nF) help reduce the switching noise peak voltage levels of C2. The pulse-generated signal is magnetically coupled to the 8Ω speaker by the audio transformer. To further analyze the bird's electronic oscillator, I built a circuit model using Multisim software. Running a simulation event produced the output signal captured on a virtual oscilloscope, as shown in Figure 1-4.

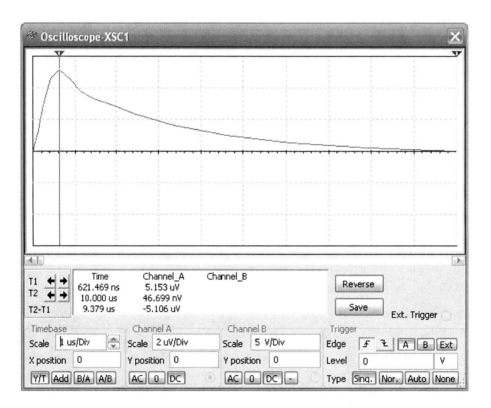

*Figure 1-4.* One cycle of a pulse wave captured on a Multisim virtual oscilloscope

---

■ **Note** Multisim is an intuitive software package capable of capturing circuit designs and testing electrical behaviors through simulation.

---

I was able to capture an actual pulsed waveform using an oscilloscope, as shown in Figure 1-5. The setup I used in capturing the pulsed signal is shown in Figure 1-6. The waveform has a frequency of approximately 1.2KHz, and it cycles approximately every 1 second. As mentioned earlier, the duration, or cycling, of the pulsed signal can be changed by adjusting the 50 K potentiometer.

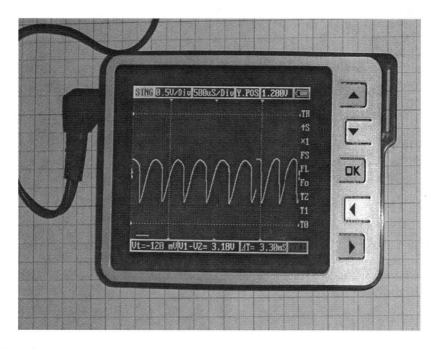

**Figure 1-5.** *The pulsed waveform signal displayed on an oscilloscope*

---

■ **Tip**   Modeling electronic circuits using simulation software will provide baseline information on the electrical behavior of the target system. Sometimes the data obtained from a simulated model may be different from the actual circuit. As shown in Figure 1-4, the signal shows the rising edge of the waveform captured on the oscilloscope pictured in Figure 1-6. The rising edge of a waveform is the transition from 0V to the peak voltage (Vp).

---

The measurement setup was made by removing the 8Ω speaker from the secondary winding of the audio transformer and attaching an oscilloscope across it to capture the pulsed waveform signal. Figure 1-7 illustrates the measurement technique I used to capture the pulse waveform signal on the virtual oscilloscope. The signal is a derivation of a *pulse width modulation*, which is used in various electronic oscillators to create special-effect sounds.

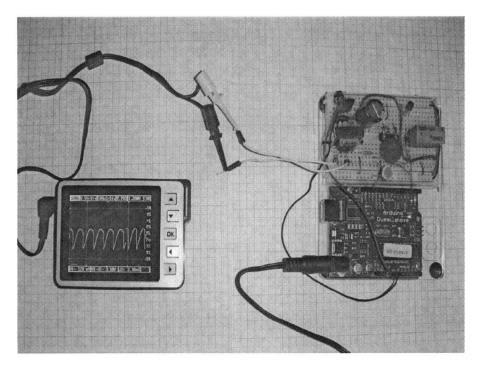

*Figure 1-6. Test setup for displaying the pulsed waveform signal from the electronic oscillator circuit*

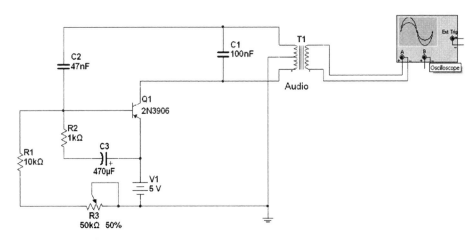

*Figure 1-7. Circuit schematic diagram showing the oscilloscope attachment to the audio transformer for capturing a pulsed waveform signal*

## Pulse Width Modulation Basics

Pulse width modulation (PWM) is commonly used for managing the power of electrical or electronic loads. You control the average value of voltage and current fed to the electrical or electronic loads by turning the output voltage supply attached to the load on and off at a fast switching rate. The longer the output voltage supply is applied to the load, the higher the power supplied to it. The PWM switching frequency must be high in order for the power management of the electrical or electronic load to take effect. The ability to manage the power of the load effectively allows the efficiency of the circuit's operation to reach up to 80 or 90 percent. The heat generated by the electrical or electronic load is very low, thereby providing longevity to the circuit. With this type of efficiency, incandescent lamps and electric motors, which are notorious for generating heat during normal operation, can function at a much lower temperature. Figure 1-8 shows a typical PWM signal for an AC electric motor. Another key electrical parameter for PWM is *duty cycle*. Duty cycle describes the proportion of "on" time to the regular interval, or *period*, of time. A low duty cycle corresponds to low power, because the power is off for most of the time. Duty cycle is expressed in percent, with 100 percent being fully on.

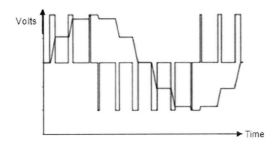

**Figure 1-8.** *A typical PWM signal for an AC electric motor*

---

■ **Tip** Duty cycle can be expressed mathematically as follows:

Duty Cycle = [Ton / (Ton + Toff)] × 100

where *Ton* is the time-on of the pulsed waveform and *Toff* is the time-off of the electrical signal.

---

This technique of switching effectively to manage the power of an electrical or electronic load can be used to create audio special effects as well. Used in this application, the PWM signal is equivalent to the difference between two sawtooth waves. The ratio between the high and low levels of the pulsed waveform is typically enhanced with a low-frequency signal. In addition, changing the duty cycle of a pulsed waveform creates unique sound effects for music applications such as synthesizers. Some music synthesizers have a duty-cycle trimmer for changing the shape of the device's square-wave output. The 50 K trimmer potentiometer for the electronic singing bird oscillator provides the similar function of changing the switching time of the circuit's output signal.

## Transistor Basics

The key electronic component of the electronic singing bird's oscillator circuit is the transistor. The main function of the transistor in this circuit application is to amplify the charging and discharging waveform produced by capacitors wired across the primary winding of the audio amplifier. The PNP transistor is biased by the 50 K potentiometer and the 10 K resistor series circuit. The duration of transistor biasing is accomplished using the 1 K (R2) and the 470uF (C3) electrolytic capacitor series circuit. The time in which the transistor stays turned on is based on the product of the R2C3 timing circuit. Changing either R2 or C3 affects the turn-on time for biasing the transistor, thereby affecting the charging of capacitors C1 (100 nF) and C2 (47 nF). When the transistor is turned off, the discharging of these capacitors is accomplished by the primary winding of the audio transformer. A circuit that can demonstrate the basic transistor-biasing operation is shown in Figure 1-9.

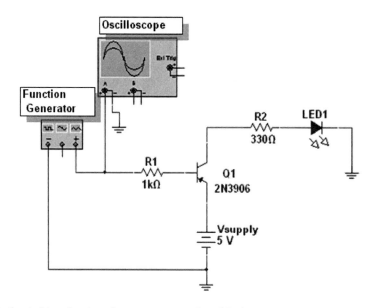

**Figure 1-9.** *A typical switching circuit to demonstrate transistor biasing*

---

▦ **Tip** For an NPN transistor, a transistor is biased (turned on) when the input signal (Vin) is greater than the base-emitter voltage (Vbe) of 700 mV. The mathematical expression for the electrical relation of Vin to Vbe is Vin > Vbe. For a PNP transistor, a transistor is biased (turned on) when the Vin is less than the Vbe of 700 mV. The expression for the electrical relation of Vin to Vbe is Vin < Vbe.

---

A *function generator* is a piece of electronic test equipment or software used to generate different types of electrical waveforms over a wide range of frequencies. The function generator can be set with the following signal parameters:

    *Signal:* Square wave

    *Frequency:* 10 Hz

    *Duty cycle:* 50 %

    *Amplitude:* 5Vp

The Multisim function generator settings are illustrated in Figure 1-10. You adjust the function generator settings by clicking the Unit text box and drop-down menu and making the appropriate changes to the values

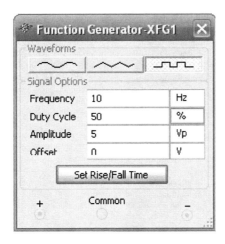

*Figure 1-10. Function generator settings for demonstrating transistor biasing*

and units. Upon powering up the circuit, you will see the LED flash at the specified frequency of the square-wave signal being applied to the base of the PNP transistor. On every falling edge transition of the square wave, the transistor's base-emitter junction will be forward biased, thereby allowing current to flow from the emitter lead through the series-limiting 330Ω resistor and the LED to ground. The LED will flash briefly based on the biasing current flowing through its anode-cathode junction when the transistor turns on.

You can increase the rate at which the LED flashes by changing the input frequency to a higher value. Although the circuit in this example was built on a virtual test bench using Multisim, a breadboard prototype can easily be constructed using the parts shown in Figure 1-9.

## Transformer Action

The pulsed waveform signal that is generated by the electronic oscillator is magnetically coupled to the 8Ω speaker by the audio transformer. The iron core of the transformer enhances the magnetic field because of its permeability (magnetic properties), thereby allowing the maximum pulsed waveform signal to be present on the secondary winding of the audio transformer. The primary and secondary windings of the transformer's pulsed waveform are inverted 180 degrees from each other. Figure 1-11 shows the transformer's inverted signals on the virtual oscilloscope. To see this inverted signal, you must use a dual-trace oscilloscope, which is quite expensive for an electronics hobbyist. However, Multisim's virtual oscilloscope can be used an alternative. To see the two waveforms simultaneously, connect the channel A scope probe across the primary winding and the channel B scope probe to the secondary winding of the audio transformer. Figure 1-12 shows the circuit schematic diagram for attaching the oscilloscope probes to the audio transformer. The two pulsed waveform signals will be inverted 180 degrees.

---

■ **Note** A transformer is a device that transfers electrical energy from one circuit to another through magnetically coupled conductors—the transformer's windings.

---

Since Multisim doesn't have an electrical symbol for a speaker, I used a standard 8Ω resistor in the circuit model during the simulation event. One key technique to remember when modeling circuits is to find

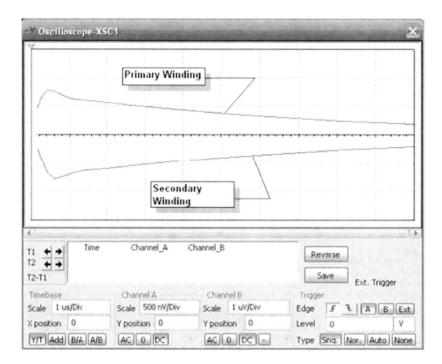

**Figure 1-11.** *Inverted pulsed waveform signals from the audio transformer*

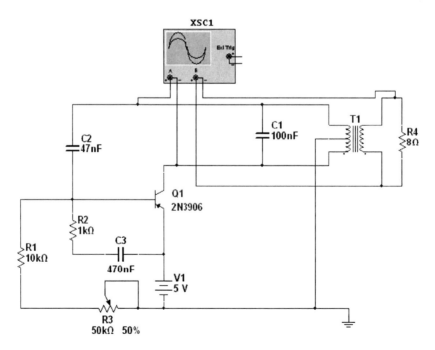

**Figure 1-12.** *Circuit schematic diagram showing oscilloscope probes attached to primary and secondary windings of the audio transformer*

components that have similar electrical behaviors to the actual devices. Although the actual component is not shown on the schematic capture diagram, its electrical behavior will be tested as if the actual part were used in the simulation circuit model. That's the reason for replacing the actual speaker with a standard fixed resistor in the circuit model. If you use a single-trace oscilloscope, the actual pulsed waveform signals can be captured from the audio transformer, as shown in Figure 1-13. In looking at the two waveforms, can you guess which signal is from the primary winding and which is from the secondary winding of the audio transformer?

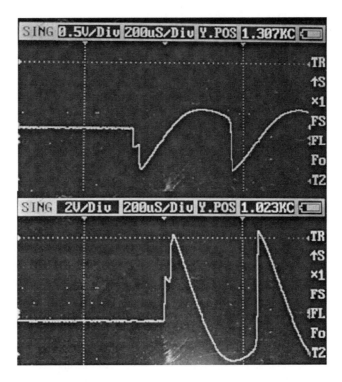

*Figure 1-13. Inverted pulsed waveform signals from the audio transformer captured on a real oscilloscope*

---

■ **Tip**  The *turns ratio* (Ns/Np) helps determine the relation between the current and voltage of the primary winding to the secondary winding of a transformer.

---

One last item to note about transformers is their ability to store electrical current within their windings. Basically, a transformer can be thought of as two inductors placed in parallel, with a piece of metal separating them. When a voltage source is applied to one coil, the energy stored (electrical current) is transferred to the other inductor through magnetic coupling. The metal piece separating them enhances the magnetic field based on its permeability (magnetic properties). If an ammeter is attached to the second inductor's coil, the electrical current can be measured and observed on it. If you add a momentary push-button switch to the first (primary) inductor's coil, you can observe the second inductor's coil-charging behavior on the ammeter. With each quick press of the push-button switch, the ammeter will show an initial charging current. Depending on how long the momentary push-button switch is held closed, the initial charging value will vary.

To show the effect of discharging the inductor's coil, I added a series discharge resistor to the second inductor's coil. Now, with each press of the switch, an initial high electrical current value will be displayed on the ammeter, followed by lower electrical current values. Again, these lower values represent the second inductor coil discharging the electrical current through the series resistor. A Multisim circuit model can easily be built for observing charging and discharging behavior of a transformer. Figure 1-14 illustrates the initial condition of the circuit completely discharged of current.

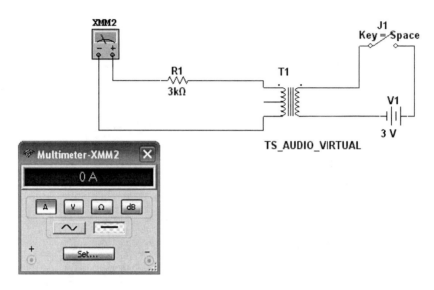

*Figure 1-14. Initial condition of the transformer with the switch open*

As shown in Figure 1-15, the transformer has charged up to a couple hundreds of microamperes (μA). When the switch is closed continuously, the electrical current starts to diminish in value, thereby displaying a discharging transformer. To automate this charging-and-discharging test, the Arduino, along with a transistor relay circuit, can be programmed to cycle the charging-and-discharging test based on a predetermined switching cycle.

---

▓ **Tip** The amount of voltage transferred in the second inductor coil as result of the first (primary) inductor coil's electrical current is relative to the *mutual inductance (Lm)* between the two inductor coils. The mutual inductance is based on the inductance of each inductor coil and the amount of coupling (k) between the two inductor coils.

---

## The Voltage Divider

The key interactive interface component for the electronic signing bird is the photocell. To assist in determining when light is present or not, a pull-up resistor is wired in series with the photocell. The two electrical components wired together make up a voltage divider circuit. With no light present, the photocell has a couple of kilo-ohms of resistance. The photocell voltage drop based on the total supply voltage is proportional to its resistance value. A high value of resistance will mean a significant voltage drop, and low resistance value will mean a small voltage drop. Figure 1-16 is a voltage divider circuit.

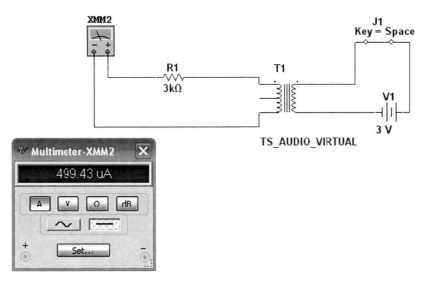

**Figure 1-15.** *The transformer charged with the switch closed*

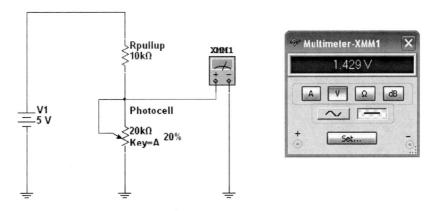

**Figure 1-16.** *Circuit simulation with light detected simulation*

---

■ **Tip** The voltage divider is a series circuit whereby the voltage drop across any resistor or combination of resistors is equal to the ratio of the target resistance to the total resistance. This ratio is multiplied by the source voltage of the circuit.

---

The photocell's resistance is set at 4KΩ. The voltage across this resistance value is determined by the voltage divider equation, as follows:

$$V4K = (V1 \times Photocell) / Rtotal$$

Substituting the appropriate values into the equation gives us the following form:

$$V4K = (5V \times 4K) / (10K + 4K)$$

$$V4K = 1.4285V$$

If no light is provided to the photocell, the voltage drop across it will be as shown in Figure 1-17.

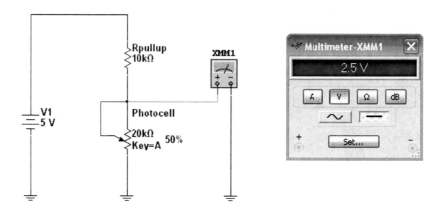

**Figure 1-17.** *Circuit simulation in which no light is detected*

We carry out the voltage drop calculation by changing the value of the photocell from 4KΩ to 10KΩ, like so:

$$V10K = (V1 \times Photocell) / Rtotal$$

$$V10K = (5V \times 10K) / (10K + 4K)$$

$$V10K = 2.5V$$

The Arduino will process a 2.5 V value as a binary logic 1, turning its output pin (D13) to +5 V. This binary logic response will bias the transistor, thereby allowing it to energize the +5VDC relay. The normally open (NO) contacts of the relay will close, allowing the electronic oscillator (i.e., the bird) to sing. The normally closed (NC) contacts will turn off the Arduino's D13 pin to go to 0 V. This will cause the transistor to turn off, which will deenergize the relay and allow the NO contacts to return to the normally closed (NC) contact position. The electronic oscillator will turn off, thereby preventing the bird's chirp from sounding through the 8Ω speaker.

## Light Detection Circuits with a Photocell

As discussed in the previous section, photocells are resistive sensors that allow light to be detected. They are packaged as small, low-cost electronic components that are used in various industrial and consumer products because of their ease of use and longevity. They are also referred to as CdS cells, light-dependent resistors, and photoresistors. A photocell, as explained in the previous section, changes its resistive value (ohms) based on the amount of light that shines on its surface. Photocells are manufactured in various sizes, and different-sized photocells function slightly differently. Because of this variation in size and function, photocells are traditional not used in critical light-measuring applications. The selection of a photocell is usually based on the following electrical parameters, traditionally listed on a datasheet (see www.ladyada.net/learn/sensors/cds.html):

> *Size:* Round, 5 mm (0.2") diameter. (Other photocells can get up to 12 mm/0.4" diameter!)

> *Resistance range:* 200 K (dark) to 10 K (10 lux brightness)

> *Sensitivity range:* CdS cells respond to light between 400 nm (violet) and 600 nm (orange) wavelengths, peaking at about 520 nm (green)

> *Power supply:* Pretty much anything up to 100 V, uses less than 1 mA of electrical current on average (depends on power supply voltage)

To use a photocell for light detection applications, such as the electronic singing bird project, you can wire a pull-up or pull-down resistor in series with electronic components so the appropriate voltage drop can be obtained for further signal processing. Depending on the size of the pull-up or pull-down resistor you use, the photocell will provide a voltage drop proportional to is resistance. If the photocell has a large resistance value, the voltage drop across it will be proportional to the ohmic value. Likewise, a small resistance value produced by the photocell will provide a small voltage drop across it. Figure 1-18 illustrates wiring a pull-up or pull-down resistor to a photocell for light detection signal interfacing.

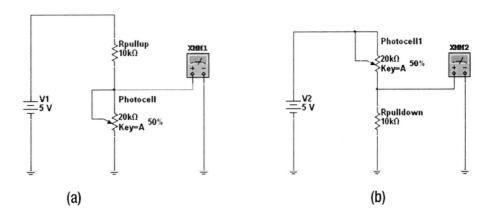

**Figure 1-18.** *Light detection circuits: A photocell wired with a pull-up resistor (a), and a photocell wired with a pull-down resistor (b)*

As an exercise, try building each circuit shown in Figure 1-18 using Multisim software and compare the electrical behaviors to each other.

## Testing the Light Detection Circuit with a Voltmeter and an Oscilloscope

You can validate the preceding exercise by using a voltmeter and an oscilloscope on a laboratory test bench. I'll discuss the test equipment arrangement I used for both instruments in the following subsections. I'll explain the individual test instruments and measurement points using simple Multisim circuit schematic diagrams, followed by the actual laboratory test bench setup.

## Using a Voltmeter

The wiring test setup for checking the electrical operation of the light detection circuit with a voltmeter is shown in Figure 1-19. Basically, the voltmeter—or digital multimeter (DMM)—test leads will be connected across the photocell. The voltmeter or DMM will be set for the appropriate measurement scale and electrical units.

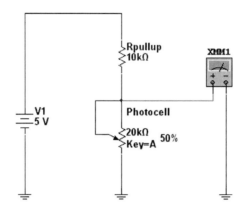

*Figure 1-19. Multisim circuit schematic diagram for testing the light detection circuit with a voltmeter or DMM*

The actual laboratory test bench setup I used is shown in Figure 1-20. I placed the DMM's test leads (red and black) across the photocell. With the DMM set to voltage I measured the photocell's voltage drop with the electronic singing bird's prototype board under ambient lighting. As pictured in Figure 1-20, the photocell's voltage drop value was low. This measurement reading coincides with the photocell's small resistance value. Next, I covered up the photocell with my hand to shield it from the ambient lighting, and another voltage drop reading was displayed on the DMM's liquid crystal display (LCD). This reading was approximately +2.5VDC, indicating a high resistance value from the photocell. Figure 1-21 shows the high voltage drop reading of the photocell shielded from the ambient light. The voltage drop readings varied based on the type of ambient light shielding and the distance of the shield from the photocell.

---

▓ **Note**   Ambient lighting is normal room light. As the light shield or hand approaches the photocell, thereby diminishing the ambient lighting, the voltage drop will increase in value, signifying that the sensor's resistance is increasing. The voltage drop of approximately +2.5VDC was measured on the Multisim circuit model shown in Figure 1-22.

---

## Using an Oscilloscope

You can also use an oscilloscope to test the light detection interface circuit by following a similar wiring convention to one discussed earlier, using a voltmeter or DMM. The oscilloscope's test probe will be attached across the photocell, similar to a voltmeter or DMM. Figure 1-23 shows a Multisim circuit schematic diagram for wiring an oscilloscope to the light detection interface circuit.

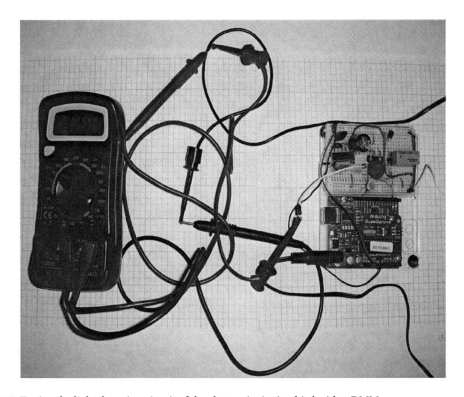

*Figure 1-20. Testing the light detection circuit of the electronic singing bird with a DMM*

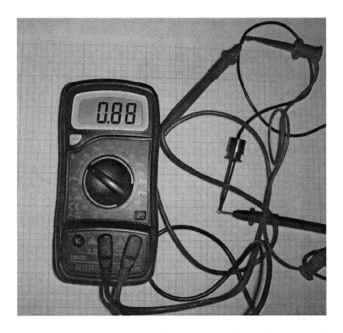

*Figure 1-21. Ambient light based on the DMM's LCD voltage drop reading of the photocell*

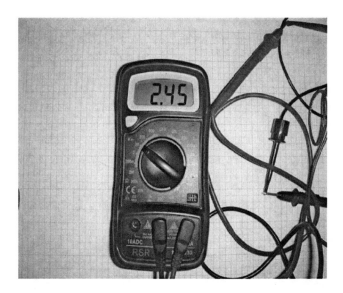

**Figure 1-22.** *No ambient light present on the photocell*

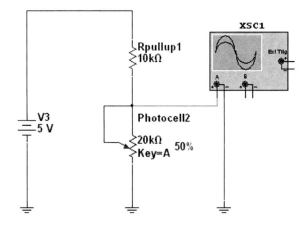

**Figure 1-23.** *Multisim circuit schematic diagram for wiring an oscilloscope to the light detection interface circuit for testing*

Figure 1-24 shows the laboratory test bench with the oscilloscope's probe attached across the photocell I used for circuit testing. To capture the ambient light and no-light-present conditions, I placed the oscilloscope in a scan mode of operation with a time base set to 100mS/div. This setting allows for the switching event of the photocell to transition from ambient light to no light present. Figure 1-25 shows the waveforms of both lighting conditions detected by the photocell.

The waveform on the left in Figure 1-25 (a) shows a 0VDC level, signifying low resistance for the photocell. This zero voltage level is indicative of the photocell being subjected to ambient lighting in the laboratory. The rise in voltage reaching a steady state value of approximately +2.4VDC indicates the photocell having high resistance based on the absence of ambient light.

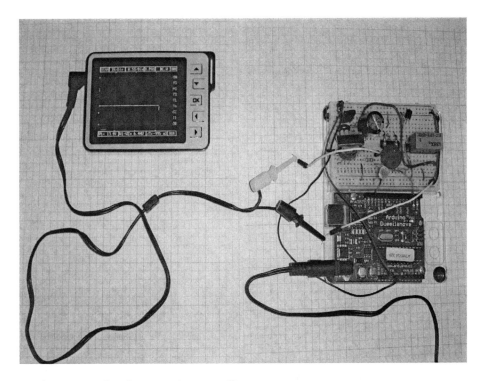

***Figure 1-24.*** *Laboratory test bench setup using an oscilloscope*

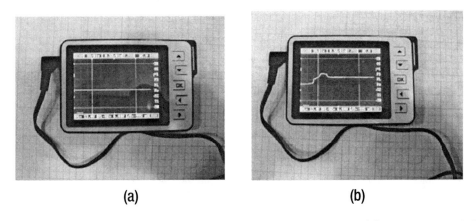

| (a) | (b) |

***Figure 1-25.*** *Oscilloscope waveforms of the light detection circuit: ambient lighting (a) and no ambient lighting (b)*

---

■ **Note**    Based on the type of oscilloscope and time base settings, the no-ambient-light-present waveform may vary in appearance slightly.

---

## Assembly of the Electronic Singing Bird Circuit on a Breadboard

In the previous sections of the chapter, I discussed key electronic concepts and principles using Multisim circuit models for visual explanation. Also, I demonstrated testing techniques to ensure that circuits will operate properly when power is applied to them. To maintain a compact size for the electronic singing bird prototype, I used a small, solderless breadboard to assemble the circuit. One approach I took to maintain proper circuit operation is to use short wiring jumper lengths on the solderless breadboard. Also, planning breadboard layout will ensure that wiring management is maintained throughout the circuit build process. Figure 1-26 illustrates the wiring circuit build of the pulsed tone oscillator on the solderless breadboard.

***Figure 1-26.*** *Wiring the pulsed tone oscillator circuit using a small, solderless breadboard*

As shown in Figure 1-26, all leads on my electronic components were cut to length, thereby maintaining tight and clean wiring for the circuit. For the relay, I used a 16-pin DIP socket to maintain good electrical connectivity on the solderless breadboard. This mounting technique helped because the pins on the relay are quite short, and eliminated intermittent operation due to improper fit into the solderless breadboard's spring terminal cavities. The pinout for the relay I used in the circuit is shown in Figure 1-27.

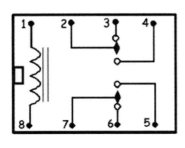

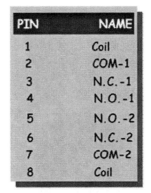

| PIN | NAME |
|---|---|
| 1 | Coil |
| 2 | COM-1 |
| 3 | N.C.-1 |
| 4 | N.O.-1 |
| 5 | N.O.-2 |
| 6 | N.C.-2 |
| 7 | COM-2 |
| 8 | Coil |

TOP OF RELAY

*Figure 1-27. Pinout for the relay used in the electronic singing bird prototype*

The two transistors (2 N3904 and 2 N3906) are complements of each other, meaning they are *bipolar* NPN and PNP devices. Transistors should be placed in a location where they can drive their respective circuits. That is, the 2 N3904 component is located close to the relay and the 2 N3906 by the audio transformer. The pinout for these transistors is the same, and is shown in Figure 1-28.

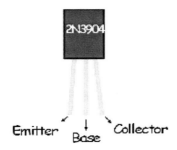

*Figure 1-28. The 2 N3904 (pictured) and 2 N3906 transistors have the same pinout*

With all of the electronic components placed on the solderless breadboard, you can complete the final circuit wiring. Figure 1-29 shows the final wiring build of the electronic singing bird prototype I built on my lab bench. Ports D2 and D13 of the Arduino are wired, using inline header connectors, to the light detection circuit and transistor relay driver circuits. The +5VDC and ground pins from the Arduino PCB power supply are wired to the + and – rows on the solderless breadboard for distributing power to the pulsed tone oscillator circuit.

---

■ **Tip**   For a robust version of the 2 N3904 NPB transistor, try using the 2N2222A component. It can handle currents as high as 50 mA.

---

*Figure 1-29. The final prototype of the electronic singing bird*

## Creating the Interactive Control Software

With the hardware prototype built, the next phase of the project is to create interactive software. The software will allow the light detection software to provide two binary events: ambient lighting and no ambient lighting triggering for the pulsed tone oscillator. Upon ambient light being detected by the photocell, the transistor relay driver circuit should be off, thereby keeping the bird asleep. Covering the photocell with an object or a hand will allow the Arduino to switch on the transistor relay driver circuit to power the electronic signing bird to chirp. The software (sketch) to allow this interaction for controlling the pulsed tone oscillator was obtained from the Arduino public domain website, at `www.arduino.cc/en/Tutorial/Button`. The sketch is shown in Listing 1-1.

*Listing 1-1.* The Button Sketch (Code) Used for Interactive Control of the Electronic Singing Bird

```
/*
Button
Turns on and off a light emitting diode(LED) connected to digital
pin 13, when pressing a pushbutton attached to pin 2.
The circuit:
* LED attached from pin 13 to ground
* pushbutton attached to pin 2 from +5 V
* 10 K resistor attached to pin 2 from ground
* Note: on most Arduinos there is already an LED on the board
attached to pin 13.
created 2005
```

```
  by DojoDave <http://www.0j0.org>
  modified 28 Oct 2010
  by Tom Igoe
  This example code is in the public domain.
  http://www.arduino.cc/en/Tutorial/Button
  */
// constants won't change. They're used here to
// set pin numbers:
const int buttonPin = 2;    // the number of the pushbutton pin
const int ledPin = 13;    // the number of the LED pin
// variables will change:
int buttonState = 0;       // variable for reading the pushbutton status
void setup() {
 // initialize the LED pin as an output:
 pinMode(ledPin, OUTPUT);
 // initialize the pushbutton pin as an input:
 pinMode(buttonPin, INPUT);
}
void loop(){
 // read the state of the pushbutton value:
 buttonState = digitalRead(buttonPin);
 // check if the pushbutton is pressed.
 // if it is, the buttonState is HIGH:
 if (buttonState == HIGH) {
 // turn LED on:
  digitalWrite(ledPin, HIGH);
 }
 else {
  // turn LED off:
  digitalWrite(ledPin, LOW);
 }
}
```

I used the code "as is" to rapidly test the interaction between an object event triggering the Arduino to switch on the external pulsed tone oscillator circuit for a bird chirp. In reviewing the code, the technique of reading a binary value, processing it, and switching the appropriate port pin on the Atmel Atmega328 microcontroller is quite easy to understand. As noted in the sketch, the authors of the code took time to comment sections of code, thereby making it easy to modify and reuse for other interactive control projects. This sketch, along with the community website presented earlier, can help make your process of learning and exploring electronics with the Arduino fun and easy. Once you enter the code into the Arduino processing editor (see Figure 1-30), you can easily upload the sketch to the Atmega328 microcontroller.

## What Is a Sketch?

For electronic hobbyists new to the world of Arduino, the Arduino team calls the embedded software of its computing platform a *sketch* because the device was created for artists interested in making their artwork or pieces interactive with the viewer or audience. Just as artists create their art pieces via sketching on a canvas or a sheet of paper, they can create visual art by downloading a small computer program (sketch) to Arduino for completing the final interactive piece.

*Figure 1-30. Example Arduino processing editor with button sketch*

---

▪ **Note**   The sketches in this book will be created using a rapid development method, whereby existing code is modified or remixed to fit the requirements of the target product. Why reinvent the wheel when you can just put new rims on it?

---

# Final Testing of the Electronic Singing Bird

Throughout this chapter, you've learned a product development process by building an electronic singing bird. . As discussed in the previous sections, each interface circuit and output driver device can be tested using basic electronics test equipment, such as a DMM and an oscilloscope.

Once you have each subcircuit working properly, the final stage of testing is to upload the sketch to the Arduino and validate the appropriate output responses of the final product. In the case of the electronic singing bird, when you place a hand over the photocell, a simulated bird chirping sound should be come from the 8Ω speaker. If there is no sound being emitted from the speaker, review the "Testing the Light Detection Circuit with a Voltmeter and an Oscilloscope" section, as well the "Transistor Basics" section, which explains how biasing assists with the control switching of an external electrical load or circuit. Also, review the sketch entered into the processing editor for typos that could be causing the Arduino to operate improperly.

# Further Discovery Methods

To keep the excitement of learning electronics with Arduino burning, explore how an additional photocell can be used to control two different bird-chirping durations. You might investigate adding a second transistor relay driver circuit to switch between two electrolytic capacitors, thereby affecting the bird-chirping duration. Keep in mind that you'll need to use a second digital output port pin of the Arduino, thereby requiring a sketch modification to be made. The light detection circuit discussed previously will serve as the design template for using another digital input port pin on the Arduino. Obtain a spiral notebook for documenting these circuit enhancements for the Arduino as well as the sketch modifications for additional I/O (input/output) control.

# CHAPTER 2

■ ■ ■

# Mini Digital Roulette Games

The Arduino makes creating simple electronic games easy. In this chapter, I will show that you can use basic digital electronic circuits to build an interactive mini casino game within two hours. With as few as nine discrete electronic components and an Arduino board, you can easily build two cool Mini Digital Roulette games. The required parts are pictured in Figure 2-1.

## Parts List

1 Arduino Duemilanove or equivalent

1 LED bar display (also called a bar graph LED display)

1 2x8 330Ω DIP resistor IC

1 big LED

1 push-button switch (tactile or equivalent)

1 10K trimmer potentiometer

1 10K resistor

1 7490/74LS90 Decade Counter IC

1 7447/74LS47 Seven-Segment Decoder Driver IC

1 Common Anode Seven-Segment LED Display (MAN 72)

1 small solderless breadboard

22 AWG solid wire

Digital multimeter

Oscilloscope (Optional)

Electronic tools

I will show you how the two devices in this chapter illustrate a design technique whereby a new product evolves from a simpler design. This "remix" design technique allows product designers and developers to get to market quicker without a major tearup to the *bill of materials* (BOM). Figures 2-2 and 2-3 show the systems block diagrams for two Mini Digital Roulette games.

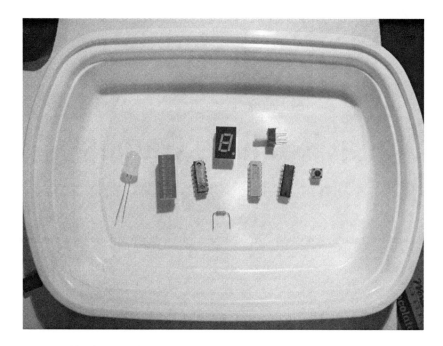

**Figure 2-1.** *Parts required for the mini digital roulette games*

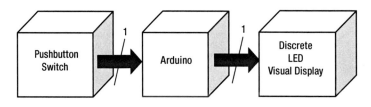

**Figure 2-2.** *A simple Mini Digital Roulette game systems block diagram*

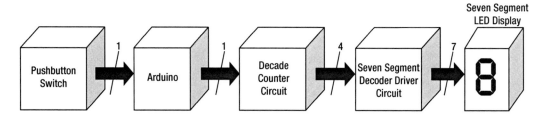

**Figure 2-3.** *A remix Mini Digital Roulette game systems block diagram*

---

▓ **Tip** In electronics design, BOM is another way of saying *parts list*.

---

A closer look at the system block diagram reveals the circuit schematic diagram of the LED roulette game, shown in Figure 2-4. The numbers located above the arrows represent the number of pins used between the two blocks. This information will become relevant with the seven-segment LED display version of the mini roulette game.

---

▓ **Note** A LED bar display is dual inline package (DIP) type IC that has multiple LEDs packaged inside of it.

---

# How It Works

The operation of the LED roulette game consists of an Arduino detecting a rising edge from a simple push-button switch. Upon receiving the +5VDC control signal, the software programmed into the Atmega328 microcontroller starts switching the three LEDs of the LED bar display in a specific sequence. The software program starts rapidly turning on the LEDs in a predetermined switching pattern, eventually slowing down and leaving only one LED lit. Each press of the push-button repeats the switching cycle with a different LED being lit. The 10K pulldown resistor is placed in series with the push-button switch, ensuring that the +5VDC will be read by the Arduino's Atmega328 microcontroller. The circuit schematic diagram shown in Figure 2-4 shows each LED of the bar display being wired in a particular orientation. The wiring convention used to assure the LEDs will light based on the appropriate switched output port (D8, D11, D13) is known as *forward biasing*.

---

▓ **Note** The rising edge of a digital control signal is basically a transition from 0V to +3.3V or +5V. The term *pulldown* refers to the supply voltage being applied across the associated resistor, thereby ensuring the microcontroller's input port pin will register it as a valid binary logic "1" data value for proper control signal processing.

---

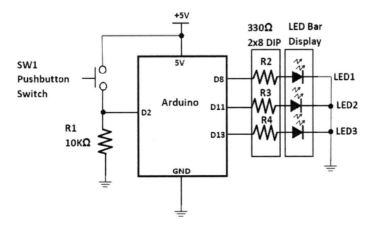

*Figure 2-4. The Arduino-based LED roulette game circuit schematic diagram*

# Forward Biasing a LED

An LED (light-emitting diode) can emit light only if you wire it properly in a circuit. To properly connect an LED to a voltage source, its positive lead (the *anode*) must be wired to the highest potential point or *electrical node* of the circuit. The negative lead (the *cathode*) is wired to the lowest potential or ground of the circuit. To prevent the LED from burning out, a series-limiting resistor is wired to it. Traditionally, the series-limiting resistor is wired to the anode of the LED but it may alternatively be attached to the cathode; the same effect of reducing current flow through it is achieved either way. If either the voltage source or the LED is wired incorrectly, current will not flow. To illustrate the basic operation and wiring configuration, Figure 2-5 shows a Multisim circuit model with the switch initially open. As displayed on the DMM, the ammeter is reading no current. In Figure 2-6, the ammeter is displaying current flow with the LED being turned on. When the LED is connected the other way around, the ammeter reads practically zero milliamperes. This condition where the LED is wired backwards, thus preventing current flow in the circuit, is known as *reverse bias*. Figure 2-7 shows reverse biasing of the LED in the simple DC circuit.

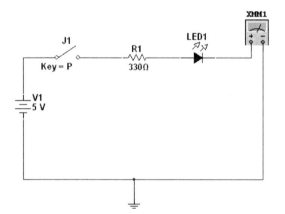

**Figure 2-5.** *Multisim circuit model for a virtual LED demonstrator*

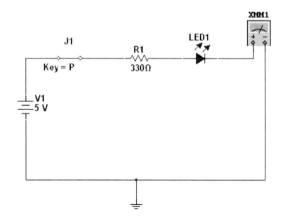

**Figure 2-6.** *Forward biasing mode illustrated by virtual LED demonstrator*

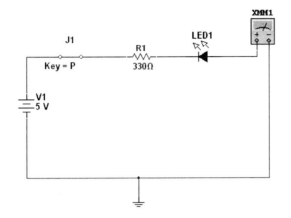

*Figure 2-7. Reverse biasing mode illustrated by virtual LED demonstrator*

## LED Circuit Analysis

The forward biasing current displayed on the virtual ammeter shown in Figure 2-6 can be manually calculated (paper and pen) using the following equation:

$$I_{FD} = (V1 - V_{FD}) / R1$$

where

- $I_{FD}$ is the forward current of the LED.
- V1 is the supply voltage.
- $V_{FD}$ is forward voltage drop of the LED (Note: 1.66 V is the value for this component parameter).
- R1 is the series limiting resistor.

So, making the appropriate substitutions into the equation

$$I_{FD} = (5V - 1.66V) / 330\Omega$$

$$I_{FD} = 3.34V / 330\Omega$$

$$I_{FD} = 0.01012A \text{ or } 10.12mA$$

Figure 2-8 shows the actual answer performed on the Windows Calculator.

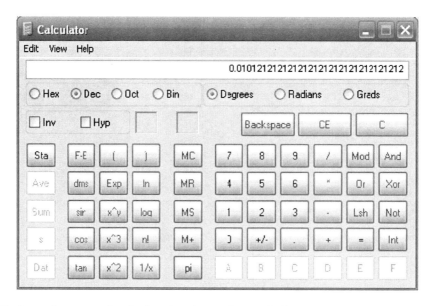

*Figure 2-8. The forward current value displayed on the Windows Calculator*

## The LED Bar Display

As shown in Figure 2-4, the visual display for the Mini LED Roulette game is a bar display package. LED bar displays come in a variety of discrete solid-state indicators ranging from 4 to 10 devices in one DIP package. The DIP IC package used in this Arduino-based electronic game has 10 discrete LEDs, as shown in Figure 2-9. The anode pins of the DIP IC package are located on the side with the part number.

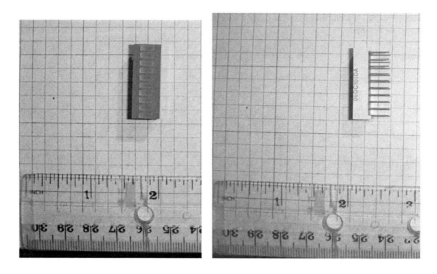

*Figure 2-9. A typical LED bar display. The anode pins are located where the part number is stamped on the component.*

You can easily test a LED bar display using a DMM set to read resistance. Modern DMMs offer a diode test function and can be used to test LEDs. By setting the DMM to test diodes, the red test lead of the measuring instrument gets attached to anode pin and the black test lead is connected to the cathode. Figure 2-10 illustrates how to connect the DMM to the LED bar display. The reading on the DMM's LCD will display an open circuit but the individual LED attached will be lit. The LED is turned ON because the ohmmeter provides a small amount current that forward biases the LED, thus lighting it.

■ **Tip** A Multisim circuit model can be built to test a virtual LED bar display using the connection setup explained. The virtual ohmmeter will read a resistance value close to 36Ω as opposed to lighting an LED (see Figure 2-11).

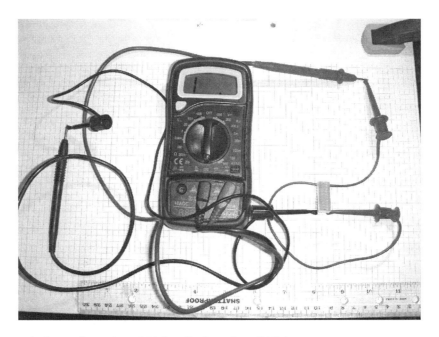

***Figure 2-10.*** *A typical setup for testing a LED bar display using a DMM*

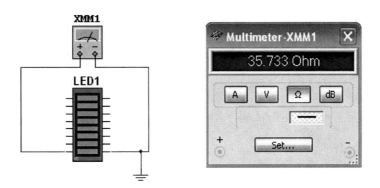

***Figure 2-11.*** *A discrete LED bar being forward biased by the ohmmeter*

You can apply the testing technique discussed here to a seven-segment LED display. As well as testing the seven-segment LED display, I will explain how the optoelectronic component works.

---

■ **Note** Optoelectronics is a technology that combines light with electronic circuits. Examples of optoelectronics include LEDs, seven-segment LED displays, and LCDs.

---

# Mini Roulette Game, Version 1

As shown in the circuit schematic diagram of Figure 2-4, the first version of the Mini Digital Roulette game is quite simple in terms of electronic design. In a way this design is experimental; the project lets you practice self discovery by adding LEDs and modifying the sketches to accommodate the additional solid state indicators. The prototype game you build uses a solderless breadboard along with the Arduino. Figure 2-12 shows the completed prototype game. In response to a momentary press of the push-button switch, the three LEDs start a lighting sequence in which each of them turns ON quickly. The sequence repeats several times before slowing down the switching rate. Upon coming to this output state, one of the LEDs remains lit, signifying the game has ended with the winning number. The LED to remain ON is based on a random switching pattern selected by the embedded sketch.

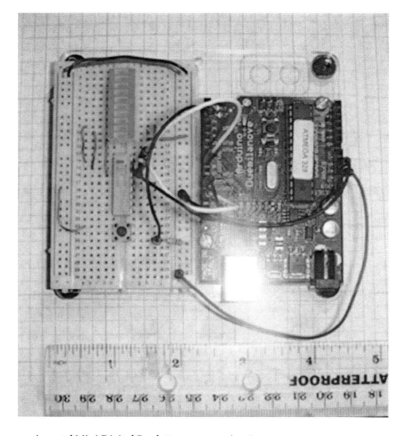

*Figure 2-12. The experimental Mini Digital Roulette game, version 1*

In the construction of the Mini Digital Roulette game, both the LED bar display and the 330 Ω DIP resistor are mounted on the mini solderless breadboard with appropriate spacing to add jumper wires. There are eight 330 Ω resistors in one DIP package. Figure 2-13 shows a typical DIP resistor pack. The resistor pack is used to limit the amount of current flowing thru each discrete LED of the bar display IC. Each resistor is placed between two parallel pins. To verify component arrangement, connect the red and black test leads of an ohmmeter to the parallel pins, as shown in Figure 2-14. The reading of one 330 Ω resistor will be displayed on the ohmmeter's LCD screen; this same measurement technique can be used to verify the other 330 Ω resistors.

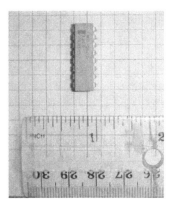

*Figure 2-13.* *A 330 Ω DIP resistor pack*

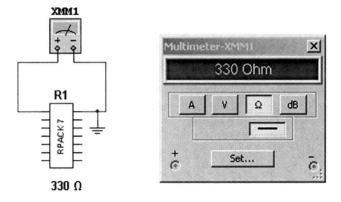

*Figure 2-14.* *The Multisim circuit model used to verify a 330Ω resistor of a DIP pack*

# Adding the Game Software

The final step for version one of the Mini Digital Roulette game is to add the sketch. Listing 2-1 shows the sketch for the mini roulette game.

*Listing 2-1.* The Mini Digital Roulette Game Sketch

```
/*Arduino LED Roulette
Posted by changb3 in Class Notes
Connect 3 LED's to digital output pins 8, 11, and 13 (with resistors in serial with each).
```

Connect a push-button to pin 2 (and don't forget the pulldown resistor).
[code]
Modified by Don Wilcher 11/17/11

```
/*
random light
*/

const int buttonPin = 2;
int lightpins[3] = {8,11,13};//Change sequence of LEDs Here!
int state=0;
void setup()
{
pinMode (buttonPin,INPUT);
pinMode (lightpins[0],OUTPUT);
pinMode (lightpins[1],OUTPUT);
pinMode (lightpins[2],OUTPUT);
digitalWrite (lightpins[0],LOW);
digitalWrite (lightpins[1],LOW);
digitalWrite (lightpins[2],LOW);
}
void loop ()
{
int reading = digitalRead (buttonPin);
int blinktime=20;
boolean done;
if (reading == HIGH)
{
if (state==0)
{
state=1;
done=false;
blinktime=20;
blinktime+= 3;
while (!done)
{
for (int j=0;j<3;j++)
{
blinktime += random(3);
digitalWrite(lightpins[j],HIGH);
if (blinktime>200)
{
done=true;
break;
}
delay(blinktime);
digitalWrite(lightpins[j],LOW);
delay(blinktime);
}
}
}
}
else
{
```

```
state=0;
}
}
```

The cool thing about the Arduino computing platform is the number of developers creating open source software for a multitude of hardware gadgets and devices. I found the remix method of software development quite easy to implement because of the great number of sketches available on the Web via forums and virtual hobbyists communities. This sketch is example of remix because of the randomness of bit selection after the game ends. The lines of code used to generate the random LED displays are as follows:

```
blinktime += random(3);
digitalWrite(lightpins[j],HIGH);
if (blinktime>200)
```

The original sketch continues to display the last bit on the LED bar display after the game stops. A new LED display sequence can be programmed by the following line of code:

```
int lightpins[3] = {8,11,13};//Change sequence of LEDs Here!
```

Changing the order of digital output pins (8, 11, 13) will produce unique visual effects for the Mini Digital Roulette game.

# The Seven-Segment LED Display Basics

Although the LED bar display provides a unique way of visualizing a ball spinning round a roulette wheel, it makes for quite a challenge to interpret the chosen number since it's in a binary format. The next improvement you will make to the Mini Digital Roulette game is replacing the LED bar display with a numeric digit. By making this design change to the electronic product, the numbers will be easily visible during the game. The seven-segment LED bar display is similar to the LED bar display except that each *segment* is arranged so that a number or character can be seen on it. Figure 2-15 shows the internal arrangements of each LED segment of the optoelectronic display.

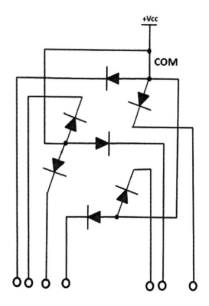

*Figure 2-15. Typical arrangement of discrete LEDs for a seven-segment LED display*

Notice that all of the anodes are connected to one electrical node or common point. Based on this single connective point, the display package is called a *common anode* seven-segment LED display. There is also a common cathode display where all of the discrete LED cathodes are wired to one electrical point or *pin* of the DIP component. Another key physical characteristic, which is quite obvious, is the number of discrete LEDs. There are seven of them in one package, thus the name *seven-segment LED display*. Figure 2-16 shows a typical seven-segment LED display component.

**Figure 2-16.** *Typical seven-segment LED display (common anode)*

## Testing the Seven-Segment LED Display

You will notice that testing a seven-segment LED display is similar to checking a basic silicon diode. When you attach the red test lead of the ohmmeter to the common anode pin and the black test lead to one of the cathode pins of the seven-segment LED display, the meter will forward bias the optoelectronic element. Figure 2-17 illustrates the setup for testing a seven-segment LED display with a DMM placed in ohmmeter mode.

By forward biasing the discrete LED segment, it will be ON. Figure 2-18 shows the bottom left segment being turned ON during testing. Another important thing about seven-segment LED displays is that each discrete LED element has a letter assigned to it. There are seven letters for each segment ranging from A-F. By wiring these letters in combinations, you can create alpha characters and numbers. In the new and improved Mini Digital Roulette game, numbers 0-9 will be displayed on the seven-segment LED display. This way of representing the ball spinning around the roulette wheel gives the game more visual appeal than seeing three LED bars scanning repeatedly.

---

■ **Note**    Before solid-state seven-segment LED displays, digital data was represented using Nixie Tubes, which looked liked mini vacuum tubes with neon light segments wired inside the glass enclosure.

---

Multisim (or equivalent circuit simulation software) can be used to illustrate how to test a seven-segment LED display. Instead of turning ON the target LED segment, the ohmmeter will display a very high resistance value (giga-ohms) for a bad LED (open). A good LED segment will display a couple hundred mega-ohms on the ohmmeter. Although the seven-segment LED display models are good in Multisim, Figure 2-19 illustrates a good LED segment (forward biasing mode) and a bad optoelement using reverse biasing mode.

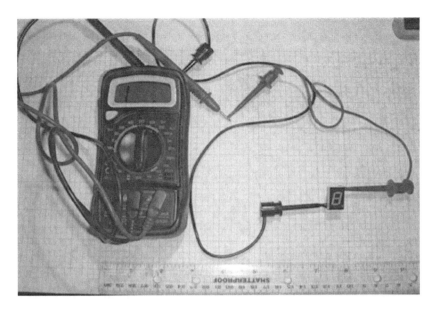

*Figure 2-17. Testing a seven-segment LED display (common anode) with a DMM set to ohmmeter mode*

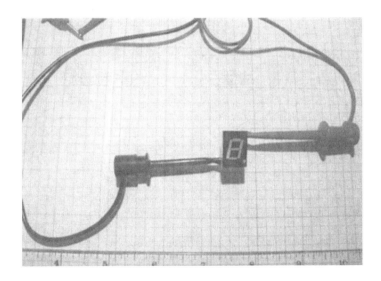

*Figure 2-18. The bottom left segment (E) is turned on during testing with a DMM set to ohmmeter mode*

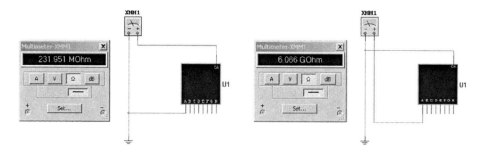

***Figure 2-19.*** *Virtually testing a good seven-segment LED display (L) using forward biasing mode and a bad display (R) using reverse biasing mode*

## Build an Arduino-based Seven Segment LED Display Flasher-Tester

The Arduino can easily be used with a simple seven-segment LED tester to create a digital clock. The pulse of flash rate of the digital clock can be adjusted using a potentiometer. By wiring the seven-segment LED display for a specific alpha (letter) character or number, target segments will be tested (flashed) on the optoelectronic component. Figure 2-20 shows the block diagram of the Arduino Flasher-Tester.

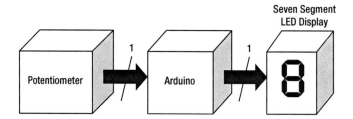

***Figure 2-20.*** *The Arduino Flasher-Tester system block diagram*

The circuit schematic for the system block diagram is shown in Figure 2-21. When you change the potentiometer resistance, a different input voltage is used to determine the flash rate of the seven-segment LED display. For Arduino's microcontroller, there are equivalent analog-to-digital count values ranging from 0 to 1024 bits that the embedded sketch of the Arduino's Atmega328 microcontroller uses to produce a unique digital clock signal flash rate at pin D13. The LED segments selected for visual display will flash at the specified rate of the sketch. By rotating the 10 K potentiometer clockwise or counterclockwise, the seven-segment LED display will flash between low and high speeds.

▓ **Note** A potentiometer is a variable resistor used to divide the applied signal across it into discrete voltage levels using an attached rotating shaft. The shaft makes electrical contact with a carbon-based ring upon variable resistance that occurs during rotation. The change in resistance affects the applied signal (voltage).

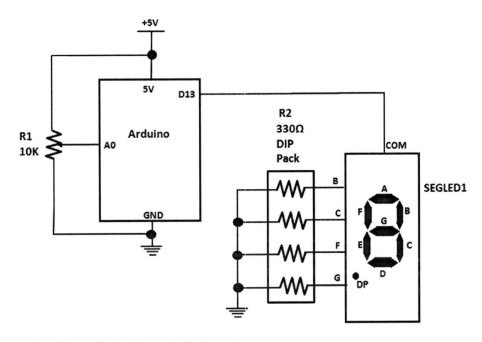

***Figure 2-21.*** *The Arduino Flasher-Tester circuit schematic*

In order to wire the common anode seven-segment LED display as shown in the circuit schematic diagram, the pinout is shown Figure 2-22. Some pins are missing; do not confuse this with a damaged or bad seven-segment LED display. The complete Arduino Flasher-Tester circuit can easily be built on a mini solderless breadboard, as shown in Figure 2-23. Just for fun, a big blue LED can be added to the circuit build, as shown in Figure 2-24. Adjusting the potentiometer for a fast flash rate makes the blue LED have a stroboscopic effect.

▓ **Note** A stroboscope is an electronic instrument used to produce a stroboscopic effect. The stroboscopic effect is where objects at a high speed can be slowed down by emitting bright and extremely brief flashes of light at regular intervals. The flash rate can be adjusting by turning a knob attached to a potentiometer wired to an electronic switching circuit.

| Pin no. | Electrical connection |
|---------|----------------------|
| 1 | Cathode A |
| 2 | Cathode F |
| 3 | Common Anode |
| 4 | No Pin |
| 5 | No Pin |
| 6 | Cathode D. P. |
| 7 | Cathode E |
| 8 | Cathode D |
| 9 | No Connection |
| 10 | Cathode C |
| 11 | Cathode G |
| 12 | No Pin |
| 13 | Cathode B |
| 14 | Common Anode |

*Figure 2-22.* *The common anode seven-segment LED display pinout*

*Figure 2-23.* *The completed Arduino Flasher-Tester*

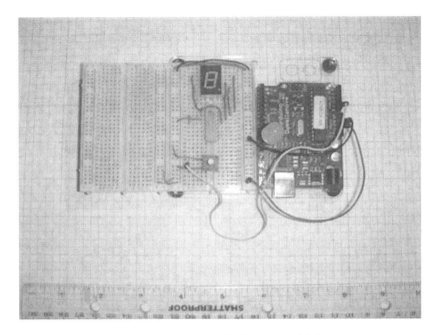

*Figure 2-24.* *The completed Arduino Flasher-Tester with a big blue LED added*

To bring the Arduino Flasher-Tester to life, you need to upload a sketch to the Arduino. As discussed in Chapter 1, the Arduino community is quite large, and contributors add new sketches and tutorials daily. The flashing control sketch shown in Listing 2-2 is from that community of volunteer software developers and contributors.

*Listing 2-2.* The Potentiometer LED Control Sketch for the Arduino Seven-Segment LED Flasher-Tester

```
/*
Analog Input
Demonstrates analog input by reading an analog sensor on analog pin 0 and
turning on and off a light emitting diode(LED) connected to digital pin 13.
The amount of time the LED will be on and off depends on
the value obtained by analogRead().

The circuit:
* Potentiometer attached to analog input 0
* center pin of the potentiometer to the analog pin
* one side pin (either one) to ground

* the other side pin to +5 V
* LED anode (long leg) attached to digital output 13
* LED cathode (short leg) attached to ground

* Note: because most Arduinos have a built-in LED attached
to pin 13 on the board, the LED is optional.
Created by David Cuartielles
Modified 4 Sep 2010
By Tom Igoe
```

This example code is in the public domain.

http://arduino.cc/en/Tutorial/AnalogInput

*/

```
int sensorPin = A0;  // select the input pin for the potentiometer
int ledPin = 13;    // select the pin for the LED
int sensorValue = 0; // variable to store the value coming from the sensor

void setup() {
 // declare the ledPin as an OUTPUT:
 pinMode(ledPin, OUTPUT);
}

void loop() {
 // read the value from the sensor:
 sensorValue = analogRead(sensorPin);
 // turn the ledPin on
 digitalWrite(ledPin, HIGH);
 // stop the program for < sensorValue > milliseconds:
 delay(sensorValue);
 // turn the ledPin off:
 digitalWrite(ledPin, LOW);
 // stop the program for < sensorValue > milliseconds:
 delay(sensorValue);
}
```

---

▨ **Note**  A little bit of Arduino trivia: David Cuartielles and Tom Igoe are members of the Arduino Team.

---

As discussed earlier, the potentiometer provides the analog-to-digital count (ADC) values using this line of instruction:

```
sensorValue = analogRead(sensorPin);
```

The Arduino pin used to obtain the potentiometer- control voltage levels is A0. Based on the ADC value, the sketch produces a delay that corresponds to the flash rate using this line of instruction:

```
delay(sensorValue);
```

Pin D13 is driven LOW based on this line of instruction and the one that follows:

```
digitalWrite(ledPin, LOW);
```

The flash rate remains at the specified switching value until the potentiometer's resistance is changed.

# The 7447 BCD-to-Decoder IC Basics

The final Mini Digital Roulette game uses a special IC that can take a four-bit binary value and convert it to the equivalent decimal number. By using a binary weighted value system of 8-4-2-1, numbers 0 to 9 can be displayed on a seven-segment LED display. Four inputs represented by letters D, C, B, and A can be converted to numbers 0 to 9. Figure 2-25 shows how four-bit binary values can easily be converted to the equivalent decimal values (binary coded decimal, or BCD).

| DECIMAL NUMBER | WEIGHTED VALUES | | | |
|:---:|:---:|:---:|:---:|:---:|
| | 8 | 4 | 2 | 1 |
| | BINARY NUMBER | | | |
| 0 | 0 | 0 | 0 | 0 |
| 1 | 0 | 0 | 0 | 1 |
| 2 | 0 | 0 | 1 | 0 |
| 3 | 0 | 0 | 1 | 1 |
| 4 | 0 | 1 | 0 | 0 |
| 5 | 0 | 1 | 0 | 1 |
| 6 | 0 | 1 | 1 | 0 |
| 7 | 0 | 1 | 1 | 1 |
| 8 | 1 | 0 | 0 | 0 |
| 9 | 1 | 0 | 0 | 1 |

*Figure 2-25. BCD-to-decimal converter table*

Note that D=8, C=4, B=2, and A=1. By adding any value that has a binary value of 1, numbers 0 to 9 can be realized easily.

Example: Convert binary 1001 to its equivalent decimal number.

Solution:

> *Step 1*. Looking at the weighted values of the BCD-to-decimal converter table, collect the numbers that have 1 under them.
>
> 8 and 1 have a binary value of 1
>
> *Step 2*. Add the weighted values together.
>
> 8 + 1 = 9

Therefore, binary 1001 is equal to decimal 9. It's that easy!

The 7447 BCD-to-Decoder driver circuit can turn on the corresponding segments of the seven-segment LED display based on the binary four-bit data value present at its input pins. The simple diagram in Figure 2-26 shows the binary coded decimal inputs and the seven-segment outputs of the 7447 BCD-to-Decode driver IC to drive a seven-segment LED display.

---

■ **Note**   The industrial name for the 7447 is *BCD-to-Seven-Segment Decoder Driver.*

---

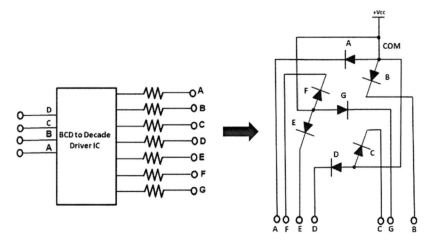

**Figure 2-26.** *The 7447 BCD-to-Decoder Driver IC*

# Build a BCD-to-Decimal Circuit with Seven Segment LED Display

Now, you can upgrade the Mini Digital Roulette game using a seven-segment LED display as oppose to the LED bar display to make reading the numbers easy for the player. The 7447 IC drives the segments based on a four-bit binary count value present at its input pins. A 7490 Decade Counter IC is used to generate the four bits needed for the BCD-to-Decoder driver chip to drive the seven-segment LED display. The 7490 Decader Counter is capable of generating a maximum of 10 count states using the four bit binary pattern shown in Figure 2-25. The Arduino provides the digital clock needed to increment the count values to be display on the seven-segment LED display. Figure 2-27 shows the circuit schematic diagram for the BCD-to-decimal circuit with seven-segment LED display.

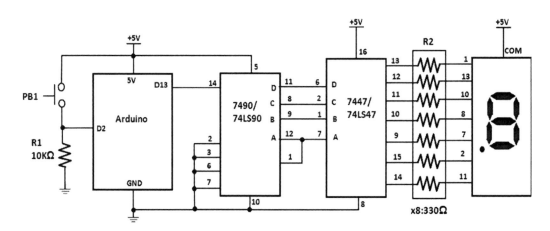

**Figure 2-27.** *Schematic diagram of the BCD-to-decimal circuit with seven-segment LED display*

A push of the PB1 momentary tactile switch starts the count sequence starting at 0. The maximum count shown on the seven-segment LED display is 9 and the count sequence continues to repeat continuously.

---

■ **Note** To make the circuit count continuously, replace the switch and pulldown resistor components with the 10K potentiometer input shown in Figure 2-12. Use the sketch from Listing 2-2. By varying the 10K potentiometer, the circuit's counting will decrease or increase in speed. Enjoy!

---

## Assembly of the Final Circuit on the Breadboard

The assembly of the improved Mini Digital Roulette game is shown in Figure 2-28. As discussed in Chapter 1, maintaining proper component and jumper wire lead lengths will provide clean wiring of the circuit. To plan for clean wiring of the circuit, place the components on the solderless breadboard for best jumper routing. As shown in Figure 2-28, an additional mini solderless breadboard was needed for the other IC components but the circuit didn't grow too extreme in size.

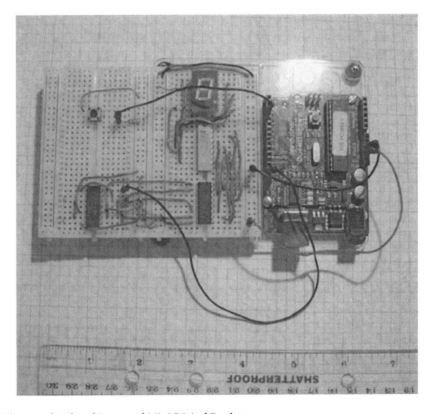

***Figure 2-28.*** *The completed and improved Mini Digital Roulette game*

---

■ **Note**    One long solderless breadboard can be used to accommodate on the ICs for this project instead of two mini boards.

---

## Adding the Mini Digital Roulette Game Software

The sketch for the improved Mini Digital Roulette game is shown in Listing 2-2. The key to using this sketch is pin 13 of the Arduino computing platform; it is used to clock the counter circuit and seven-segment LED display. The speed at which the game can be executed is controlled by the following line of instruction:

```
int blinktime = 20;
 delay(blinktime);
```

By changing the integer value of the variable blinktime, the delay instruction will provide the appropriate switching pulsing needed to drive the 7490 and 7447 digital ICs. As a self discovery exercise, create various switching schemes and record the effects via changing the value for the blinktime variable.

## Final Testing of the Mini Digital Roulette Game

In this chapter, I outlined a product development process such that the Arduino becomes a tool of instruction for learning electronics. As you learned in the previous sections, each interface circuit and output driver device can be tested using basic electronics test equipment such as a DMM and oscilloscope. When each subcircuit works properly, the final stage of testing (with the sketch uploaded to the Arduino) involves validating the appropriate output responses of the final product.

In the case of the Mini Digital Roulette games, the speed in which the LED bar and seven-segment LED displays change the displayed data is dependent upon specific instructions to create delay-based clock pulses. The key feature to observe when testing is the randomness of numbers displayed when the game ends. It's important the same number isn't displayed on both visual displays. Also, the speed at which the game ends should be observed and modified accordingly. A game that ends too quickly will not keep the player interested. On the other hand, if the device is slow in coming to a stop, the player will lose interest with the game. Timing is everything! If the seven-segment LED display shows breaks in segments, check the wiring to assure the IC pins are connected to the optoelectronic device properly. Also, review the sketch entered into the Processing Editor for typos that will cause the Arduino to operate improperly.

## Further Discovery Method Suggestions

To keep the excitement of learning electronics with Arduino burning, I suggest adding a potentiometer to allow the player to adjust the speed at which the game is executed. Figure 2-29 shows the block diagram of the new feature for the game. By pressing the button, the game should execute by incrementing count values on the seven-segment LED display. Releasing the button should result in a number displayed on the optoelectronic device.

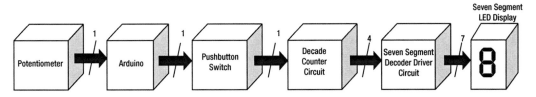

**Figure 2-29.** *New Mini Digital Roulette system block diagram with button feature*

The pressing and releasing of the button should show a different number on the seven-segment display. The self discovery exercise is to create a circuit schematic diagram using the system block diagram shown in Figure 2-2. The sketch in Listing 2-1 can be used to test the new circuit design. Remember to document the design in a spiral notebook along with any sketch modifications you make for the new Mini Digital Roulette game you've created! Good luck!☺

# CHAPTER 3

■ ■ ■

# An Interactive Light Sequencer Device

Creating special effects with the Arduino is fun and easy. By remixing four basic discrete components, you can build two interactive light sequencer devices within an hour and a half. The electronic concepts discussed in the previous chapters will be applied in this chapter along with new items to be discussed. Additional remix techniques in electronics prototyping and software development will be explained in this chapter as well. The required parts are pictured in Figure 3-1.

## Parts List

Arduino Duemilanove or equivalent

LED bar display

2 × 8 330Ω DIP resistor IC

10K trimmer potentiometer

10K resistor

Small solderless breadboard

22AWG solid wire

Digital multimeter

Oscilloscope (optional)

Electronic tools

*Figure 3-1. Parts required for building two interactive light sequencer devices*

# Remix Revisited

As discussed in Chapter 2, the two devices in this chapter illustrate a design technique whereby a new product evolves from a simpler design. This remix design technique allows product designers and developers to get to market quicker without a major tear-up to the BOM. Figures 3-2 and 3-3 show system block diagrams for two interactive light sequencer devices. Also, the software code(sketch) used in the two interactive electronic devices will allow lighting sequence operation of the LED bar display, either by manual or automatic methods of human control.

---

■ **Tip**   Analogous to remix in hardware design is code reuse for software development. We say modified, you say recycled!

---

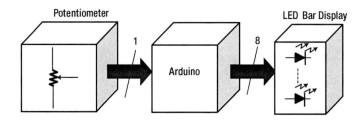

*Figure 3-2. Systems block diagram for an interactive light sequencer device*

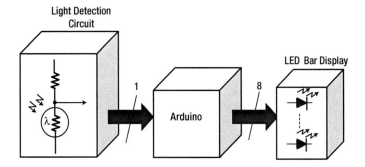

***Figure 3-3.*** *System block diagram for a remixed interactive light sequencer device*

As in Chapters 1 and 2, conducting a deep dive into the system block diagram reveals the circuit schematic diagram of the light sequencer device shown in Figure 3-4 .The control that allows human interaction with the device is the 10KΩ potentiometer. Figure 3-5 shows a remixed interactive light sequencer device version. The light detection circuit used in the electronic singing bird project of Chapter 1 will allow for non-contact interaction with the light sequencer device. The numbers located above the arrows represent the number of pins used between the two blocks.

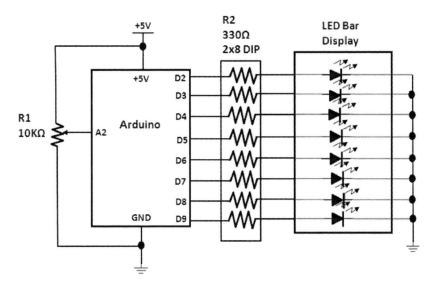

***Figure 3-4.*** *Circuit schematic diagram for a simple interactive light sequencer*

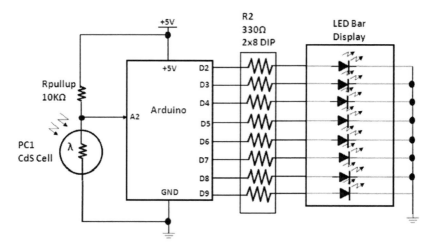

**Figure 3-5.** *Circuit schematic diagram for a remixed interactive light sequencer*

# How It Works

The operation of the interactive light sequencer device consists of an Arduino detecting discrete voltage levels from a simple potentiometer. Upon receiving these continuous analog control signals, the integrated ADC (analog-to-digital converter) will switch the varying input voltage signal to an equivalent digital value consisting of binary digits (1 s and 0s). The sketch programmed into the ATmega328 microcontroller will display the binary data on the LED bar display. The sequence in which the binary data is shown visually on the bar display is part of the programmed software code uploaded to the Arduino using the IDE (integrated development environment) editor. In addition, the potentiometer allows control over the LED bar display patterns. The speed at which the binary data is displayed is controlled by the analog values interpreted from the potentiometer's resistance via shaft position. The higher the potentiometer's resistance value, the slower the switching speed for displaying the binary data sequence. The smaller the potentiometer's resistance value, the faster the binary data will be displayed on the LED bar display. Adjusting the potentiometer's resistance by one-half would provide half-speed switching of binary data displayed by the optoelectronic component.

# The Potentiometer

Before proceeding, the potentiometers' analog input voltage to the ATmega328's ADC will need to be measured with DC voltmeter, I will provide a brief explanation of what a potentiometer is and how it works. Basically, a potentiometer is a variable resistor. Its value can be changed by moving a sliding contact or wiper along its resistive element. A simple schematic symbol of the potentiometer is shown in Figure 3-6. The schematic symbol shows that you can obtain different values of resistance by rotating the mechanical wiper arm along the resistive element. If you rotate the mechanical wiper arm counterclockwise, the resistance values get smaller. If you rotate the mechanical wiper arm clockwise, the resistance values increase.

To help you further understand how the potentiometer works, the Multisim circuit model in Figure 3-7 demonstrates the passive component's operation. If you attaching a DMM and set it to ohmmeter mode, you can read the potentiometer's resistance quite easily. If you connect the black and red tests leads at opposite pins of the component, it will display the total resistance. Keeping the black test lead on the potentiometer's current pin, moving the red test lead to the center pin, and adjusting the mechanical wiper arm (shaft) will cause various resistance values to be displayed on the ohmmeter. If you provide a range of resistance values with one passive electronic component, the Arduino's ATmega328 microcontroller will be able to interpret discrete analog input voltages. In order to provide discrete analog input signals for the Arduino to process, a voltage supply source connected across the potentiometer is required.

As shown in Figure 3-8, the voltage supply source is connected to the outer pins of the potentiometer. The output signal is read between the shaft (traditionally the center pin) and one of the outer pins. When you connect a voltmeter between these respective measuring pins and adjust the shaft, all the discrete voltage levels between the minimum and maximum signal values will be displayed by the voltmeter.

A final key concept behind the potentiometer is its ability to allow interaction between a human and an electronic device. When you twist the potentiometer's shaft, a physical computing action takes place because of a human interacting with the variable resistor's mechanical wiper arm.

Therefore, the potentiometer's shaft becomes the physical extension of the electronic device, allowing interaction with it.

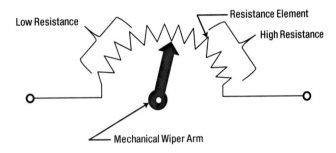

*Figure 3-6. A simple schematic symbol of a potentiometer*

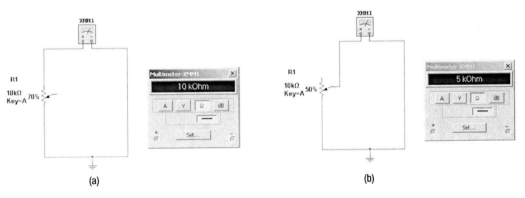

*Figure 3-7. Operation of a potentiometer measuring total resistance with an ohmmeter (a) and adjusted for half range of total resistance (b)*

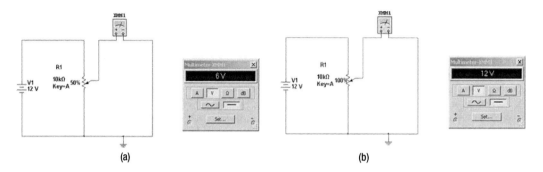

**Figure 3-8.** *Potentiometer used as a voltage divider circuit adjusted for 50 percent of V1 (a) and adjusted for 100 percent of V1 (b)*

---

■ **Tip**  Instead of using a series of resistors to create a voltage divider, use a potentiometer instead.

---

In Chapter 4, physical computing will be explained in more detail. As an experiment and validation for the application of providing analog data to the Arduino's ATmega328 microcontroller using a potentiometer, the following measurement exercise can be performed on the simple interactive light sequencer device.

# Measurement Setup Procedure

The following steps will outline the procedure for obtaining resistance vs. voltage data as it relates to the function of the interactive light sequencer device.

1.  Build the circuit schematic diagram shown previously in Figure 3-4 using the appropriate electronic parts. See Figure 3-9 for a reference prototype.

2.  Create a data table as shown in Figure 3-10.

3.  With the interactive light sequencer device powered on, adjust the sequence switching using the potentiometer for slow LED visual display.

4.  Turn off or remove the power to the device and use an ohmmeter to measure the resistance of the potentiometer across the mechanical wiper arm (center pin) and ground (see Figure 3-11).

5.  Record the measured value (resistance) in the data table.

6.  Turn on or apply power to the device and use a voltmeter to measure the voltage across the mechanical wiper arm (center pin) and ground (see Figure 3-12).

7.  Record the measure value (voltage) in the data table.

8.  Repeat steps 3 through 7 until the data table is complete.

9.  Plot the results from the data table to get a graphical relationship between resistance vs. voltage and the impact on the LED sequence speed (see Figure 3-13).

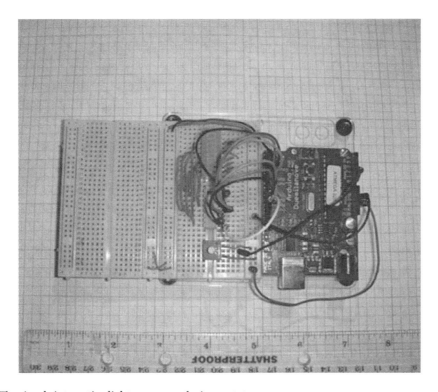

**Figure 3-9.** *The simple interactive light sequencer device prototype*

| Resistance (Ω) | Voltage (V) |
|---|---|
| 10000 | |
| 9000 | |
| 8000 | |
| 7000 | |
| 6000 | |
| 5000 | |
| 4000 | |
| 3000 | |
| 2000 | |
| 1000 | |

Sequence Speed

Slow

Fast

**Figure 3-10.** *Data table: Resistance vs. voltage*

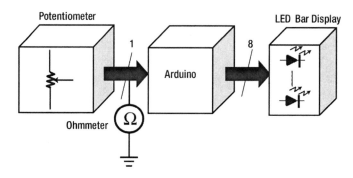

**Figure 3-11.** *Resistance measurement setup (power off)*

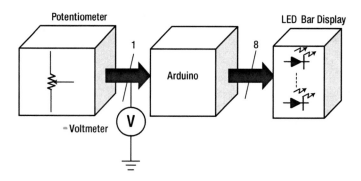

**Figure 3-12.** *Voltage measurement setup (power on)*

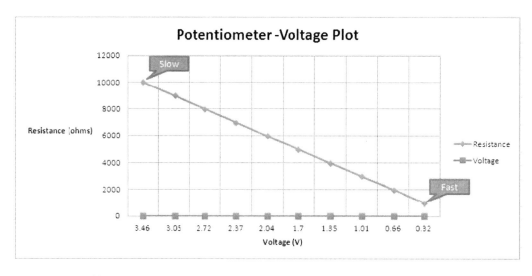

**Figure 3-13.** *Data table results plotted in Excel*

If additional data points are plotted, the LED bar display will reach a point where all segments are visible at the same time. The LEDs are on because of the fast switching speed (frequency) of the Arduino's output ports. Figure 3-14 shows a 54Hz signal generated by one of the microcontroller's digital output pins. As shown in the plot, low voltage relates to fast LED sequence switching and high voltage correspond to low switching speeds.

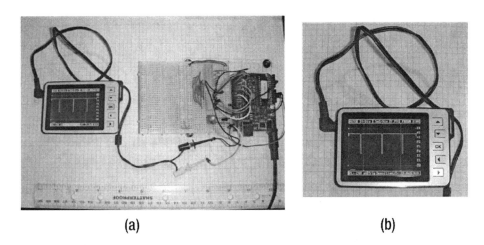

(a)                                                      (b)

*Figure 3-14. Output frequency: Measurement setup (a) and a 54 Hz signal displayed on an oscilloscope (b)*

---

■ **Note**    The LED bar segments being on simultaneously based on a switching frequency of 54Hz is an example of a duty cycle in which the on time is longer than the off time, as shown in Figure 3-14 (b).

---

# How to Drive Multiple LEDs with a Microcontroller

The Arduino is capable of driving LEDs using one output port pin. The ability to drive multiple devices using one pin is known as *fan-out*. The Arduino's ATmega328 microcontroller has a drive current capability of 40mA per I/O pin. Typical LED forward current ratings range from 1 to 20mA. Thus, one output port pin on the ATmega 328 microcontroller can drive two LEDs. If additional LEDs are required, as with the interactive LED sequencer device, the easiest method is to use more output port pins. The secret behind the 40mA drive is a high-current-sourcing output buffer. The output buffer is strong enough to drive 2 LEDs per pin, giving it the ability to operate 16 LEDs using 8 output port pins. The typical circuit used per output port pin of the ATmega328 microcontroller is shown in Figure 3-15. To further increase the output current drive of the ATmega328 microcontroller, a transistor driver circuit can be wired to the respective port pin. See the "Transistor Basics" section of Chapter 1 for more information on biasing and building an LED driver circuit.

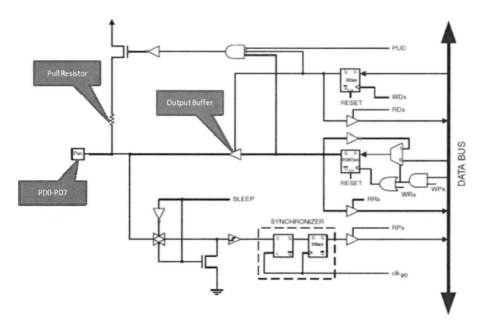

**Figure 3-15.** *Typical output port pin of the ATmega328 microcontroller (courtesy of Atmel datasheet)*

---

■ **Note**   The output buffer is a circuit that prevents an electrical device from loading its input and output pins. Also, the output buffer has the ability to drive an electrical load based on current sourcing. Talk about multitasking!

---

To wire additional LEDs to the Arduino ATmega328 microcontroller, a 1 × 8 single inline header connector is soldered to the PCB (printed circuit board). The microcontroller port used (not only for general digital outputs but inputs) is PD (port D). You can use 22AWG solid wire to easily wire LEDs and transistors to this port. Figure 3-16 shows the wiring diagram of the ATmega328 microcontroller's connection from port D to the 1× 8 single inline header connector.

The technique of building this circuit follows the same principles as explained in the first two chapters of this book: keep the wires short and place the components close to each other. Now, that doesn't mean that the electronic parts should be kissing each other, which can cause short circuits. Wire routing can be achieved using short path lengths. Two prototyping materials that can easily accomplish the wiring requirements mentioned are a *jumper wire kit* and *stranded core wires*. Figure 3-17 shows prototyping wiring products.

---

■ **Tip**   Stranded core wire and precut jumper wires allow prototyping electronic circuits to be built quickly and easily.

---

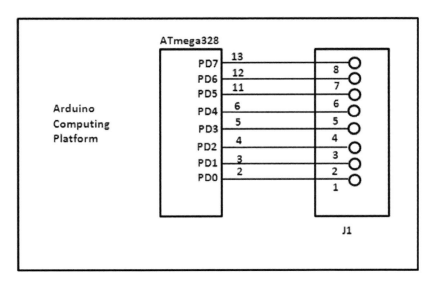

**Figure 3-16.** *Wiring diagram of the Arduino 'sconnection to the J1 connectorAssembly of the Light Sequencer Circuit on a Breadboard*

(a)                                             (b)

**Figure 3-17.** *Wiring prototyping tools for rapid circuit breadboarding: Stranded core wires (a) and a jumper wire kit (b)*

The technique of rapid circuit breadboarding using these two wiring products consists of making electrical connections between the LED bar display and the 330Ω DIP resistor pack with the jumper wire kit. Because the leads are precut and formed, correct placement of these parts on the solderless breadboard requires a little preplanning via a hand-sketch drawing. Figure 3-18 illustrates this preplanning.

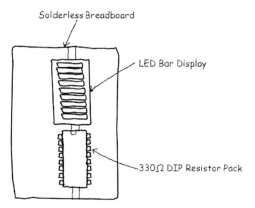

**Figure 3-18.** *A hand sketch of the parts layout The stranded core wires are used to connect the 330Ω DIP resistor to the Arduino. Figure 3-19 illustrates the two wiring techniques used to build the simple interactive LED sequencer device. This is only one example of maintaining good wiring practices; with a little creativity, other techniques can be found.*

**Figure 3-19.** *The simple interactive LED sequencer device built with stranded core wires and a jumper wire kit*

# Building the Remixed Interactive LED Sequencer Device

The remix design of the interactive LED sequencer device has the same core electronic components as the original device, with one exception: the potentiometer is replaced with a light detection circuit. The light detection circuit, discussed in Chapter 1, is used to remove the manual control of the potentiometer, and in its place is an automatic method of operating the device. So, the circuit breadboard build is the same as the original device, but the potentiometer is substituted for a voltage divider circuit consisting of a 10K pull-up resistor in series with a CdS photocell. The operation is the same as the simple LED sequencer device. The bar display will move back and forth like the robotic eyes of a Cylon in the *Battlestar Galactica* TV series (I used to watch TV). With ambient light present, the scan, or switching-sequence, rate is moderate. As the light increases, the rate also increases. Placing an object in front of the CdS photocell will decrease the scan speed of the LED bar display. This method of fast and slow scan-sequence behavior follows the same functional trend shown in the Excel plot shown previously in Figure 3-13. Figure 3-20 shows the prototype build of the remixed interactive LED light sequencer device. Refer to Figure 3-5 for the complete circuit schematic diagram.

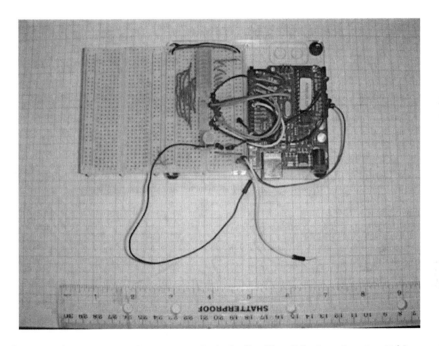

***Figure 3-20.*** *The remixed interactive LED sequencer device built with a light detection circuit (shown at the bottom of the solderless breadboard)*

---

■ **Note** The ATmega328 microcontroller has an ADC that takes the continuously variable analog voltages generated by the light detection circuit and digitizes them (converts them into a bit stream). The sketch uploaded to the microcontroller will turn on the right output port (PD) pins to operate the LED bar display. The ATmega328 is a beast!

---

# Creating the Sequential-Switching Software

Now that you have built the hardware, it's time to bring your electronic creation to life with some embedded software. As discussed in the "How It Works" section of this chapter, the sketch will read the analog voltage value of either the potentiometer or the CdS photocell, and will convert or digitize it into an equivalent binary bit pattern. Also, the sketch will use this data to create the appropriate delay for switching each discrete LED segment of the bar display. Therefore, the sketch is a dual-purpose piece of embedded software with the ability to read analog devices such as potentiometers and CdS cells and control digital outputs of the Arduino's ATmega328 microcontroller. Listing 3-1 is the interactive LED light sequencer sketch for both prototype circuits.

***Listing 3-1.*** The Interactive LED Light Sequencer Sketch (Code)

```
// Create array for LED pins
byte ledPin[] = {2, 3, 4, 5, 6, 7, 8, 9};
int ledDelay; // delay between changes
int direction = 1;
int currentLED = 0;
unsigned long changeTime;
int potPin = 2; // select the input pin for the potentiometer

void setup() {
// set all pins to output
for (int x = 0; x < 10; x++) {
pinMode(ledPin[x], OUTPUT); }
changeTime = millis();
}

void loop() {
// read the value from the pot
ledDelay = analogRead(potPin);
// if it has been ledDelay ms since last change

if ((millis() - changeTime) >
ledDelay) {
changeLED();
changeTime = millis();
}
}
void changeLED() {
// turn off all LEDs
for (int x = 0; x < 10; x++) {
digitalWrite(ledPin[x], LOW);
}
// turn on the current LED
digitalWrite(ledPin[currentLED], HIGH);

// increment by the direction value
currentLED + = direction;
// change direction if we reach the end

if (currentLED == 9) {direction =
-1;}
if (currentLED == 0) {direction = 1;}
}
```

Key sketch snippets to experiment with are explained following.

The following section of code defines all the variables related to the GPIO (general-purpose inputs/outputs) of the Arduino's ATmega328 microcontroller:

```
// Create array for LED pins
byte ledPin[] = {2, 3, 4, 5, 6, 7, 8, 9};
int ledDelay; // delay between changes
int direction = 1;
int currentLED = 0;
unsigned long changeTime;
int potPin = 2; // select the input pin for the potentiometer
```

The first line of code defines what digital pins of the microcontroller are used for controlling the LED bar display.

```
byte ledPin[] = {2, 3, 4, 5, 6, 7, 8, 9};
```

The sequence or order is based on how the pins are read into the array ledPin[ ]. By changing the order of the pins, you can create various lighting-sequence patterns with the Arduino.

---

■ **Note** An array is a software collection of variable data that can be obtained through an index. The index is the number inside of the brackets that stores the target data.

---

You can get the analog data from the potentiometer or CdS photocell by following this line of code:

```
int potPin = 2; // select the input pin for the potentiometer
```

If a different analog pin is needed, simply change it within the int potPin code. The delay between each discrete instance of the LED of the bar display switching on and off is controlled by the following code:

```
ledDelay = analogRead(potPin);
```

The ATmega328 microcontroller has eight ADC channels, but only six of them are accessible on the Arduino computing platform PCB inline header connector. The ADC is a 10-bit circuit capable of reading a range of voltages from 0 to 5V. Therefore, a 10-bit ADC has an integer range of 0 to 1023. The low value of 0 represents 0V, and the integer 1023 represents 5V. The *resolution*, or number of digitized steps, represented in volts per unit, can easily be calculated by taking the maximum input voltage that the ADC can read and dividing it by its integer value equivalent. Thus, the ATmega328 microcontroller has a resolution of 4.9 mV per unit. The calculation is shown here:

Resolution = volts / units

Known:

volts = 5 V

units = 1023

Therefore:

Resolution = 5 / 1023

Resolution = 0.0049 V or 4.9 mV/units

The circuit schematic block diagram for the ADC is shown in Figure 3-21.

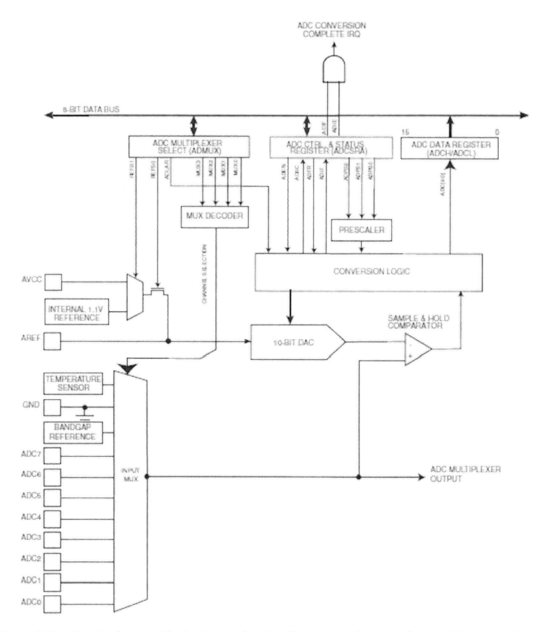

***Figure 3-21.*** *Circuit schematic block diagram for the ATmega328 microcontroller ADC (courtesy of Atmel datasheet)*

---

■ **Note**   The maximum integer value for the ATmega328 microcontroller ADC is calculated by $2^n$, where $n$ equals 10. Therefore, $2^{10}$ equals 1028. Imagine that!

---

The scan-sequence direction of the LED bar display can be changed by reversing the original lines of code instruction:

```
if (currentLED == 9) {direction = -1;}
if (currentLED == 0) {direction = 1;}
```

to the following:

```
if (currentLED == 0) {direction = 1;}
if (currentLED == 9) {direction = -1;}
```

In the chapters to follow, I will present a style guide that explains in detail how all the Arduino sketches on the Web are written. So for now, experiment with the code snippets you've examined and document the effects on the Arduino in a lab notebook.

# Final Testing of the Interactive Light Sequencer Device

This chapter outlined a series of mini activities to illustrate the ease of building an interactive light sequencer device. You can use a DMM to obtain voltage data for plotting the potentiometer's resistance to the scan rate of the LED Bargraph display. An oscilloscope wired to the circuit will show you the scan rate signal. Make sure the wiring is correct prior to applying voltage to the Arduino and supporting circuits.

- Use proper wiring methods.

- Verify that the circuit breadboard is working correctly (the "How it Works" section of this chapter is a great reference).

- Review the sketch entered into the Arduino IDE editor for typos that could cause the hardware device to operate improperly.

# Further Discovery Methods

There are quite a few activities that you can investigate for the two projects in this chapter. The first is changing the functional behavior of the remixed interactive LED sequencer device so that its scan speed increases in darkness, instead of when light is present. Second, as shown in Figure 3-5, you can change the wiring positions of the 10K resistor and the CdS photocell to have the LED sequence speed slow down in ambient (normal) light. The scan sequence speed should increase when the ambient light is removed. Third, you can create new lighting patterns by changing the order of how the array reads the digital data from the Arduino pins, as discussed earlier in the chapter. Finally, you can change the direction of the new lighting pattern. Remember to document the design in a lab notebook along with the sketch modifications you made for the new sequence lighting patterns you created.

■ ■ ■

# CHAPTER 4

# Physical Computing and DC Motor Control

Controlling a DC motor is quite easy using an Arduino. There are various ways to interact with a motor besides using an electric switch. Also, you can easily replace the conventional electromechanical relay with a suitably chosen transistor, allowing the speed to be controlled by software. This chapter will explore various ways of controlling a DC motor using conventional electromechanical switching by a relay, as well as solid state control using a transistor. Also, the conventional method of varying speed using a potentiometer will be investigated, along with a force sensitive resistor. Both the potentiometer and the photocell can be categorized as *physical computing* input devices. Therefore, I'll present a discussion in this chapter as well. I'll apply the electronic concepts discussed in the previous chapters in this unit along with the new items to be discussed. I'll also explain additional remix techniques in electronics prototyping and software development in this chapter. The required parts are listed following and pictured in Figure 4-1.

## Parts Lists

Arduino Duemilanove or equivalent

TIP31C NPN Power Transistor or TIP120 NPN Darlington Transistor

2N2222 NPN Transistor

10K trimmer potentiometer

2 10K resistors

1K resistor

CdS photocell

Tactile push-button switch

1N4001 diode

3VDC or 6VDC motor

16-pin IC socket

+5VDC electromechanical relay

Small solderless breadboard

22 AWG solid wires

Digital multimeter

Oscilloscope (optional)

Electronic tools

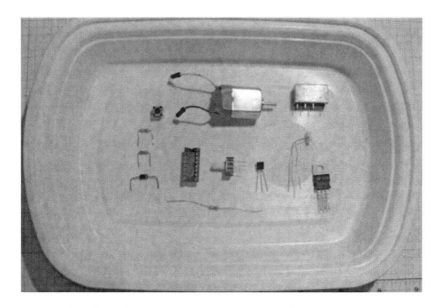

*Figure 4-1. Parts required for phyiscal-computing and DC motor control projects*

# Remixing Revisited

As discussed in Chapter 2, the two devices in this chapter illustrate a design technique where one new product evolves from a simpler design. This *remix* design technique allows product designers and developers to get to market quicker without a major tear-up to the BOM. Figures 4-2 and 4-3 show systems block diagrams for two physical-computing DC motor controllers. Also, the sketch used in the two interactive electronic devices will allow speed control operation of the DC motor by either manual or automatic methods for human control.

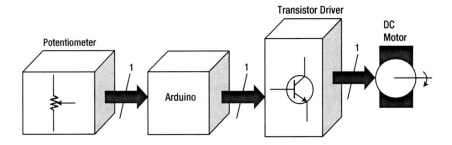

**Figure 4-2.** *A physical-computing DC motor control systems block diagram*

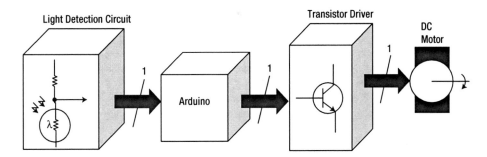

**Figure 4-3.** *A remixed physical-computing DC motor control systems block diagram*

# How It Works

Before transistors were used as direct electronic circuit drivers, electromechanical relays provided the means to control heavy current-drawn electrical loads. I will begin the discussion of physical-computing DC motor control with a hands-on exploration of a transistor relay driver circuit. Figure 4-4 shows a system block diagram of a basic transistor relay driver circuit.

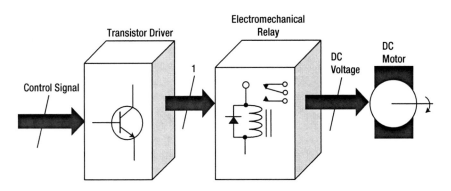

**Figure 4-4.** *A typical transistor relay driver block diagram*

A circuit schematic diagram for a typical transistor relay driver block diagram is shown in Figure 4-5.

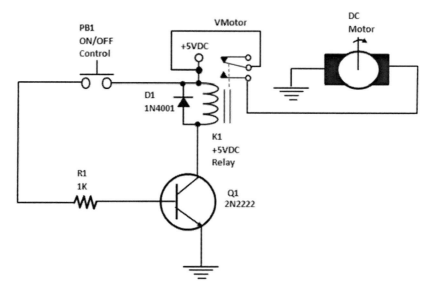

**Figure 4-5.** *Circuit schematic diagram for a typical transistor relay driver*

---

■ **Tip**   An electromechanical relay is an electrically operated switch. Awesome!!!

---

## A Base Biasing Transistor Driver Circuit

When you press switch PB1, current flows through resistor R1, allowing the transistor to be biased. This type of transistor current management is known as *base biasing*. This biasing scheme is quite simple because of a single resistor connected in series with a +5VDC power supply and the base circuit of the transistor. The current flowing through the resistor is sufficient to turn the NPN transistor on or put it into a saturation mode of operation. To calculate the biasing or base current for the transistor driver circuit, the following analysis equation may be used:

$$I_B = (V_{CC} - V_{BE}) / R_B$$

where

- $I_B$ is the base current.
- $V_{CC}$ is the collector supply voltage.
- $V_{BE}$ is the base-emitter junction voltage.
- $R_B$ is the base resistor ($R_1$ is equal to $R_B$ in this design).

Using Figure 4-5 and the preceding equation, you can determine $I_B$. The following exercise demonstrates the steps you need to take to do this:

1. First, write down the original analysis equation:

$$I_B = (V_{CC} - V_{BE}) / R_B$$

2. Next, substitute circuit parameter values into the analysis equation:

$$I_B = (5VDC - 0.7V) / 1K$$

3. Finally, solve for $I_B$:

$$I_B = 4.3VDC / 1K$$

$$I_B = 0.0043A \text{ or } 4.3mA$$

Using Multisim circuit simulation software, you can easily build a virtual transistor circuit. With the electrical switch opened, the base current is very small (in the magnitude of picoAmperes [pA]), keeping the electromechanical relay deenergized, as shown in Figure 4-6 (a). The 69.8Ω resistor represents the electromechanical relay coil's resistance if measured with an ohmmeter. Closing the electrical switch allows the transistor to be biased and the electromechanical relay to be energized. Figure 4-6 (b) illustrates base biasing of the transistor.

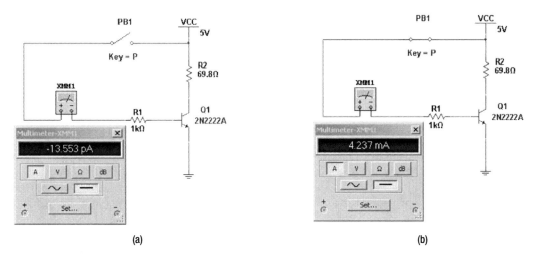

(a)                                    (b)

*Figure 4-6.* *Multisim circuit transistor driver models: Unbiased transistor (a) and base-biased operation (b)*

---

■ **Tip** Based on the electromechanical relay manufacturer, the coil's resistance value will vary.

---

With the transistor in saturation mode, current from the+5VDC power supply will flow through the electromechanical relay's coil and the collector-emitter leads of the NPN transistor (2N2222) to ground. The current flowing through the electromechanical relay's coil will put it in a conductive mode known as *energization*. The current flowing through the electromechanical relay coil windings establishes a magnetic field, thereby allowing it to attract the armature (moveable contact) of the component. The relay coil's magnetic field is enhanced with a solid iron core, allowing it to provide strong contact attraction with the armature. Because the armature is attracted by the coil's magnetic field, it makes contact with the NO contact of the electromechanical relay. The Vmotor power supply (+5VDC) is now switched into the external control circuit, allowing current to flow through the DC motor, turning it on.

Releasing switch PB1 will provide an open circuit to the base, allowing removal of current biasing to the NPN transistor. As the electric current is removed from the coil, the electromechanical relay's contacts will be switched off, or deenergized. The magnetic field produced through the energizing is now removed, thus allowing the armature to return to its NC position contact. The external control circuit is switched off, stopping the DC motor from rotating. A last note about the electromechanical relay is that contacts have an *ampacity* rating, which allows them to switch high-current devices such as incandescent bulbs and low-horsepower motors. The electromechanical relay contacts have ampacity ratings as low as 1A and can go as high as 10A. Therefore, the Arduino can be used in implementing industrial control applications on the bench quite easily.

## D1: Flyback Diode

The electromechanical relay coil is basically an inductor capable of storing electric current through its windings. Upon energizing and deenergizing the coil, the inductor charges and discharges accordingly. When the electromechanical relay coil is deenergized, the energy (electric current) that's stored must be released or discharged through a grounding circuit. The grounding circuit in the case of a relay driver circuit is the transistor. The magnitude of electric current stored in the relay coil is maximum in value ($I_p$ [peak current]) and can cause severe damage to sensitive electronic components when discharging or releasing the energy to a grounding surface.

The transistor is providing a ground path for the electromechanical relay and therefore can be damaged by this maximum $I_p$ value. The diode placed across the coil helps to redirect this electrical energy back through the relay windings using a *flyback* method for electric current suppression. The flyback method allows the diode to absorb the peak current created by the inductor during the charging cycle, as well as that of the coil during deenergization of the electromechanical relay. At the moment the transistor turns off, during the deenergization mode of the electromechanical relay, the diode becomes forward biased, redirecting the peak current away from the transistor and allowing it to flow through the coil of the electromechanical switch.

Other names for a flyback diode are *snubber, freewheeling, suppressor,* and *catch* diode. Figure 4-7 shows the Multisim circuit model of an electromechanical relay coil with a flyback diode wired in parallel with it. Figure 4-7 (a) shows the relay being energized (inductor charging) while Figure 4-7 (b) shows it in the deenergized condition (the inductor discharging). The peak current is significant in magnitude and electrical units (in mA) compared to energization of the coil (in nA).

---

■ **Note** Flyback is the return to the starting or original point, and ampacity is the maximum amount of current flowing in a conductor (wire) before it causes damage.

---

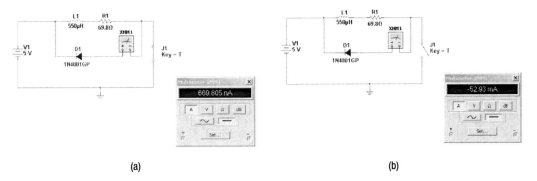

*Figure 4-7.* Multisim circuit transistor driver models: inductor charging (relay coil energized), inductor discharging (relay coil de-energized).Unbiased transistor (a) and based-biased operation (b).

## Experimenting with a Transistor Relay Driver DC Motor Control Circuit

A transistor relay driver DC motor control circuit is quite easy to build using the Arduino. The Arduino will provide the intelligent processing interface between receiving a control signal from a tactile push-button switch and commanding the transistor relay driver to operate a DC motor. Figure 4-8 shows the circuit schematic diagram of the simple DC motor control device. The circuit is a remix of the transistor relay driver circuit used in the electronic singing bird from Chapter 1, with the exception of the input interface. As stated, the tactile push-button switch is used to provide the control signal to the Arduino instead of the light detection circuit used in the bird project. The button sketch used in the bird project is uploaded to the Arduino, allowing the DC motor to be switched on by the transistor relay driver circuit.

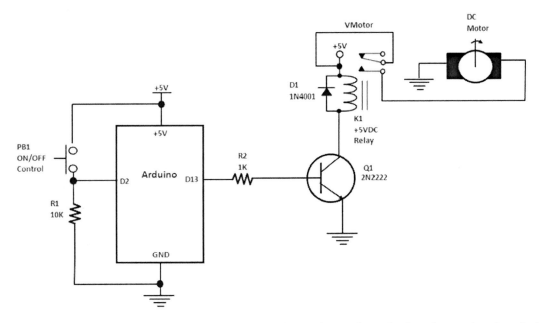

*Figure 4-8.* The Arduino computing platform provides the electrical control signal to bias the transistor-based relay driver to turn on the DC motor.

It's time to further elaborate on the physical-computing attributes of the DC motor control circuit. The resistor, along with tactile push-button switch, is considered an input *transducer*, or *sensor*, because of the conversion between *mechanical action* (pressing the internal contacts of the switch with a mini-plunger-spring assembly) and generating a digital-level *electrical* control signal (+5VDC or binary 1 logic level). Upon release of the button on the tactile switch, the mini-plunger-spring assembly allows it to return to its normal position, and the binary 1 logic level control signal transitions to a 0 logic level signal.

The arrangement of the tactile push-button switch preceding the 10K resistor is known as an *active-high* digital input circuit. If the inverse or opposite transducer function is needed, switching the push-button switch and the 10K resistor will achieve this requirement. The name for this inverted electrical control signal function is known as an *active-low* digital input circuit.

Figure 4-9 shows the Multisim circuit model analysis via output voltage results displayed on a digital voltmeter. Figure 4-10 shows an Arduino-based physical-computing DC motor control with an active-low digital input circuit. An active-high digital input circuit for the Arduino-based physical-computing DC Control is shown in Figure 4-11.

---

■ **Note**    The electromechanical relay is classified as a potential digital output transducer because it converts electrical energy into a mechanical switch.

---

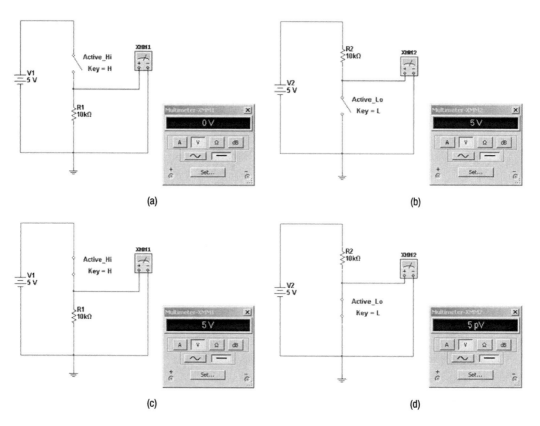

(a)                                                (b)

(c)                                                (d)

*Figure 4-9. An active-high digital input circuit voltage with the switch open and an active-low digital input circuit voltage with the switch open (b). The measured voltages are inverted between an active-high and an active-low digital input circuit.*

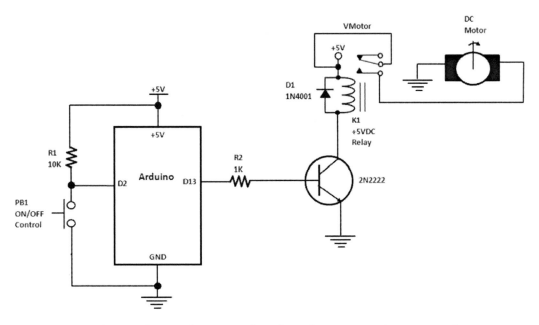

**Figure 4-10.** *Circuit schematic diagram for an active-low physical-computing DC motor control*

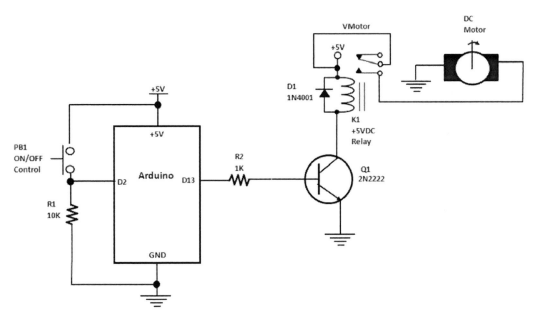

**Figure 4-11.** *Circuit schematic diagram for an active-high physical-computing DC motor control*

## Electromechanical Relay Preparation

A method that will aid in wiring the electromechanical relay is to write the pinout on both sides of the component with a black marker, as shown in Figure 4-12. The pinout of the electromechanical relay is shown in Chapter 1. While prototyping the basic physical-computing DC motor control circuits on the solderless breadboard, you can improve the +5VDC electromechanical relay pins' contact insertion with the embedded spring terminals. By inserting the electromechanical relay into an IC socket, you enhance the electrical pins' contact force and remove the possibility of circuit intermittence from the project build. Figure 4-13 illustrates this technique.

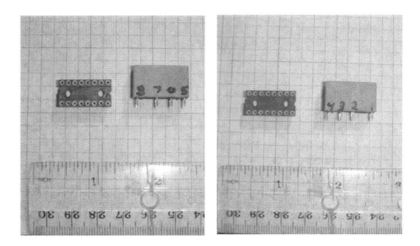

*Figure 4-12. Pinout written on both sides of the electromechanical relay*

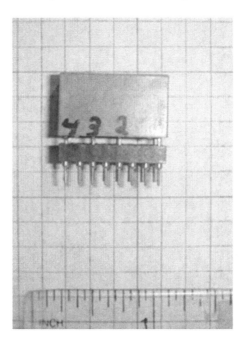

*Figure 4-13. An IC socket used to improve the insertion of the electromechanical relay onto the solderless breadboard*

Since few components are required for the project build, you can place them close together, as shown Figure 4-14. The technique of using stranded core wire and preformed jumper wires helps to manage the wiring of the circuit on the breadboard and to the Arduino. The Arduino board provides the +5VDC supply to power both the control circuit and the DC motor.

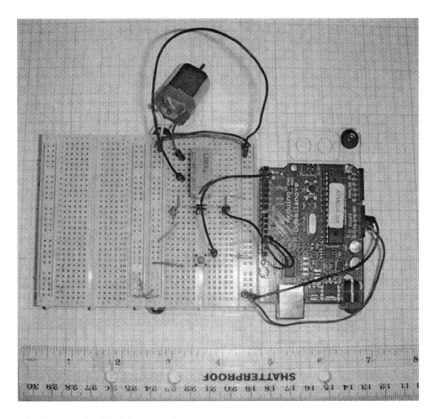

***Figure 4-14.*** *The final project build of the control circuit*

The project shown in Figure 4-14 is wired as an active-high digital input circuit. Press and hold the tactile push-button switch, allowing the Arduino to provide an output control signal (approximately +5VDC); this will bias the 2N2222 NPN transistor to drive the electromechanical relay. The contacts of the electromechanical relay will switch from the NC position to NO, allowing the +5VDC power supply to switch on the DC motor. Releasing the button will remove the biasing current from the transistor relay driver circuit, and the +5VDC power supply source will be interrupted from the DC motor, stopping it from rotating. As mentioned earlier, the button sketch from the electronic singing bird project from Chapter 1 is uploaded to the Arduino for input monitoring and output switching (biasing) control for this physical-computing device.

---

■ **Note**    Before wiring the circuits schematic diagrams shown, go to the section "The 2N2222 Transistor Pinout" in this chapter for the 2N2222 NPN transistor pinout information.

---

# The Basics of Physical Computing with Electric Motors

In the first several pages of this chapter, the concept of controlling a DC motor with a transducer (or sensor), microcontroller, and transistor relay driver was illustrated with simulated circuits and a physical control project. Using an electromechanical relay is a traditional approach to driving electric motors because they relay's switching contacts are capable of handling several amperes of current. Electric motors are really electromechanical devices because they take an electrical signal (voltage and/or current) and convert it to mechanical motion. To overcome the mechanics of rotation, a high *inrush* current is required from the power supply driving the electromechanical part.

In the example of the simple physical-computing DC motor control project discussed, the electromechanical relay had the burden of providing the power supply current using a pair of high-ampacity-rated contacts. But there is another alternative for controlling an electric motor: using a power transistor instead of an electromechanical relay. Torque and speed are two important parameters associated with electric motors, and the device that drives them must be capable of controlling these elements efficiently. A microcontroller, along with a power transistor, provides an efficient and clean approach to maintaining constant torque and speed control for electric motors.

The embedded software inside the Arduino has a specialized computing/mathematical approach, using a tested procedure (algorithm) for maintaining torque and speed control for electric motors. An algorithm is simply a step-by-step procedure for calculations The output of the electric motor is constantly monitored by the microcontroller using a feedback transducer/sensor, which provides voltage or current signal data as it relates to the electromechanical device's torque and/or speed. The embedded software of the microcontroller constantly checks to see if the signal data has deviated, and if so, makes adjustments to the output signal that's controlling the circuit driving it. So, to some extent, the transducer or sensor that's monitoring the output parameters of the motor is providing indirect physical-computing activity to the electric motor. Figure 4-15 shows a typical system block diagram for a physical computing–based DC motor controller.

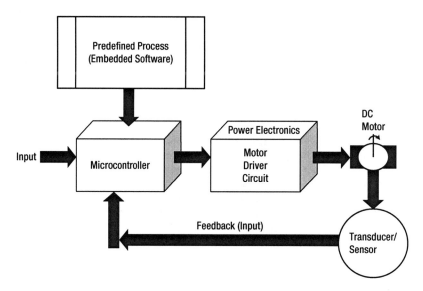

***Figure 4-15.*** *System block diagram for the DC motor control*

■ **Note** Physical computing deals with building devices that can sense and respond to their environment using software and hardware.

# Achieving Motor Speed Control with Physical Computing

The discussions in this chapter have been on simple control of DC motors—basically turning them on and off. The remainder of this chapter will explore controlling the speed of the motor using physical-computing techniques. You will be using potentiometer and photocell as input sensor circuits for interacting with the DC motor.

## Potentiometer Input Control

The first technique requires using a potentiometer (discussed in Chapter 3) to provide an input signal that directs the microcontroller to adjust its output control signal to bias the transistor through modulation. The modulation is accomplished by changing the pulse width of the output control signal generated by the Arduino's ATmega328 microcontroller. The technique of pulse width modulation (PWM; discussed in Chapter 1) allows for controlling the speed of a DC motor through a transistor. Switching the base at a predetermined frequency allows for the transistor to provide an average sourcing current to the DC motor's stator for efficient speed control of the electromechanical component. Figure 4-16 shows a typical DC motor speed control technique using the Arduino as the PWM signal generator.

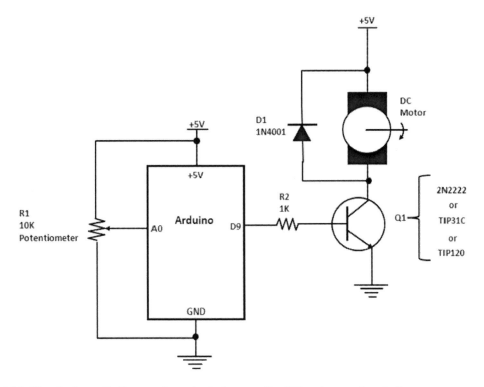

***Figure 4-16.*** *Circuit schematic diagram for a physical-computing DC motor speed controller*

The construction of the circuit on the solderless breadboard has minimum component and wiring content. Also, there are only two jumper wires from the potentiometer and the base of the 2N2222 to the Arduino single inline header connectors. Figure 4-17 shows the final motor speed controller prototype.

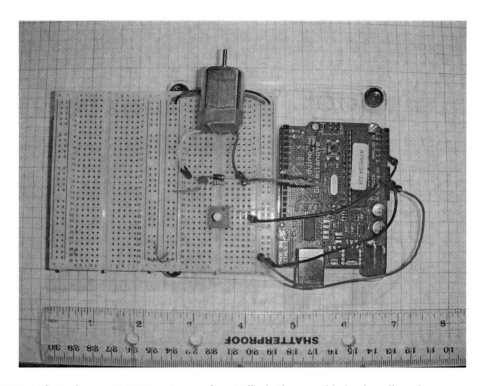

*Figure 4-17. A physical-computing DC motor speed controller built on a solderless breadboard*

The motor speed control, as discussed earlier, takes place through the 10KΩ potentiometer. Adjusting it will allow the Arduino's ATmega328 microcontroller to provide a smooth string of pulses that will bias the 2N2222 transistor to efficiently drive the small DC motor. To see the PWM signal, you must connect an oscilloscope at the base of the transistor driver and attach the other test lead to ground. Figure 4-18 illustrates how an oscilloscope is connected to the 2N2222 NPN transistor's base lead. The actual measurement setup is shown in Figure 4-19. The duty cycle (discussed in Chapter 1) for the adjusted motor speed was measured at 38.81 percent. When the potentiometer's shaft is rotated, the duty cycle value changes proportional to the amount of resistance. As the potentiometer's resistance increases, the duty cycle value becomes larger. At full resistance (10KΩ), the duty cycle value is at 100 percent with the small DC motor running at full-rated speed.

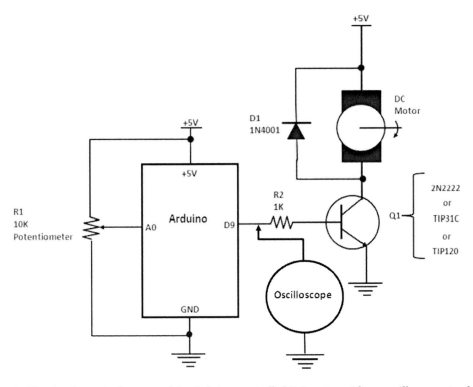

**Figure 4-18.** *Circuit schematic diagram of the Arduino controlled DC motor with an oscilloscopes to observe the PWM signals*

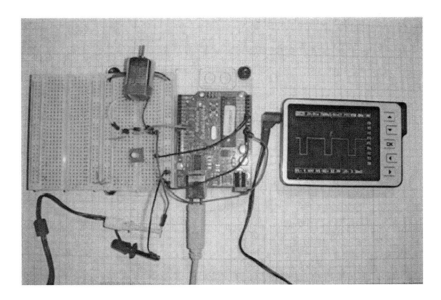

**Figure 4-19.** *Circuit schematic diagram showing how to attach an oscilloscope to observe the PWM signals generated by the Arduino*

Figure 4-20 shows a close-up of the Arduino-produced PWM control signal in which you can see a series of clean, square-wave pulses.

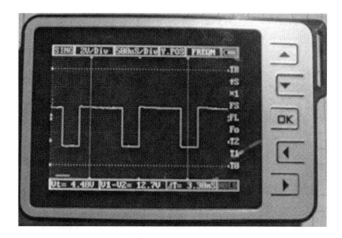

***Figure 4-20.*** *The Arduino-produced PWM control signal for motor speed control*

## The 2N2222 Transistor Pinout

An important item to note is that all NPN transistors are not created equal. The 2N3904 NPN transistor's pinout (from the "Assembly of the Electronic Singing Bird Circuit on a Breadboard" section of Chapter 1) consists of the emitter being located to the *left* of the three-pin device. The base is the *center* lead, and the collector is located to the immediate *right*. For the 2N2222 transistor, the emitter is on the right side and collector is on the left side. Figure 4-21 shows the pinout for the 2N2222 transistor that will ensure proper operating function of this speed control circuit, as well as the simple motor control project.

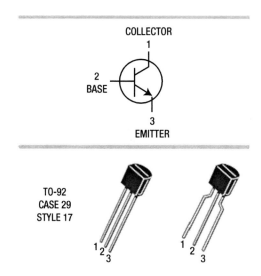

***Figure 4-21.*** *Pinout diagram for the 2N2222 NPN transistor (courtesy of ON Semiconductor datasheet)*

# The Motor Speed Control Software

With the electronics hardware in place, the sketch is needed to complete the project build. The sketch allows the Arduino to read the potentiometer's analog position and generates a PWM signal that is proportional to the angular location of the wiper arm. The sketch is well commented, so changes to the analog or digital port pins can easily be made. Listing 4-1 shows the motor speed control sketch.

***Listing 4-1.*** The Motor Speed Control Sketch

```
int motorPin = 9;    // motor connected to digital pin 9
int analogPin = 0;   // potentiometer connected to analog pin 0
int val = 0;         // variable to store the read value
void setup()
{
  pinMode(motorPin, OUTPUT);  // sets the pin as output
}
void loop()
{
  val = analogRead(analogPin);  // read the input pin
  analogWrite(motorPin, val / 4); // analogRead values go from 0 to 1023, analogWrite ➥
  values from 0 to 255
}
```

Here's a final note regarding the operation of the physical computing–based controller: after uploading the motor speed control sketch to the Arduino, depending on the position of the 10KΩ potentiometer, the electromechanical device may start at low, medium, or high speed.

## Light Detection Input Control

In the final project build in exploring human interaction and control with the physical world, we'll adjust the DC motor's speed using a light. The light detection input control is similar to the potentiometer shown in Figure 4-3, with one exception: no contact with a sensing device is required in order to change the speed of the DC motor. A proportional voltage based on the CdS photocell resistance provides the appropriate duty cycle of the PWM output control signal from the Arduino computing platform. With ambient light present, placing an object (such as hand) over the CdS photocell will increase the DC motor's speed. If the light sensor detects no object, the DC motor will spin at a medium rate. If a light source shines on the sensor, the DC motor will stop completely. Figure 4-22 shows the circuit schematic diagram of the light-activated DC motor speed controller.

The motor speed control sketch remains the same, with the exception that the 10KΩ potentiometer is replaced by the light detection circuit shown in the circuit schematic diagram of Figure 4-22. The final project build is shown in Figure 4-23. The placement and orientation of the CdS photocell is optimum because of the quick response the Arduino computing platform provides in adjusting the DC motor speed based on varying light levels detected. The speed ramp-up and ramp-down based on the change in ambient lighting is quite smooth, with little to no hesitation in motor acceleration adjustment.

---

■ **Note** As shown in the circuit schematic diagrams, the only difference between the TIP31C NPN transistor and the TIP120 Darlington NPN transistor is that in the latter, the semiconductor device collector can manage current as high as 8A peak, while the former component can only handle up to 5A peak. The TIP120 is a tiger!

---

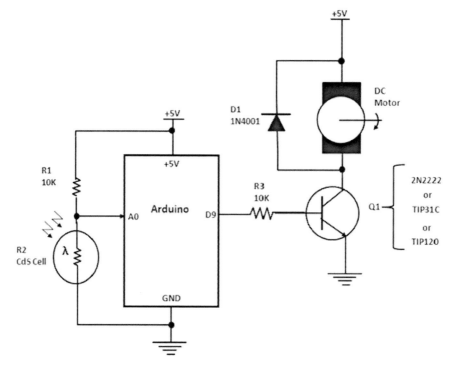

*Figure 4-22.* *Circuit schematic diagram for a light-activated DC motor speed controller*

*Figure 4-23.* *Final project build of the light-activated DC motor speed controller*

# Final Testing of the Devices

This chapter outlined a series of testing activities for capturing bugs in building the hardware circuits. Using a DMM and an oscilloscope, the testing techniques described can be validated on the bench. Depending on the type of vendor of the testing instruments, the results may vary by +/-10 percent. While testing, make sure the wiring is correct prior to applying voltage to the Arduino and supporting circuits. Use proper wiring methods, as discussed in Chapter 3. The "How it Works" section of this chapter is a great reference to help you verify that the circuit breadboard is working correctly. Also, review the sketch entered into the Arduino IDE editor for typos that could cause the hardware device to operate improperly as well.

# Further Discovery Methods

There are quite a few activities that you might investigate for the two projects in this chapter. The first is to change the functional behavior of the simple DC motor control using a transistor relay driver circuit. Instead of controlling the device with an active-high switch, use an active-low digital input configuration. Figure 4-10 earlier in the chapter shows the wiring roadmap for the investigation.

In the second activity, change the wiring positions of the 10K resistor and the CdS photocell to have the motor speed increase in ambient (normal) light as shown in Figure 4-21. Also change the 2N2222 transistor to either a TIP31C or TIP120 transistor, and use a higher operating current and voltage-rated DC motor, and note the speed control behavior. Remember to document the design in a lab notebook along with sketch modifications you made for the new DC motor speed controller you've created.

# CHAPTER 5

■ ■ ■

# Motion Control with an Arduino: Servo and Stepper Motor Controls

As explained in Chapter 4, there are several control schemes for operating a DC motor using an Arduino. This chapter extends the discussion of electric motor control to servo and stepper electromechanical devices. The Arduino's ATmega328 microcontroller has dedicated port pins for providing digital signals to control the speed and direction of servo and stepper motors. In this chapter, I explain the conventional method of varying speed using a potentiometer or joystick, along with an introduction to the FlexiForce sensor. The potentiometer, joystick, and the FlexiForce sensor are important tools in many Physical Computing projects and are used here to introduce the concept of motion control. You will use remix techniques in prototyping and writing software for the electronic projects in this chapter. The required parts you will need to build the experiments and projects are pictured in Figure 5-1.

## Parts List

1 Arduino Duemilanove or equivalent

1 10K potentiometer

1 470K resistor

1 FlexiForce sensor

3 servo motors (1small, 1 medium, 1 continuous [not shown])

1 ULN2803A Darlington Array IC

1 unipolar stepper motor (six-wire type)

1 joystick

1 small solderless breadboard

22 AWG solid wire

Digital multimeter

Oscilloscope (optional)

Electronic tools

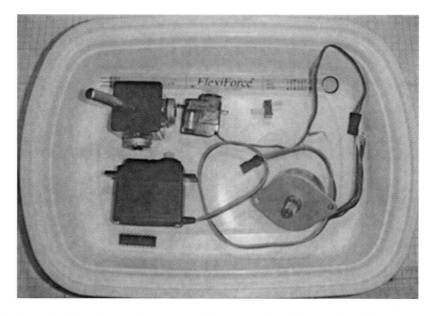

*Figure 5-1. Parts required for motion control servo and stepper motor projects and experiments*

# Remixing Motion Controls

I am continuing with the technique of remix, and I am using four motion control devices with two input controls to illustrate how to create motion controls with the Arduino. The potentiometer and FlexiForce sensor are used to vary the speed and/or direction of both the stepper and servo motor components. The Arduino provides the intelligence to the motion control platforms by reading the input voltage level from either the potentiometer or FlexiForce sensor and providing the appropriate output control signal to drive either the stepper or servo motor device. Figures 5-2 through 5-5 show the system block diagrams for the four stepper and servo motor controllers. Note that the sketch for the interactive electronic devices allows speed control operation of the stepper and servo motor by manual method; in other words, you can control the speed manually via the potentiometer or the FlexiForce sensor.

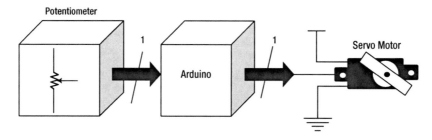

*Figure 5-2. An Arduino-based servo motor control system block diagram*

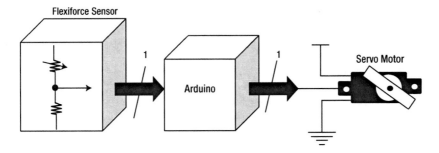

*Figure 5-3.* *A remixed FlexiForce sensor-activated servo motor control system block diagram*

■ **Note**   A FlexiForce sensor is a piezoresistive sensing device. The sensor's resistance changes based on the amount of force applied to it. This sensing device is also referred to as a tactile force sensor. A tactile force sensor is capable of the detection and measurement of a contact force at a defined point. May the force be with you!

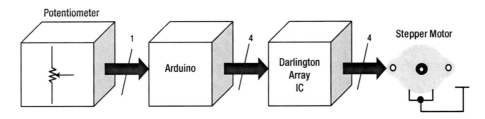

*Figure 5-4.* *An Arduino-based stepper motor control system block diagram*

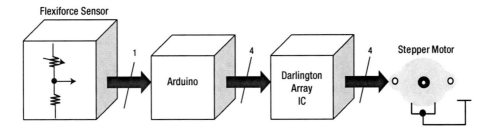

*Figure 5-5.* *A remixed FlexiForce sensor-activated servo motor control system block diagram*

# How It Works

As discussed in Chapter 4, transistors and electromechanical relays are used as direct electronic circuit drivers to control medium-to-heavy current-drawn electrical loads. With the aid of the Arduino's ATmega328 microcontroller, digitally operated motors like a servo and stepper can be controlled quite easily. Referencing the block diagram in Figure 5-6, to operate a servo motor digitally, an output port pin from the ATmega328 microcontroller drives the command control signal lead of the electromechanical component. The command control signal lead receives digital data in the form of pulses that correlate to the angle in which the servo motor will rotate. The pulse has a specific ON time duration that represents an angle. For example, the starting or neutral position to command the servo motor is 1.5ms. An angle of 0° is accomplish using a 1.25ms pulse. To rotate the servo motor to 180° a 1.75ms pulse from the Arduino is needed. Figure 5-7 shows the primary pulses and the angular position of the servo motor.

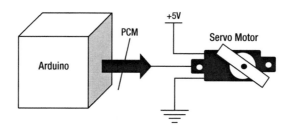

***Figure 5-6.*** *An Arduino-based computing platform used to control a servo motor*

---

■ **Note**   PCM, or pulse code modulation, is the control signal applied to the servo motor by the Arduino. The angular position is the code or data within the pulse width of the PCM signal. Digital control theory is truly awesome!

---

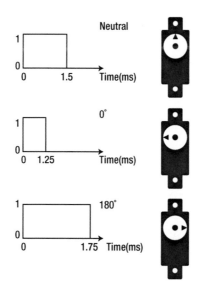

***Figure 5-7.*** *Typical pulse widths with angular positions for controlling a servo motor*

# Experimenting with a Servo Motor

The Arduino computational platform provides the command control signal (PCM) to drive a typical servo motor. A servo motor is an electromechanical device that uses error-sensing negative feedback to correct the operation of a mechanism. Negative feedback is a small amount of energy taken from a voltage- or current-detecting component and looping it back for proper adjustment to the error-correcting device. In Figure 5-6, the circuit schematic diagram consists of the Arduino and the servo motor illustrated in Figure 5-8. When you upload the sketch in Listing 5-1, the servo motor starts a sweep from neutral position to 180° and back to its original starting point. This motion is continuous, which allows the Arduino to be an automated tester for other suspect servo motors.

The servo motor wiring to the Arduino is quite simple. The wiring consists of the command control signal wire of the servo motor going to D9 of the Arduino PCB. The brown wire goes to ground with the red wire terminating at the +5VDC on the board. A wiring alternative is to use a solderless breadboard for the servo-to-Arduino connections, as shown in Figure 5-9 on the Fritzing circuit build.

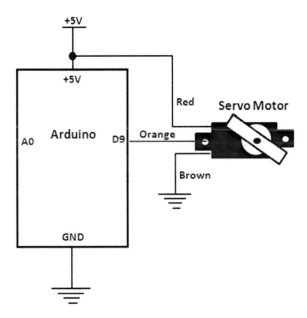

***Figure 5-8.*** *Controlling a servo motor with an Arduino*

---

■ **Note**   Fritzing software allows electronic circuits to be laid out for actual prototyping and testing on solderless breadboard, experimenter boards, and printed circuit boards (PCBs) by hobbyists, professionals, and artists. You can find the software, along with help and background information, at http://fritzing.org.

---

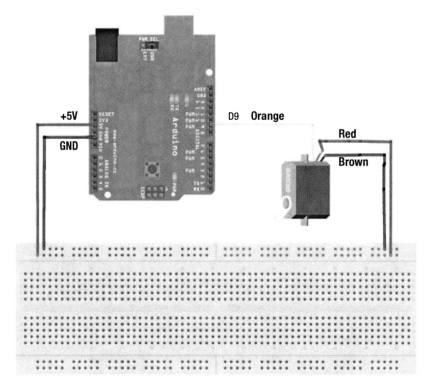

*Figure 5-9. Fritzing circuit build of an Arduino-based servo motor controller*

# Fritzing Software

The Fritzing circuit build serves as prototype guide for the actual construction of the Arduino-based servo motor controller. Although the prototyping tools used by the author are slightly different, the wiring shown in Figure 5-9 is quite similar to the actual build. Figure 5-10 shows the prototype of the servo motor controller. The process of designing a product virtually using graphics or modeling software and then building with real components is practiced daily in electronics manufacturing. Fritzing software is free and provides a wealth of resources online for taking a solderless prototype and turning it into a functional PCB-based product. So if you are a hobbyist, a student, an artist, or even a professional engineer, Fritzing software lets you adopt an electronics design automation (EDA) approach to your Arduino projects. The library of parts is quite substantial and provides technical resource for learning electronics with the Arduino.

---

■ **Note**　Electronics design automation is a category of software tools for designing circuits, systems, integrated circuits (ICs), and PCBs. Fritzing software falls into the EDA category because of its ability to create circuit schematic diagrams and printed circuit boards based on the prototype board layout. Multisim is another EDA software package with the ability to create printed circuit boards from a circuit schematic diagram captured by the tool's IDE (integrated development environment).

---

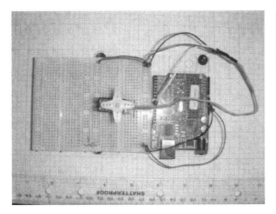

***Figure 5-10.*** *The actual Arduino-based servo motor controller prototype*

To make the servo motor stationary on the solderless breadboard, a small jumper wire is secured across its wiring pigtail, as seen in Figure 5-10 on the right.

---

■ **Tip**    If an electrical/electronic or small electromechanical component needs to be secure on a solderless breadboard during prototyping build, a small jumper wire can do the trick. MacGyver strikes again!

---

***Listing 5-1.*** The Servo Sweep Sketch

```
// Sweep
// by BARRAGAN <http://barraganstudio.com>
// This example code is in the public domain.

#include<Servo.h>

Servo myservo; // create servo object to control a servo
        // a maximum of eight servo objects can be created

int pos = 0;  // variable to store the servo position

void setup()
{
 myservo.attach(9); // attaches the servo on pin 9 to the servo object
}

void loop()
{
 for(pos = 0; pos < 180; pos += 1) // goes from 0 degrees to 180 degrees
 {                  // in steps of 1 degree
  myservo.write(pos);       // tell servo to go to position in variable 'pos'
  delay(15);             // waits 15 ms for the servo to reach the position
 }
 for(pos = 180; pos >= 1; pos- = 1)   // goes from 180 degrees to 0 degrees
```

```
  {
   myservo.write(pos);          // tell servo to go to position in variable 'pos'
   delay(15);                   // waits 15 ms for the servo to reach the position
  }
}
```

The Sweep sketch shown in Listing 5-1 is located in the ArduinoIDE at File ➤ Examples ➤ Servo ➤ Sweep. Figure 5-11 shows the Sweep sketch within the Examples directory. When you upload the code to the Arduino computational platform, the servo motor begins to sweep between the established rotational angles of 0° to 180°. As mentioned, this sweep motion is continuous.

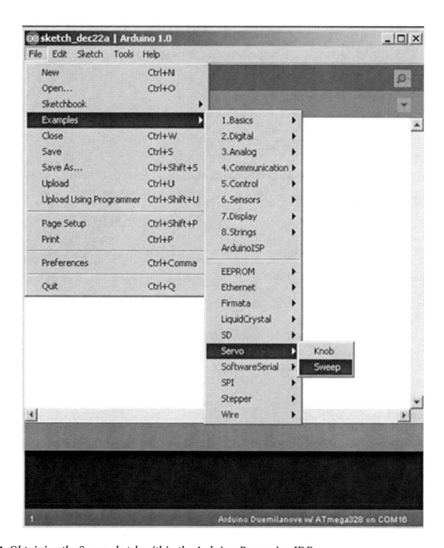

***Figure 5-11.*** *Obtaining the Sweep sketch within the Arduino-Processing IDE*

■ **Tip** The new Arduino 1.0 Processing software is now available for download. It includes the latest computational platforms, such as the Arduino Uno, and the Android Accessory ADK board. The Getting Started page of the Arduino web site has the latest software version (1.0) available for download; go to `http://arduino.cc/en/Guide/ HomePage`.

# Try It!

The Sweep sketch is commented quite well, which allows for experimentation with the code. With commented code, it's easier to learn the programming style and the technique of operating motors, lights, and LEDs because the various functions are explained. Here are the two lines of code that affect the sweep speed; feel free to change the values to see what happens. That's the philosophy behind experimentation!

```
for(pos = 0; pos < 180; pos += 1) // goes from 0 degrees to 180 degrees
for(pos = 180; pos >= 1; pos -= 1)  // goes from 180 degrees to 0 degrees
```

By changing the +1 and -1 values in each of these lines of code, the servo motor sweep speed will increase, thereby creating new motion patterns for the electromechanical actuator. Change the values of both lines of code to 5 and observe the sweep speed being five times faster than the original setting! If one line of code is changed to 5 and the other to -1, the servo motor will sweep quickly in the clockwise direction but will move slowly in the reverse direction. Also, note that the motion of the servo motor is still smooth and precise, which makes it great for robotics applications. Try some changes and record your observations!

# Physical Computing: A Servo Motor with a Potentiometer

If you add a potentiometer to the servo setup you have now, you can accommodate easy human interaction with the electromechanical components. By adding a potentiometer, manual control of the servo motor is possible. The potentiometer allows the servo motor's angular position to be dialed in precisely. By rotating the potentiometer's shaft (wiper arm), the servo motor's degree of motion can be changed. Discrete angles such as 35°, 45°, 60°, and 110° can easily be dialed in using the potentiometer. The wiring to the Arduino's PCB inline header connectors is accomplished as shown in Figure 5-12. The circuit schematic diagram is illustrated in Figure 5-13 with the actual prototype shown in Figure 5-14. The sketch for controlling the servo motor with a potentiometer is obtained from the Arduino-Processing IDE by clicking File ➤ Examples ➤ Servo ➤ Knob. Figure 5-15 shows the Knob sketch within the Examples directory. The Knob sketch is shown in Listing 5-2.

■ **Tip** The other sketches for performing Physical Computing experiments with the Arduino can be obtained within the Examples directory inside of the Arduino Processing IDE toolbar.

■ **Note** In keeping with the Arduino concept of software code being called a sketch, a Fritzing Circuit Build is also know as a sketch. Long live consistency!

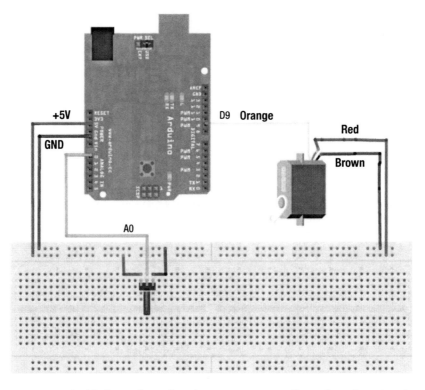

*Figure 5-12. Fritzing circuit build of an Arduino-based servo motor controller with angle-positioning potentiometer*

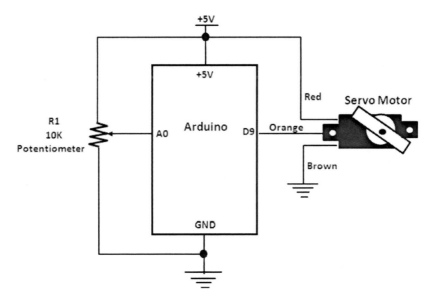

*Figure 5-13. Circuit schematic diagram for the Arduino-based servo motor controller with angle-positioning potentiometer*

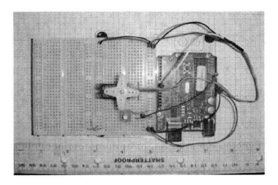

*Figure 5-14. Prototype of the Arduino-based servo motor controller with angle-positioning potentiometer*

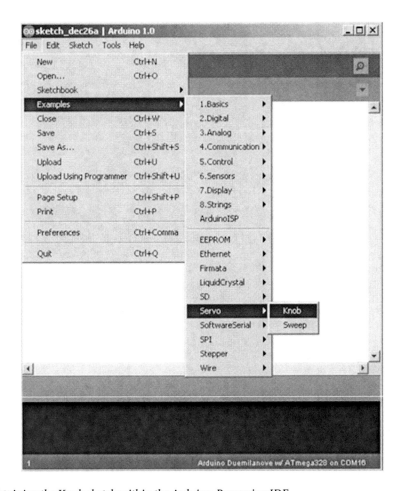

*Figure 5-15. Obtaining the Knob sketch within the Arduino-Processing IDE*

With the code uploaded to the Arduino, turning the shaft of the 10K potentiometer allows the servo motor to move in precise angular increments (or *steps*) with the variable resistor. The faster the potentiometer's shaft is turned, the quicker the servo motor responds. Besides the angular positions hard-coded in Listing 5-1, discrete movements of the servo motor can be commanded by the potentiometer quite easily. Once again, a well-commented sketch allows you to experiment with the servo motor's operation easily.

*Listing 5-2.* The Knob Sketch

```
// Controlling a servo position using a potentiometer (variable resistor)
// by Michal Rinott <http://people.interaction-ivrea.it/m.rinott>
#include<Servo.h>
Servo myservo; // create servo object to control a servo
int potpin = 0; // analog pin used to connect the potentiometer
int val;  // variable to read the value from the analog pin
void setup()
{
 myservo.attach(9); // attaches the servo on pin 9 to the servo object
}
 void loop()
{
 val = analogRead(potpin);       // reads the value of the potentiometer (value ↵
 between 0 and 1023)
 val = map(val, 0, 1023, 0, 179);   // scale it to use it with the servo (value ↵
 between 0 and 180)
 myservo.write(val);        // sets the servo position according to the ↵
 scaled value
 delay(15);          // waits for the servo to get there
}
```

# Physical Computing: A Servo Motor with a Joystick

A joystick can also be used to operate a servo motor's angular motion. A joystick consists of two potentiometers packaged into a single unit. Wiring either the x or y potentiometer into the Arduino computing platform allows control of the angular position of the servo motor by movement of a handle instead of knob. Both the x and y potentiometers are attached to the handle using a mechanical linkage assembly that allows for either individual or simultaneous control of both variable resistors. Figure 5-16 shows a typical joystick and the mechanical linkage assembly. The circuit schematic diagram for wiring a joystick to the Arduino computing platform is illustrated in Figure 5-17.

Additional wires are soldered to the joystick (as shown in Figure 5-16) to make it easier to replace the 10 K potentiometer from the previous experimental lab build using the solderless breadboard. Figure 5-18 shows the attached wires to the terminals on the x potentiometer of the two-axis joystick.

The completed project build on the solderless breadboard shows both the joystick and servo motor wired to the Arduino via jumper wires. The Knob sketch allows the joystick to change angular position of the servo motor. Moving the handle on the joystick from right to left (x direction of control) to operate the servo motor provides accuracy in motion control for the small electromechanical component. Figure 5-19 shows the final build of the joystick-operated servo motor controller.

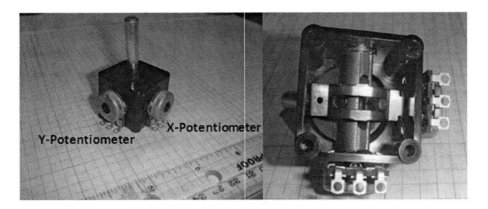

**Figure 5-16.** *On the left, a typical joystick consisting of x and y potentiometers. On the right, the mechanical linkage assembly of a joystick.*

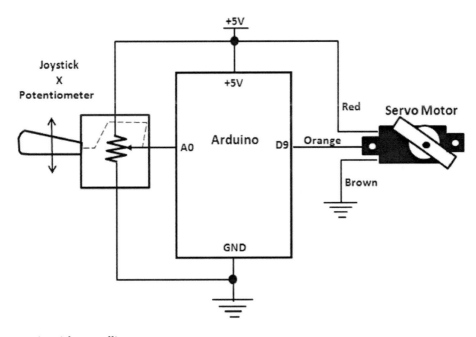

**Figure 5-17.** *A joystick controlling a servo motor*

---

■ **Note**    In addition to Physical Computing devices, the joystick has become common in many industrial and manufacturing applications, such as cranes, assembly lines, and heavy equipment trucks used in mining and excavation jobs.

---

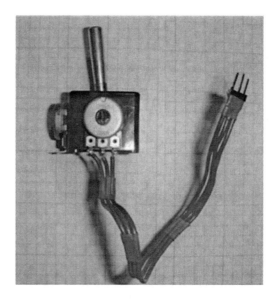

**Figure 5-18.** *Soldered pigtail wire harness for joystick*

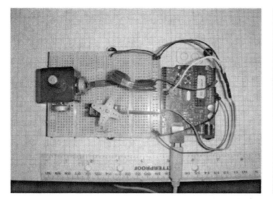 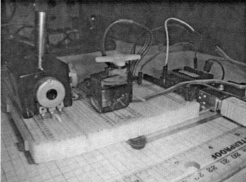

**Figure 5-19.** *Prototype of a joystick-operated servo motor controller*

# Physical Computing: A Servo Motor with a FlexiForce Sensor

Another technique used to control a servo motor is applying a force to a targeted area's sensing surface, allowing it to provide a proportional signal to the Arduino. Based on the magnitude of the force applied to the targeted area, the sensing device's internal resistance will change. In essence, the sensing device will act as a variable resistor. There is such a component that can change its resistance based on a *tactile force* being applied to its sensing surface area: a FlexiForce sensor. The FlexiForce sensor is capable of detecting forces up to 1000 lbs, which allows applications in object detection and control to be implemented quite easily. With its internal resistance to change, the sensor can be used in a voltage divider circuit where the output voltage is monitored and used to provide an input signal to the Arduino. The ATmega328's ADC (analog-to-digital converter) provides an equivalent digital value representing the force being applied to the FlexiForce sensor.

■ **Note** A tactile force sensor is capable of detection and measurement of a contact force at a defined point.

To interface a FlexiForce Sensor to an Arduino is quite simple and requires only a pull-down resistor. The two components wired in series form a voltage divider circuit, as discussed in Chapter 1. In Figure 5-3, the system block diagram for controlling a servo motor with a FlexiForce sensor was introduced. As shown in the first block, a voltage divider circuit illustrates how the input detection signal is created with the two series-wired components. Figure 5-20 is a look into the first block, illustrating the FlexiForce sensor input interface circuit.

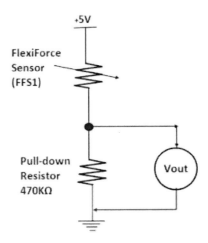

*Figure 5-20. The FlexiForce sensor input interface circuit*

In Figure 5-20, Vout can range from +0 to +5VDC based on the the amount of force applied to the sensor's target surface area. Wiring this circuit to the Arduino provides a method of controlling the servo motor's angular rotation by the amount of force applied to the FFS. The more force applied to the FFS sensing surface, the greater the angular rotation by the servo motor. Figure 5-21 shows the circuit schematic diagram of the FFS input interface circuit wired to the Arduino. The Fritzing circuit build showing solderless breadboard layout of components is illustrated in Figure 5-22.

■ **Note** The FFS input interface circuit allows for a simple method of building a low-cost electronic scale, based on its ability to detect and measure weight of objects. How cool is that?!

■ **Note** The amount of force applied to the sensor allows the servo motor to move in discrete rotational angles. Applying full amount of force to it allows the servo motor to rotate 180°.

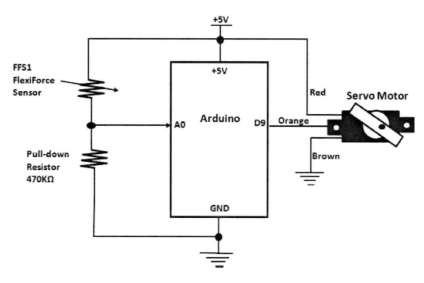

***Figure 5-21.*** *The FlexiForce-operated servo motor controller*

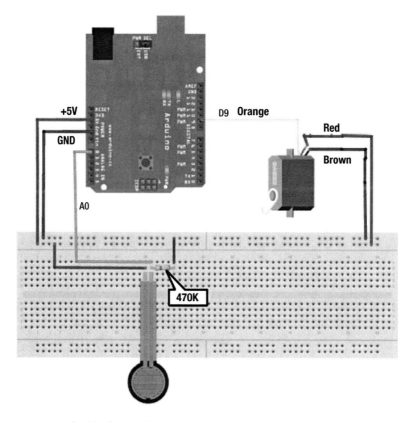

***Figure 5-22.*** *Fritzing circuit build of an Arduino-based servo motor controller with angle-positioning FlexiForce sensor*

The actual prototype build of the FlexiForce sensor is shown in Figure 5-23. To make the prototype build, compact jumper wires are used to secure both the sensor and the servo motor onto the solderless breadboard. The Knob sketch is used to read the applied force level, process the discrete input signal into an angular position, and provide a command drive signal to operate the servo motor.

*Figure 5-23. Prototype a FlexiForce sensor-operated servo motor controller*

■ **Note**    One of the advantages of using a FlexiForce sensor is its ability to bend in various shapes for packaging into unique enclosures. The sensing elements of the sensor are printed on a flexible plastic material, allowing it to bend in many shapes without affecting its internal resistance. Mr. Fantastic, move over!

# Motion Control Basics

Basically, motion control requires the movement of an object from one location to another. In manufacturing, a motion control system provides precision in automation equipment with emphasis on positioning, velocity, and torque control. Examples of motion control applications include, but are not limited to, robotics, conveyor systems, automobiles, and toys. Although servo motors are the main electromechanical *actuators* used in motion control applications, stepper motors are capable of maintaining precision in moving an object a given distance by the use of electrical pulses. The microcontroller is capable of generating electrical pulses for commanding a stepper motor's positioning, as you just saw.

# The Darlington Transistor

As illustrated in Figures 5-4 and 5-5, the microcontroller provides step-positioning electrical pulses to four windings of the stepper motor. A binary code associated with the position of the stepper motor is received by a Darlington transistor array IC. The Darlington transistor IC provides the appropriate *sink* drive current to switch ON the windings of the stepper motor. The Darlington transistor is capable of handling up to 8A of Ipk (peak current) or 5A of steady state current. The key electrical parameter of the Darlington transistor is its high current gain ($h_{FE}$). A nominal value for $h_{FE}$ is 1000. The reason behind this high current gain is because of the wiring of two NPN transistors. With one transistor having an amplification factor (current gain) wired to another one, the overall gains of each semiconductor component are multiplied, thus creating a transistor with a significant $h_{FE}$ value. Figure 5-24 shows the circuit configuration of a typical Darlington transistor.

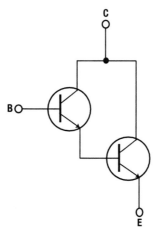

**Figure 5-24.** *Darlington transistor circuit*

The Darlington array IC (ULN2803) has eight transistors conveniently packaged into an 18-pin dual inline package (DIP). Four transistors are used to drive the windings of the stepper motor. The base of each transistor is commanded by the Arduino's ATmega328 microcontroller to turn ON based on a binary code. The binary code provides the phase sequence for positioning the stepper motor. Either a full or half-step phase sequence can be used to command the angular position of the stepper motor. Figure 5-25 shows the phase sequence for full and half-step positioning of a unipolar stepper motor.

---

▓ **Tip**  A Darlington transistor is also known as a Darlington pair.

---

---

▓ **Note**  Servos and steppers are types of electromechanical actuators used to move or control a mechanism or system.

---

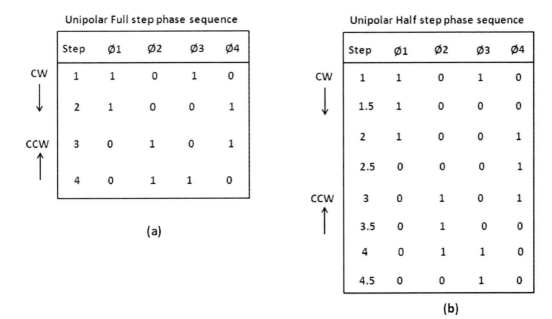

Figure 5-25. *Unipolar stepper motor phase sequences (a) full step (b) half step*

# The Unipolar Stepper Motor

The unipolar stepper motor is a special type of DC motor that can rotate in both directions and move in precise angular steps. It can also sustain a holding torque at zero speed and can be controlled using digital circuits. The other electrical characteristic of the unipolar stepper motor is it requires only one power supply source.

---

■ **Tip** A bipolar stepper motor requires two DC power supplies or a split power supply (+-Vsupply).

---

The unipolar stepper motor doesn't require a feedback control but the use of an encoder or other type of position sensor will ensure accuracy when exact positioning control is required. As mentioned, operating the unipolar stepper motor requires a binary code that provides the switching sequence or phase control for turning ON or OFF the windings of the electromechanical actuator. The unipolar stepper motor has four windings that require an equivalent number of switching devices, such as transistors, to sink the driving current for proper operation and control. Figure 5-26 illustrates the typical schematic diagram of a sink driver circuit using four discrete transistors.

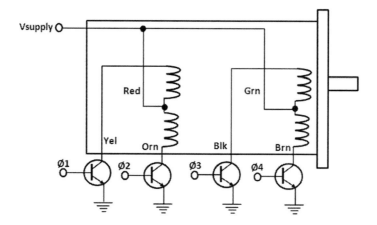

*Figure 5-26. Unipolar stepper motor sink driver circuit*

# A Multisim Digital Controller Model for a Unipolar Stepper Motor

As mentioned, a unipolar stepper motor can easily be operated by using a digital circuit. The digital circuit is responsible for providing the binary phase sequence to switch the transistors in proper order to control the unipolar stepper motor. The basic discrete digital ICs needed for implementing the unipolar stepper motor controller are 74191 up/down synchronous binary counter, 7408 exclusive OR (EXOR) logic gate, and 7414 Schmitt trigger. The digital controller circuit schematic diagram is shown in Figure 5-27.

As shown in the Multisim circuit model, a logic analyzer is wired to the circuit for the purpose of capturing the phase sequence binary bit patterns produced by the digital controller. The function generator is set with the signal generation parameters shown in Figure 5-28. Upon executing a simulation event in Multisim, the timing diagrams displaying both clockwise (CW) and counterclockwise (CCW) directions are captured on the logic analyzer. Further analysis of these diagrams will positively correlate to Figure 5-25. Figure 5-29 shows the CW/CCW timing diagrams of the digital controller. The 7414 Schmitt trigger generates sharp one-shot square wave pulses for commanding CW/CCW motor direction. The 74191 up/down synchronous 4-bit counter along with the 7486 EXOR logic gate provide the proper phase sequence for switching the correct transistor to energize the appropriate winding, in sequence, of the unipolar stepper motor. Each square wave pulse received from the function generator causes the unipolar stepper motor to rotate a full step in the direction established by the CW/CCW switch. The motor will come to a complete stop upon closing the reset switch.

---

■ **Note** A logic analyzer is a special type of an oscilloscope capable of using multi I/O (input/output) pins and signals from a microcontroller or digital circuit.

---

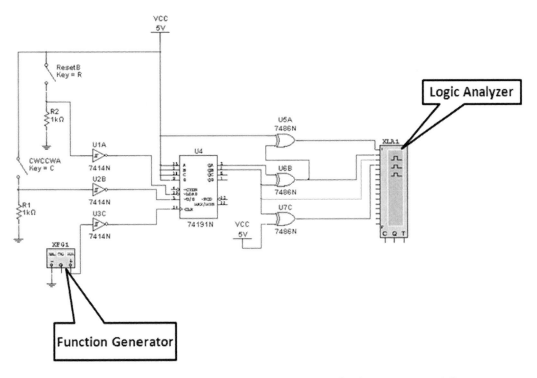

*Figure 5-27. A digital controller for operating a unipolar stepper motor (Multisim circuit model)*

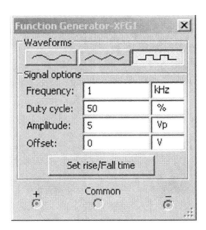

*Figure 5-28. The setup of a virtual Function Generator instrument for operating the digital controller*

▪ **Note**   To see an example of the stepper motor digital controller, go to `http://video_demos.colostate.edu/`
`mechatronics/index.html#PIC_PROJECTS`. Under the actuator section, click the *stepper motor PIC-based position
and speed controller* link to see an awesome demonstration. I like hot butter on my popcorn, please!

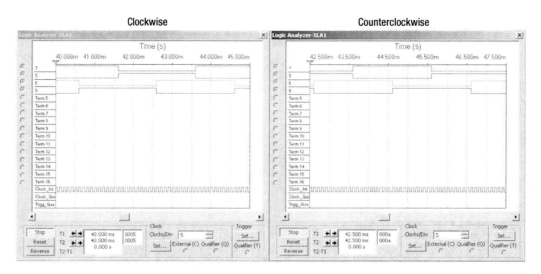

*Figure 5-29.* *CW/CCW timing diagrams produced by the Multisim-based stepper motor digital controller circuit
model*

# Build an Arduino Unipolar Stepper Motor Controller

The best way to start exploring stepper motor control is to build a basic driver circuit for operating a unipolar
electromechanical device. Figure 5-30 shows the basic building blocks for such a driver circuit.

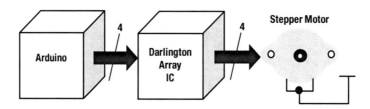

*Figure 5-30.* *An Arduino-based stepper motor controller with Darlington transistor driver*

The system block diagram of Figure 5-30 reveals the actual circuit schematic diagram shown in Figure 5-31.

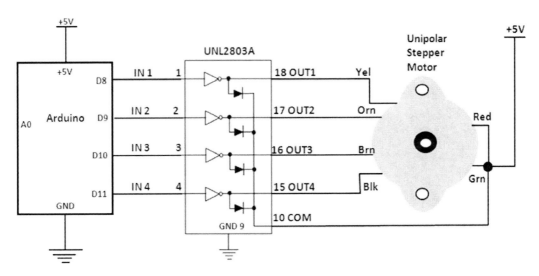

**Figure 5-31.** *Circuit schematic diagram of an Arduino-based stepper motor controller with Darlington transistor driver*

Although the ATmega328 microcontroller is capable of sourcing and sinking 40mA of continuous drive current, the ULN2803A Darlington array IC can provide 500mA of current, which is sufficient to operate a unipolar stepper motor. The diodes shown in the Darlington array IC provide transient protection when the winding (inductor coil) of the stepper motor is de-energized, thus preventing the internal transistor of the IC package from being damaged. For a refresher on how this transient process works, review Chapter 4. Figure 5-32 shows the actual build of the Arduino-based stepper motor controller.

**Figure 5-32.** *Actual build of the Arduino-based stepper motor controller with Darlington transistor driver*

Once the circuit is built, a test program can be used to validate the stepper motor operation. The sketch for controlling the stepper motor can be obtained from the Arduino-Processing IDE by going to File ➤ Examples ➤ Stepper ➤ stepper_oneRevolution. Figure 5-33 shows the stepper_oneRevolution sketch within the Examples directory. The stepper_oneRevolution sketch (code) is shown in Listing 5-3.

***Listing 5-3.*** The stepper_oneRevolution Sketch

```
/*
 Stepper Motor Control - one revolution

 This program drives a unipolar or bipolar stepper motor.
 The motor is attached to digital pins 8 - 11 of the Arduino.

 The motor should revolve one revolution in one direction, then
 one revolution in the other direction.

 Created 11 Mar. 2007
 Modified 30 Nov. 2009
 by Tom Igoe

 */

#include<Stepper.h>

const int stepsPerRevolution = 200; // change this to fit the number of steps per revolution
                    // for your motor

// initialize the stepper library on pins 8 through 11:
Stepper myStepper(stepsPerRevolution, 8,9,10,11);

void setup() {
 // set the speed at 60 rpm:
 myStepper.setSpeed(60);
 // initialize the serial port:
 Serial.begin(9600);
}

void loop() {
 // step one revolution in one direction:
 Serial.println("clockwise");
 myStepper.step(stepsPerRevolution);
 delay(500);

 // step one revolution in the other direction:
 Serial.println("counterclockwise");
 myStepper.step(-stepsPerRevolution);
 delay(500);
}
```

After you upload the sketch to the Arduino board, the stepper motor makes one revolution and reverses direction continuously. An *Easter egg* in the sketch is the message it displays on a serial monitor with each directional revolution the stepper motor makes. Figure 5-34 shows the messages displayed on the serial monitor with each directional revolution pass made by the stepper motor.

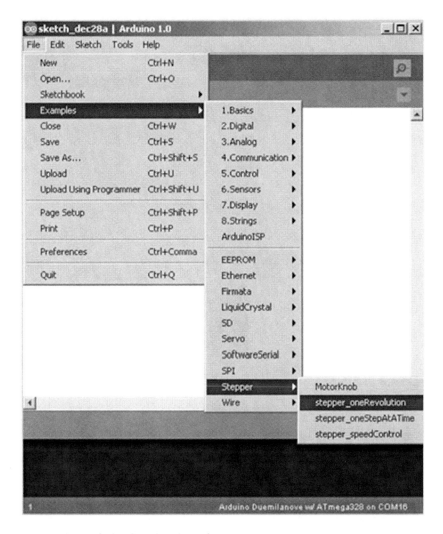

**Figure 5-33.** *Obtaining the Knob sketch within the Arduino-Processing IDE*

---

▓ **Note**　Once you have a functional unipolar stepper motor controller, other motors can be tested—an awesome electronics application of built-in testability system (BITs).

---

The lines of code within the sketch responsible for generating these messages are as follows:

```
Serial.println("clockwise");
:
Serial.println("counterclockwise");
```

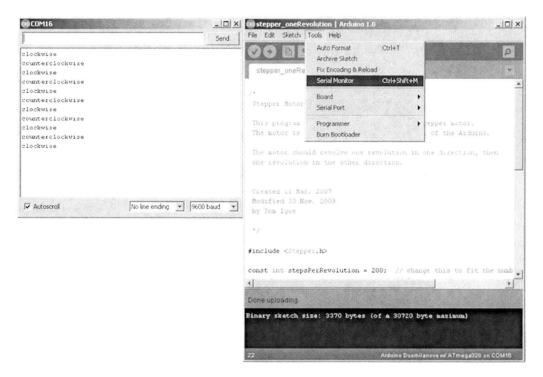

**Figure 5-34.** *Gaining access to the Serial Monitor for viewing messages within the Arduino Processing IDE*

The `println` instruction is used quite often in the C programming language to display text messages or reveal the content of variables for numerical analysis or debugging code. Therefore, in this example test code, whatever text message the embedded system wants to display in the Serial Monitor can be easily accomplished using this basic programming instruction.

## Adding a Speed Control Function

With a modification to the sketch and the addition of a potentiometer to the Arduino's analog port pin A0, a speed control function can be added to the unipolar stepper motor. Referencing the system block diagram of Figure 5-4, looking at the individual blocks will reveal the circuit schematic diagram shown in Figure 5-35.

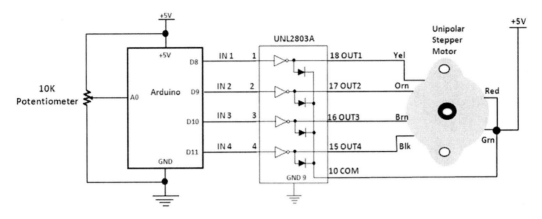

***Figure 5-35.*** *Speed control added to the unipolar stepper motor controller*

By increasing the resistance of the 10KΩ potentiometer, the stepper motor's speed increases proportionally. The stepper motor controller circuit is truly an example of a remix design. The sketch for controlling the stepper motor with a potentiometer is found in the Arduino-Processing IDE by going to File ➤ Examples ➤ Stepper ➤ stepper_speedControl. The stepper_speedControl sketch is shown in Listing 5-4.

***Listing 5-4.*** The stepper_speedControl Sketch

```
/*
Stepper Motor Control - speed control

This program drives a unipolar or bipolar stepper motor.
The motor is attached to digital pins 8 - 11 of the Arduino.
A potentiometer is connected to analog input 0.

The motor will rotate in a clockwise direction. The higher the potentiometer value,
the faster the motor speed. Because setSpeed() sets the delay between steps,
you may notice the motor is less responsive to changes in the sensor value at
low speeds.

Created 30 Nov. 2009
Modified 28 Oct 2010
by Tom Igoe

*/

#include<Stepper.h>

const int stepsPerRevolution = 200; // change this to fit the number of steps per revolution
// for your motor

// initialize the stepper library on pins 8 through 11:
Stepper myStepper(stepsPerRevolution, 8,9,10,11);

int stepCount = 0;      // number of steps the motor has taken
```

```
void setup() {
 // initialize the serial port:
 Serial.begin(9600);
}
void loop() {
 // read the sensor value:
 int sensorReading = analogRead(A0);
 // map it to a range from 0 to 100:
 int motorSpeed = map(sensorReading, 0, 1023, 0, 100);
 // set the motor speed:
 if (motorSpeed > 0) {
  myStepper.setSpeed(motorSpeed);
  // step 1/100 of a revolution:
  myStepper.step(stepsPerRevolution/100);
 }
}
```

When you have uploaded the sketch to the Arduino board, the stepper motor may be turning at some predetermined speed set by the potentiometer. Rotate the potentiometer in a CW/CCW direction and the unipolar motor will increase or decrease its speed accordingly.

---

■ **Tip** The Arduino Processing IDE makes it quite easy to start developing embedded system devices because of several examples provided with the tool. Anyone for a journey to the center of the Earth?

---

## Final Testing of the Servo and Stepper Motor Controllers

In this chapter, a series of subsection testing activities have been outlined to capture bugs in building the hardware circuits. Using a DMM and an oscilloscope, the testing techniques described can be validated on the bench. Depending on the type of vendor of the testing instruments, the results may vary by +/−10 %. Key elements to keep in mind while testing are

- Make sure the wiring is correct prior to applying voltage to the Arduino and supporting circuits.

- Use the proper wiring methods discussed in Chapter 3.

- The "How It Works" section of this chapter is a great reference to verify that the circuit breadboard is working correctly.

- Review the sketch entered into the Arduino IDE Editor for typos that will cause the hardware device to operate improperly.

# Further Discovery Method Suggestions

For the unipolar stepper motor controller, try changing the speed with a FlexiForce sensor or joystick. Also, experiment with print text messages for diagnostics/testing of both servo and stepper motor controllers using the Serial Monitor. Try a continuous-mode servo motor, and record and compare its behavior to a non-continuous device. In addition to the Power ON LED located on the Arduino PCB, add an external indicator to the controllers. Remember to document your designs in a lab notebook (spiral or three ring binder type) along with any sketch modifications you made for the new servo and stepper motor controllers you've created!

# CHAPTER 6

■ ■ ■

# The Music Box

The Arduino has the ability to generate a multitude of sounds and tones, and a combination of them can produce snippets of musical melodies. Creating sounds or tones is relatively easy using the tone( ) instruction along with its *code library*. This chapter will show how you can use the tone instruction and its library to generate sounds and melodies. This chapter will use the physical-computing techniques discussed in previous chapters in the creation of a human-interactive electronic music box. Figure 6-1 shows the parts required for the hands-on projects and experiments.

## Parts List

Arduino Duemilanove or equivalent

10K potentiometer

470K resistor

4 10K resistors

FlexiForce sensor

CdS photocell

4-bit DIP switch

2 N3904 NPN transistor

IFR630A N-channel MOSFET

Keypad

8Ω speaker

Piezo-buzzer

Small solderless breadboard

22AWG solid wire

Digital multimeter

Oscilloscope (optional)

Electronic tools

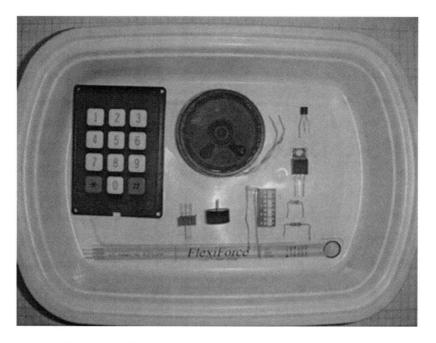

***Figure 6-1.*** *Parts required for the music box projects and experiments*

# Remixing Physical-Computing and Driver Interface Circuits

Continuing with the technique of remixing, we'll use the following components for creating human interaction with the electronic music box: a FlexiForce sensora 4-bit DIP switch, a CdS photocell, a speaker, and a keypad. The BJT (bipolar junction transistor) and PMOSFET (power metal oxide semiconductor field effect transistor) electronic components will be used to drive a piezo-buzzer, and a speaker will be used to enhance the audible output of the Arduino by providing sufficient sourcing current to the audio output components. The Arduino will provide the audible sound based on the tone instruction and its associated software library components. Figures 6-2, 6-3, 6-4, and 6-5 show variations of system block diagrams for four physical-computing music box controllers. Also, the sketch used in the interactive electronic devices will allow audible tone control operation for the piezo-buzzer and speaker audio output components.

---

■ **Note**   The original music boxes of the 19th and 20th centuries were musical instruments that produced sound by a set of pins placed on a revolving cylinder that plucked the tuned teeth of a steel comb. Today's music boxes produces sound with the help a microcontroller and embedded software. All hail to the mighty electron!

---

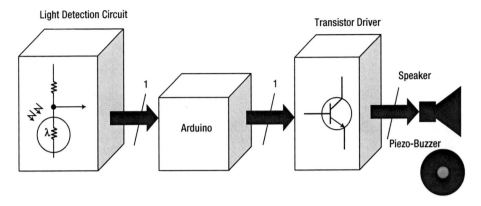

*Figure 6-2. System block diagram for an Arduino-based physical-computing music box controller*

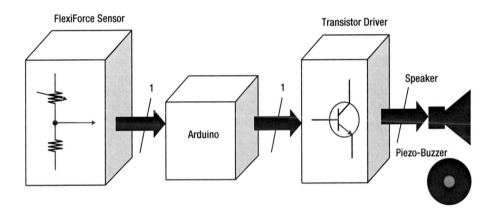

*Figure 6-3. Systems block diagram for a remixed FlexiForce sensor–activated music box controller*

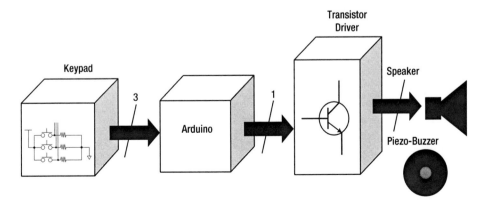

*Figure 6-4. Systems block diagram for a keypad-activated music box controller*

121

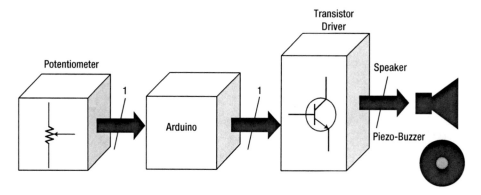

*Figure 6-5. Systemblock diagram for a potentiometer-activated music box controller*

## How It Works

The piezoelectric element of the buzzer is made from either a crystal or ceramic material packaged inside a small cylinder. It produces a small electric voltage when subjected to mechanical stress. When a piezoelectric element is stressed, its structure is distorted and it produces a clicking sound. By pulsing the piezoelectric element several times per second, you can make it emit an audible tone or sound. Pulsing the element at distinct frequencies makes the element produce different tones or sounds. Using the Arduino's ATmega328 microcontroller's PWM output port and a small amount of code, you can create a piezo-buzzer to generate snippets of sound to create music. Figure 6-6 shows a typical piezo-buzzer, along with an equivalent Fritzing model.

*Figure 6-6. A typical piezo-buzzer and a Fritzing model: (L) Front of piezo-buzzer, (R) Back of piezo-buzzer (B) Fritzing piezo-buzzer*

■ **Note**    The piezo-buzzer works via a piezoelectric effect, which involves linear electromechanical interaction between the mechanical and the electrical state in crystalline materials. Isn't material science wonderful?

# Experimenting with PWM

The Arduino computational platform can provide the tone signal to drive a typical piezo-buzzer directly. PWM (pulse width modulation, discussed in Chapter 1) is the technique behind signal generation. In this chapter PWM will be used in the application of waveform generation, allowing the Arduino to produce different tones for the music box controller device. The Arduino has three PWM output ports. PWM port 9 will be used for the tone signal in this miniature lab experiment. Figure 6-7 shows the pinout of the ATmega328 microcontroller and the electrical interface to the 1×8 inline header connector for the PWM signal.

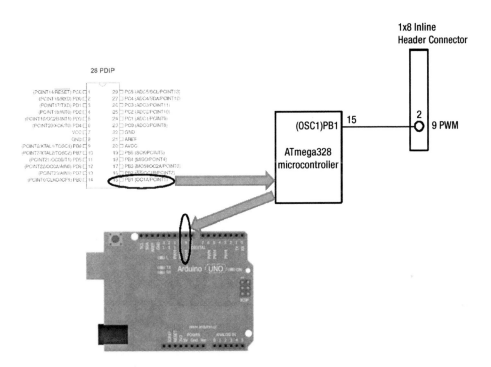

***Figure 6-7.*** *The ATmega328 Microcontroller PWM output port connecting to output 9 of the Arduino computational platform's 1 × 8 inline header connector*

Internally, the ATmega328 microcontroller has a waveform generator capable of creating switching signals for motor control, lighting, and frequency synthesis applications. The waveform generator output synthesis is based on setting the operating mode WGM2:0 and the COMnx1:0 using either the C or Assembly Language. There is also an internal counter inside the PWM circuit that alternates between *top* (high byte) and *bottom* (low byte) counting to assist in the signal creation by the waveform generator. A prescale number (*n*) is used with the waveform generator to determine the output frequency of the signal. The equation is shown following. It too is programmed in either C or Assembly Language. The waveform generator block diagram is illustrated in Figure 6-8.

$$Focn = fclkIO/n \times 256$$

Again, $n$ is the prescale factor, with values of 1, 8, 256, or 1024 and *Focn* is the oscillator frequency counter.

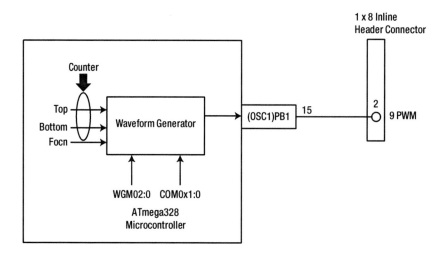

***Figure 6-8.*** *The ATmega328 microcontroller's waveform generator for producing PWM signals*

---

■ **Note**   The tones and sounds that can be created from the Arduino's PWM output port are based on the ATmega328 microcontroller's waveform generator, which can arbitrarily create or define any tone or sound through software.

---

You can easily build a Multisim circuit model to experiment with PWM and waveform generation. As shown in Figure 6-9, all that's required is a controlled one-shot, two DC power supplies, a SPDT electric switch, a function generator, and a 1K potentiometer.

To configure the one-shot component, the following setup is required. Double-click the component and select the Value tab. The "Clock trigger value" fields are used to set the clock pin threshold value. When the voltage at this pin reaches the defined value, it will trigger the component. The input voltage at the control pin is used to determine the output pulse width. In the circuit model shown in Figure 6-9, the values shown in Table 6-1 were entered.

Figure 6-10 shows the configuration dialog box for entering the control array and pulse width array values for the one-shot component.

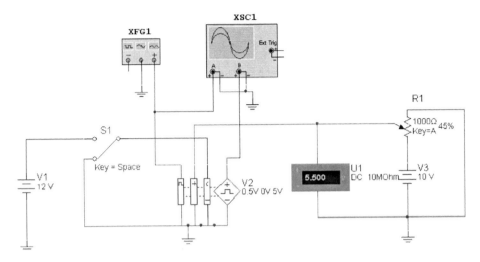

**Figure 6-9.** *A Multisim PWM virtual circuit*

**Table 6-1.** *Values  Entered*

| Control Array | Pulse Width Array (Seconds) |
| --- | --- |
| 1 | 0.0001 |
| 3 | 0.0003 |

■ **Note**    The 74LS123 TTL IC has dual one-shot outputs capable of creating a PWM circuit.

When the voltage to the control pin is 1 V, the output pulse is 1 ms. When the input is at 3 V, the output pulse will be 3 ms. Since Table 6-1 has a piecewise property, when the input to the control pin is 2 V, the output pulse will be 2 ms, and when it is 4 V, the pulse will be 4 ms. When simulating the Figure 6-9 circuit, please note the following:

Press the space bar on your keyboard. When the input is set to high, the output should be zero. When set to low, the circuit will be in operation mode.

The function generator outputs a triangle wave. The setup of the function generator is shown in Figure 6-11. When it passes 0.5 V, it will trigger the one-shot.

Pressing A on the keyboard changes the potentiometer wiper position, which controls the voltage at the control pin, controlling your pulse width.

The results of the setup are shown on the virtual oscilloscope in Figure 6-12. Experimenting with a 10 K potentiometer will allow various PWM duty cycles to be displayed on the oscilloscope. See the "Pulse Width Modulation Basics" section of Chapter 1 for calculating duty cycle values.

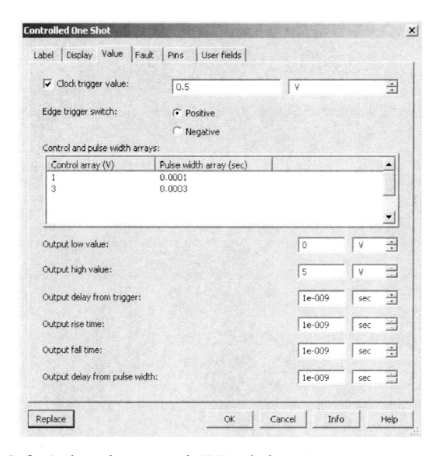

*Figure 6-10. Configuring the one-shot component for PWM mode of operation*

*Figure 6-11. The Multisim function generator setup for a triangle wave*

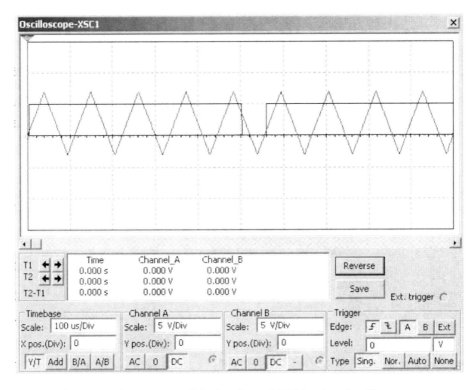

*Figure 6-12. A triangle wave and a PWM signal displayed on a Multisim virtual oscilloscope*

# Building and Testing a Basic Music Box Controller

Building a basic music box controller is quite simple and only requires an Arduino and a piezo-buzzer, as shown in the system block diagram of Figure 6-13. Figure 6-14 shows the Fritzing sketch. The Fritzing software makes it convenient to plan a solderless breadboard layout of components for optimum spacing quite easily. Although hand-sketching is the original technique for parts placement on a breadboard (see the "Assembly of the Light Sequencer Circuit on a Breadboard" section of Chapter 3), Fritzing software provides a clean way of placing components on a breadboard. Also, it allows you to change the design quite easily and save it digitally, preventing you from having to redraw the prototype from scratch. You will upload Twinkle, Twinkle, Little Star sketch to the Arduino as the musical melody.

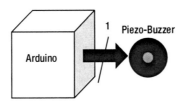

*Figure 6-13. System block diagram for a basic music box controller*

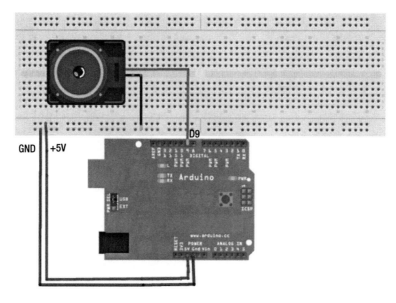

**Figure 6-14.** *A Fritzing music box controller sketch*

The circuit schematic diagram for the basic music box controller is shown in Figure 6-15.

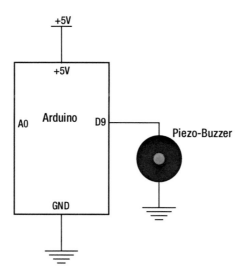

**Figure 6-15.** *Circuit schematic diagram for the Arduino-based music box controller*

The prototype controller circuit is built on a solderless breadboard using the circuit schematic diagram of Figure 6-16. The prototype build is shown in Figure 6-16.

**Figure 6-16.** *The physical prototype of the music box controller*

The code (Arduino sketch) used to test the prototype is shown in Listing 6-1.

**Listing 6-1.** The Code for Playing "Twinkle, Twinkle, Little Star"

```
/* Melody
 * (cleft) 2005 D. Cuartielles for K3
 *
 * This example uses a piezo speaker to play melodies. It sends
 * a square wave of the appropriate frequency to the piezo, generating
 * the corresponding tone.
 *
 * The calculation of the tones is made following the mathematical
 * operation:
 *
 *     timeHigh = period / 2 = 1 / (2 * toneFrequency)
 *
 * where the different tones are described as in the table:
 *
 * note       frequency    period   timeHigh
 * c          261 Hz       3830     1915
 * d          294 Hz       3400     1700
 * e          329 Hz       3038     1519
 * f          349 Hz       2864     1432
 * g          392 Hz       2550     1275
 * a          440 Hz       2272     1136
 * b          493 Hz       2028     1014
 * C          523 Hz       1912     956
 *
 * http://www.arduino.cc/en/Tutorial/Melody
 */
 int speakerPin = 9;
int length = 15; // the number of notes
```

```
char notes[] = "ccggaagffeeddc "; // a space represents a rest
int beats[] = { 1, 1, 1, 1, 1, 1, 2, 1, 1, 1, 1, 1, 1, 2, 4 };
int tempo = 300;

void playTone(int tone, int duration) {
 for (long i = 0; i < duration * 1000 L; i + = tone * 2) {
  digitalWrite(speakerPin, HIGH);
  delayMicroseconds(tone);
  digitalWrite(speakerPin, LOW);
  delayMicroseconds(tone);
 }
}

void playNote(char note, int duration) {
 char names[] = { 'c', 'd', 'e', 'f', 'g', 'a', 'b', 'C' };
 int tones[] = { 1915, 1700, 1519, 1432, 1275, 1136, 1014, 956 };

 // play the tone corresponding to the note name
 for (int i = 0; i < 8; i++) {
  if (names[i] == note) {
   playTone(tones[i], duration);
  }
 }
}

void setup() {
 pinMode(speakerPin, OUTPUT);
}

void loop() {
 for (int i = 0; i <  length; i++) {
  if (notes[i] == ' ') {
   delay(beats[i] * tempo); // rest
  } else {
    playNote(notes[i], beats[i] * tempo);
  }

  // pause between notes
  delay(tempo / 2);
 }
}
```

Once the sketch is uploaded to the Arduino, it will play the "Twinkle, Twinkle, Little Star" melody. The melody keeps playing until power is removed from the Arduino.

## Try It!

To see the tones electrically, attach an oscilloscope (if one is available) across the piezo-buzzer, as shown in Figure 6-17. A close-up of the waveform data displayed on the oscilloscope is shown in Figure 6-18. As the melody plays, various PWM signals flash on the screen. The frequencies for each note are visible as well. This method of seeing the music play, in terms of notes, on the oscilloscope, is a quick way to validate the sketch.

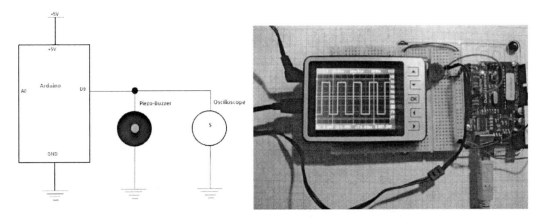

***Figure 6-17.*** *Attaching an oscilloscope to see the PWM signal as the sketch is executing on the Arduino*

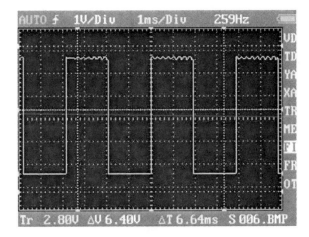

***Figure 6-18.*** *Saved image from a digital storage oscilloscope of the music box controller PWM output playing "Twinkle, Twinkle, Little Star"*

If you'd like to play a different melody is desired, you can change the sketch by modifying the int length variable, char notes[], and the int beats[] arrays. Try changing these three lines of code to the following:

```
int length = 13; // the number of notes
    char notes[] = "ccdcfeccdcgf "; // a space represents a rest
    int beats[] = { 1, 1, 1, 1, 1, 2, 1, 1, 1, 1, 1, 2, 4 };
```

After making the modifications to the "Twinkle, Twinkle, Little Star" sketch with these three lines of code, upload the new program to the Arduino. The music box controller will now play a new song instead of the original one. The note pattern will change, and you can observe this on the oscilloscope. Figure 6-19 shows the new PWM waveform based on the three lines of modified code.

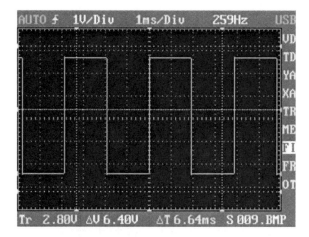

**Figure 6-19.** *Saved image from a digital storage oscilloscope of the music box controller PWM output playing "Happy Birthday." Notice the smooth on time vs. that of the PWM waveform for "Twinkle, Twinkle, Little Star."*

You can find other musical tone sketches by clicking File ➤ Examples ➤ Digital in the Arduino-Processing editor. If the melody playing is becoming a nuisance while validating the sketch, leave the oscilloscope attached to the Arduino' s PWM port pin and remove the piezo-buzzer from the circuit. After you remove the piezo-buzzer, note that the oscilloscope will no longer display a ripple the on time, as shown in on the right in Figure 6-20.

You can add another hardware component to adjust the volume of the piezo-buzzer if leaving the oscilloscope attached is not an option. A potentiometer can be wired to the Arduino's PWM port pin 9 using the circuit schematic diagram shown on the left in Figure 6-20.

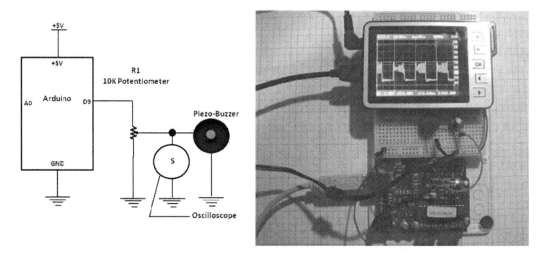

**Figure 6-20.** *Circuit schematic diagram for attaching an oscilloscope to see the PWM signal (left) and the oscilloscope showing the sketch executing on the Arduino (right). Volume control is provided by a 10Kpotentiometer.*

A close-up of the PWM signal generated from the "Happy Birthday" melody is shown in Figure 6-21.

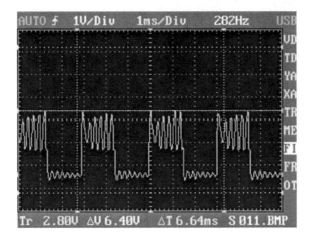

***Figure 6-21.*** *Saved image of PWM output adjusted to one-half volume using a 10 K potentiometer. Notice the oscillations on both the peak voltage and off time of the PWM output signal.*

The oscillations on both the peak voltage and off time of the PWM output signal are caused by the piezo-buzzer's internal crystallization behavior being stimulated by the switching of the ATmega328's OSC1 port. You can consider the oscillations to be small amounts of electrical noise being induced by the piezo-buzzer onto the PWM output signal generated by the ATmega328. Removal of the piezo-buzzer will allow clean pulses to be produced by the ATmega328 microcontroller.

## Driving a Speaker

Besides allowing melodies to be played through a piezo-buzzer, the Arduino is capable of driving an 8Ω speaker. In this case, the output does not sound as digitized as it does with the piezo-buzzer. In observing the waveforms on an oscilloscope, notice that the top peaks have fewer ripples on the PWM output signal from the speaker as compared to the piezo-buzzer output. Figure 6-22 illustrates the PWM output signal from the Arduino's ATmega328 microcontroller with the ripple removed from the waveform. The speaker has an intrinsic inductance of the coil that surrounds the cone, which provides a little filtering to the PWM output signal. The piezo-buzzer is somewhat noisy in operation because of the crystalline structure and voltage signal it generates when disturbed by a switching source (in this case, the PWM signal) applied to it. To limit the amount of current flowing thru the coil of a speaker, a 100 Ω resistor is added to one of the leads. Figure 6-23 shows the Fritzing sketch of a speaker replacing the piezo-buzzer in the original music box controller. The circuit schematic diagram and physical prototype is illustrated in Figure 6-24.

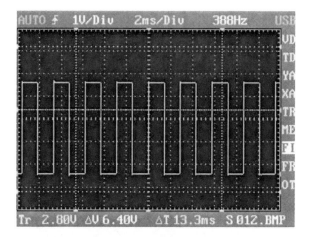

*Figure 6-22. The PWM output signal from an 8Ω speaker. Notice that there is no ripple on either the peak voltage or the off time of the PWM output signal.*

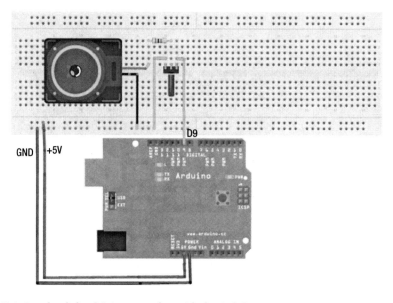

*Figure 6-23. The Fritzing sketch for driving a speaker with the Arduino*

---

■ **Note**    The Fritzing software has the ability to create circuit schematic diagrams and printed circuit boards (PCBs).

---

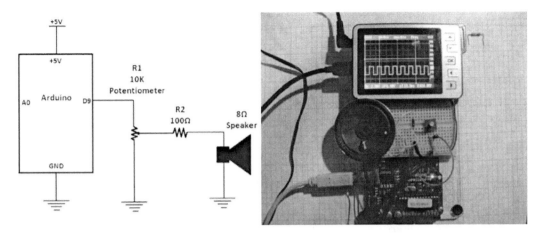

*Figure 6-24. Circuit schematic diagram with prototype build of a music box controller with speaker*

The volume of the speaker can be controlled using the 10K potentiometer. As discussed, the ripple on the PWM output signal has been minimized tremendously as compared to that of the piezo-buzzer. The adjusted speaker volume waveform is shown in Figure 6-25.

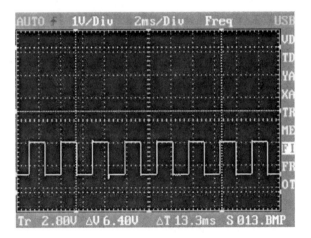

*Figure 6-25. An adjusted PWM output signal driven by the Arduino*

# Physical Computing and the Music Box Controller

The music box controller can easily be made interactive by interfacing sensors to the Arduino computational platform, thus creating a physical-computing layer to the musical device. As discussed in Chapter 3 (the ATmega328 microcontroller ADC circuit schematic diagram), the ATmega328 microcontroller has eight ADC channels, of which six are used for the Arduino, thereby making sensory-interfacing expansion easy and seamless. The physical-computing device's system block diagrams shown in Figures 6-2 through 6-5 will be investigated in this section. Also, the operation of the PMOSFET will be explained as it pertains to providing a power driver circuit for both a piezo-buzzer and a speaker.

## What Is a PMOSFET?

A PMOSET is designed to handle high-current electrical loads. It has high input impedance (AC resistance) with an electrically insulated gate, making it a voltage-controlled device. Because of this, it doesn't have the problem of current leakage like a bipolar junction transistor making it unstable for frequency response–based applications such as amplifiers. Also, the drain-to-source resistance (Rds) is low—in the milliohm (mΩ) range. Because of this range, its power dissipation is quite low compared to the BJT, making it an excellent electronic switch for directly driving electromechanical loads that demand high-current, such as light bulbs, small DC motors, and solenoids. It's a *majority-carrier* (electron) device that stores no electrical charge, making it switch faster than a BJT. A majority carrier is the electrons that move freely in electronic circuit. The PMOSFET can be used in amplifier and switching applications, just like the BJT, allowing it to be a direct high power-substitute component. Figure 6-26 shows a typical PMOSFET component with a pinout, along with its electrical symbol.

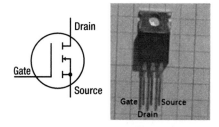

*Figure 6-26. Pinout for an N-channel PMOSFET (IRF630A) with its electrical symbol*

---

■ **Note**    Just like the BJT, the PMOSFET has two types of devices: an N-channel and a P-channel component.

---

The N-channel PMOSFET is labeled as shown in Figure 6-26 because the arrow tip, which is negative, touches one of the dashed lines making up part of the channel. The channel allows migration of electrons received from the gate, thereby turning on the PMOSFET. Current flows between the *drain* and *source*, allowing the PMOSFET to switch on any electrical load connected to it. The drain, gate, and source are the pins of a PMOSFET. As mentioned, the Rds is very low, allowing the current to flow easily between the two pins. With such a low Rds, more current can flow, making it ideal for switching high-current electrical loads, as compared to the BJT. The metal tab attached to the PMOSFET can serve as a thermal transfer mechanism when driving high-current electrical loads. An external heat sink attached to this tab, along with thermal conductive paste, will allow the PMOSFET to stay cool when switching high-current devices. There is also a P-channel MOSFET component that can be used in amplifier or circuit-switching applications. The arrow for the P-channel PMOSFET points away from the channel, thereby allowing the positive material to make contact with the channel. Figure 6-27 shows the electrical symbol for a P-channel MOSFET component.

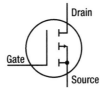

**Figure 6-27.** *The electrical symbol for a P-channel PMOSFET*

## A PMOSFET Multisim Circuit Model

Figure 6-28 shows a Multisim circuit model to illustrate the operation of a PMOSFET as an electronic driver. The operation of the circuit is such that turning on the electronic driver with the SPST (single-pole, single-throw) switch and changing the 1MΩ potentiometer resistance value will change the brightness of the LED from off to on.

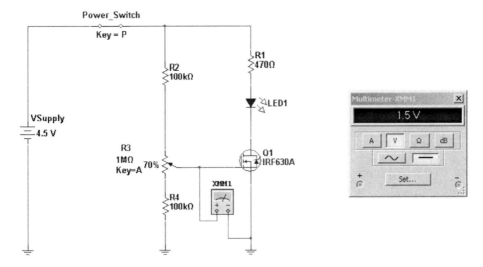

**Figure 6-28.** *A Multisim PMOSFET LED driver demonstration circuit (Forrest Mims Basic Electronics Lab Manual)*

The LED turns on based on the gate-threshold voltage (Vgs-th), which typically is 3VDC. The minimum Vgs-th voltage value is 2VDC. In Figure 6-29 the LED is off because the Vgs-th value is 1.5VDC. By adjusting the 1MΩ potentiometer to 2VDC, the LED will turn on. Figure 6-30 illustrates controlling the PMOSFET based on Vgs-th.

---

■ **Note** The Vgs-th value is similar to biasing a BJT. The challenge of switching the PMOSFET is overcoming the internal gate capacitance (Cg). Although in the Multisim circuit model, an increase of Vgs-th was able to overcome the internal Cg, for sensitive or crucial high-speed switching circuits, an electronic circuit known as an f is used to provide a high gate voltage (Vg) to surpass Cg voltage, thereby allowing the PMOSFET to switch on/off at the appropriate switching time. Now that's how to flex muscles in electronics!

---

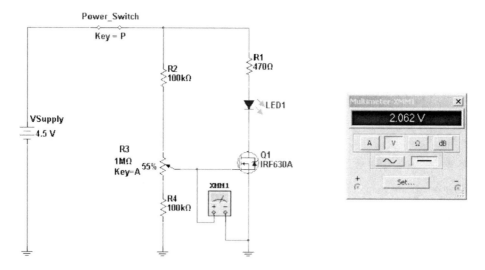

**Figure 6-29.** *A Multisim PMOSFET LED driver demonstration circuit (left), and the proper Vgs-th signal for switching on the LED (right)*

With the PMOSFET capable of driving electrical loads as high as 200VDC at 9A, an 8 Ω speaker driver circuit can be realized quite easily. Figure 6-30 shows a remixed system block diagram of Figure 6-2 with a PMOSFET speaker driver circuit with a volume control.

---

■ **Note**  Due to the driving power that the PMOSFET provides in outputting sound to the speaker, the volume control allows you to adjust the PWM signal down to a reasonable level.

---

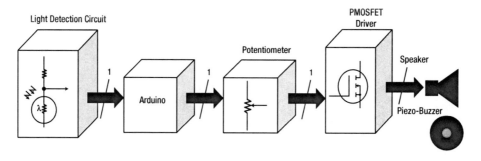

**Figure 6-30.** *System block diagram for the remixed interactive music box controller*

Using the systems block diagram as a design guide, the Fritzing circuit build/model is shown in Figure 6-31. The circuit schematic diagram and the actual prototype build of the interactive music box controller are shown in Figure 6-32. The sketch uploaded to the Arduino will allow you to interact with the music box controller by waving a hand over the CdS photocell.

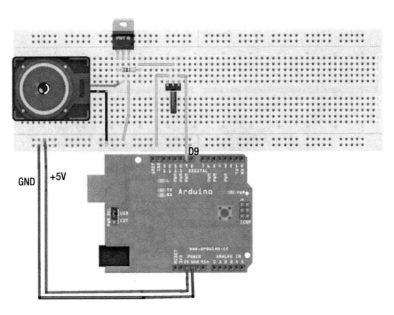

*Figure 6-31.* *The Fritzing circuit build of the interactive music box controller with a PMOSFET speaker driver circuit*

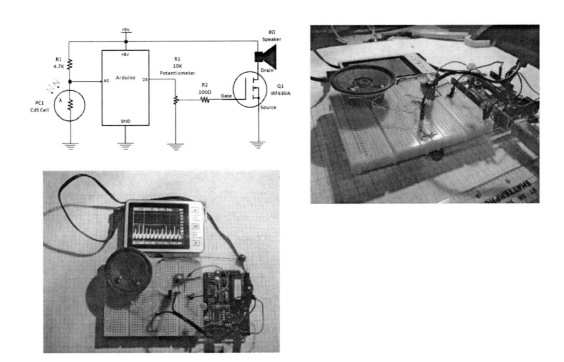

*Figure 6-32.* *Prototype build of the interactive music box controller with a circuit schematic diagram*

Initially, the music box controller will have a 2.77KHz buzzing sound without human interaction. Placing your hand over the light detection circuit sensor will allow it to blare out a 625 Hz PWM signal. Continued waving of the hand over the photocell will cause the music box controller to generate different sounds with unique frequencies. Figure 6-33 shows the waveform pattern with the music box controller's photocell under ambient light.

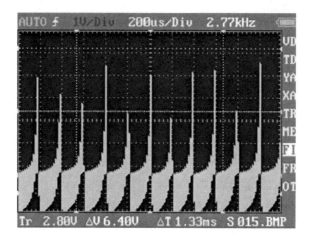

***Figure 6-33.*** *PWM output signal from interactive music box under ambient lighting*

By waving a hand over the CdS cell, the tone/pitch is changed, as well as the frequency, as shown in Figure 6-34. Notice the sharp spike in Figure 6-34—the transient (electrical noise) on the positive, or rising, edge of the PWM signal is caused by the PMOSFET switching on quite fast and hard. The PMOSFET on-switching time is quite fast and can produce noisy positive edges. These noisy signal peak edges can be reduced either through software or by adding a few nanofarads (nF) of capacitance at the gate of the switching component.

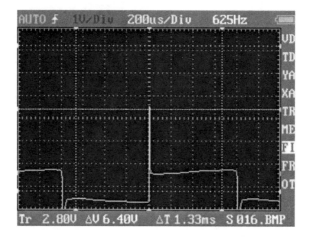

***Figure 6-34.*** *PWM output signal from the interactive music box with a hand passing over the photocell*

To obtain a different set of tones, you can replace the 8Ω speaker with the piezo-buzzer. Figure 6-35 shows the music box controller PWM output under two lighting conditions: ambient light and passing a hand or object over the photocell. Although this device is more of a sound-effects generator than a music box, with a little practice, basic musical tunes can be made by the wave a hand!

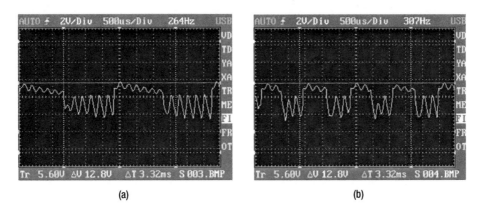

(a)　　　　　　　　　　　　　　　(b)

*Figure 6-35. Piezo buzzer PWM output signal from interactive music box in ambient light (a) and with a hand passing over the photocell (b). The 10K potentiometer was adjusted to approximately half volume. Waveforms may vary slightly based on the type of ambient lighting (e.g., incandescent vs. CFL).*

---

■ **Note**    This music box controller is patterned after the famous theremin musical instrument. It was patented in 1928 by physics professor Lev Sergeivich Termen (aka Leon Theremin). The basic operating principle behind his invention is the heterodyning (i.e., combining) of two radio frequency signals to produce audio tones using oscillators. One oscillator is fixed while the other controls the pitch of the tone by using an antenna. The body of the performer is grounded by standing on a metal plate. The performer's hand, which is an extension of the metal plate, acts as a grounded plate of a variable capacitor in an LC (inductor-capacitor) oscillator circuit of the theremin. This LC oscillator circuit establishes one frequency. The other hand changes the frequency of the first oscillator by movement near the antenna. The difference between the two frequencies creates a new audio tone.

---

## Sketch for the Interactive Music Box Controller

The sketch to be uploaded to the interactive music box controller is within the Examples folder of the Arduino IDE software. To obtain the sketch for the interactive music box within the Arduino IDE, go to File ➤ Examples ➤ Digital ➤ tonePitchFollower. Figure 6-36 shows the tonePitchFollower sketch within the Examples directory.

---

■ **Note**    A quick method of developing software is to remix it to suit the new application.

---

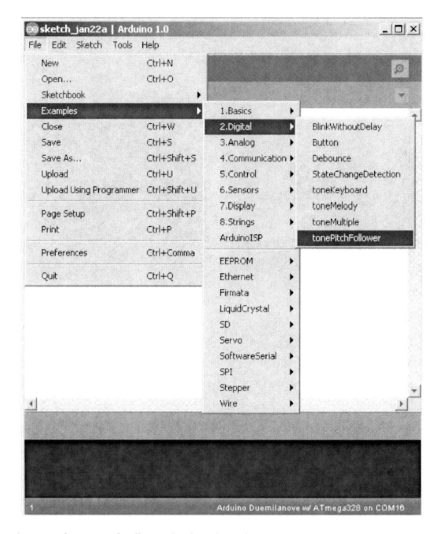

**Figure 6-36.** *Obtaining the tonePitchFollower sketch in the Arduino IDE*

The tonePitchFollower sketch is shown in Listing 6-2.

**Listing 6-2.** The tonePitchFollower Sketch

```
/*
Pitch follower
Plays a pitch that changes based on a changing analog input
```

```
circuit:
* 8-ohm speaker on digital pin 9
* photoresistor on analog 0 to 5 V
* 4.7 K resistor on analog 0 to ground

created 21 Jan 2010
modified 30 Aug 2011
by Tom Igoe

This example code is in the public domain.

http://arduino.cc/en/Tutorial/Tone2
*/
void setup() {
 // initialize serial communications (for debugging only):
 Serial.begin(9600);
}
void loop() {
 // read the sensor:
 int sensorReading = analogRead(A0);
 // print the sensor reading so you know its range
 Serial.println(sensorReading);
 // map the pitch to the range of the analog input.
 // change the minimum and maximum input numbers below
 // depending on the range your sensor's giving:
 int thisPitch =  map(sensorReading, 400, 1000, 100, 1000);

 // play the pitch:
 tone(9, thisPitch, 10);
}
```

An embedded feature of the sketch is the ability to see the analog data generated by the sensor wired to A0 of the Arduino's inline header connector. The serial monitor of the Arduino-Processing IDE is called based on this single line of code:

```
Serial.println(sensorReading);
```

This line of code is a built-in debug feature that allows the sensor-interfacing circuit to be validated prior to adding either the piezo-buzzer or speaker for audio feedback. The serial monitor can be obtained as shown in Figure 6-37.

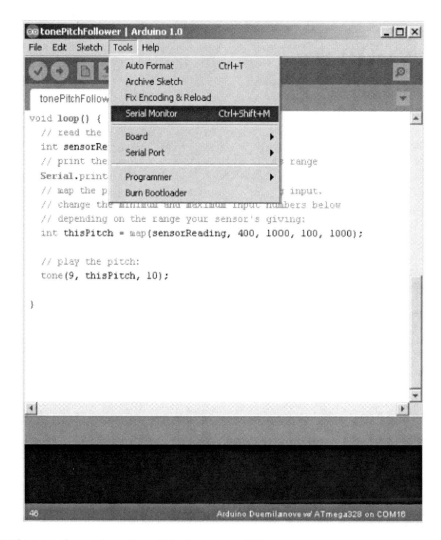

**Figure 6-37.** *Obtaining the serial monitor within the Arduino IDE*

The output of the serial monitor based on the CdS photocell interfacing circuit is shown in Figure 6-38.

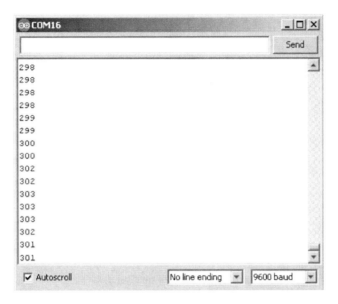

*Figure 6-38. CdS photocell data being displayed on the serial monitor within the Arduino IDE*

Notice COM16 at the top left of the serial monitor. This is the communication port that the Arduino is plugged into or attached to. This value will vary based on the communication port you use during microcontroller-electronics development.

# Building and Testing a Basic Music Box Controller with a Keypad

The final project in this chapter is to build a music box controller capable of generating tones using a keypad. Three distinct tones will be heard through the 8Ω speaker using three keys on a keypad. The systemblock diagram for this device was shown previously, in Figure 6-4. The circuit schematic diagram for the three-tone music box controller is shown in Figure 6-39.

---

■ **Tip** Tones were generated on old telephone keypads using a 567 Tone Decoder IC. The Arduino makes generating tones easy.

---

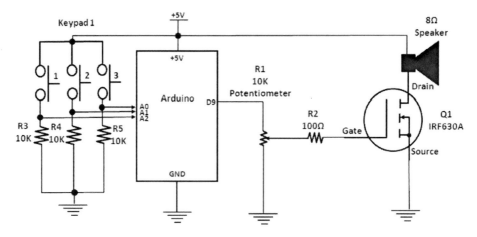

**Figure 6-39.** *Circuit schematic diagram for the three-key music box controller*

Pressing keys 1, 2, and 3 generates distinct frequencies heard as tones through the 8Ω speaker. The keypad shown in the circuit schematic diagram can easily be replaced with three tactile switches or a 4-bit DIP switch. The actual prototype build for the circuit schematic diagram shown in Figure 6-39 is shown in Figure 6-40.

**Figure 6-40.** *The prototype build of the three-key music box controller*

You can find the toneKeyboard sketch by going to Examples ➤ Digital ➤ toneKeyboard in the Arduino IDE. The sketch listing for uploading to the Arduino is shown in Listing 6-3.

***Listing 6-3.*** The toneKeyboard Sketch

```
/*
 keyboard

 Plays a pitch that changes based on a changing analog input

 circuit:
 * 3 force-sensing resistors from +5V to analog in 0 through 2
 * 3 10 K resistors from analog in 0 through 2 to ground
 * 8-ohm speaker on digital pin 9

 created 21 Jan 2010
 modified 30 Aug 2011
 by Tom Igoe
 modified 23 Jan 2012
 by Don Wilcher

This example code is in the public domain.

 http://arduino.cc/en/Tutorial/Tone3

 */

#include "pitches.h"

const int threshold = 10;  // minimum reading of the sensors that generates a note

// notes to play, corresponding to the 3 sensors:
int notes[] = {
 NOTE_A4, NOTE_B4,NOTE_C3 };

void setup() {
}
void loop() {
 for (int thisSensor = 0; thisSensor < 3; thisSensor++) {
  // get a sensor reading:
  int sensorReading = analogRead(thisSensor);

  // if the sensor is pressed hard enough:
  if (sensorReading > threshold) {
   // play the note corresponding to this sensor:
   tone(9, notes[thisSensor], 20);
  }
 }
 Serial.println();
}
```

Upon uploading the sketch to the Arduino, pressing keys 1, 2, 3, or any combination of them on the keypad will produce unique tones.

# Final Testing of the Music Box Controllers

This chapter outlined a series of activities for visually looking at the operation of the Arduino circuits. Using an oscilloscope, the circuit waveforms maybe used to validate proper operation of the Arduino music box devices. Depending on the vendor and type of testing instruments, the results may vary by +/-10 percent. Here are some things to keep in mind while testing:

- Make sure the wiring is correct prior to applying voltage to the Arduino and supporting circuits.

- Use proper wiring methods as discussed in Chapter 3.

- Refer to the "How It Works" section of this chapter for details on verifying that the circuit breadboard is working correctly.

- Review the sketch entered into the Arduino IDE editor for typos that could cause the hardware device to operate improperly.

# Further Discovery Methods

For the music box controller, try experimenting with a FlexiForce sensor or joystick. The system block diagram for the FlexiForce sensor was shown in Figure 6-3. The tonePitchFollower sketch will work with both the FlexiForce sensor and the joystick. Also, experiment with print text messages for diagnostics/testing of the tonePitchFollower and toneKeyboard sketches using the serial monitor, as discussed earlier in this chapter. Try adding additional key buttons to the circuit schematic diagram shown in Figure 6-39 Last, replace the IRF630A PMOSFET with a 2N3904 NPN transistor and note the difference in audio output gain. Remember to document your designs in a lab notebook along any modifications you made to the sketch.

# CHAPTER 7

■ ■ ■

# Fun with Haptics

Haptics is the sensing and manipulation of objects using touch. The Arduino has the ability to monitor and control devices using sensors and electromechanical actuators. Sensory devices that can be interfaced or wired to the Arduino include CdS photocells, tactile switches, thermistors, and temperature ICs. Electromechanical actuators (such as solenoids) and motors (such as servos, steppers, and DC motors) can be used to manipulate or change the orientation of objects either in a linear or angular direction.

There are several areas of haptics research (human, machine, and computer) being conducted in university and corporate research labs. In this chapter, the fundamentals of machine haptics will be explored through basic lab experiments and projects using off-the-shelf or junk box electronic components. A 1 DOF (1 degree of freedom) robot is used to illustrate a simple feedback technique. To help in the discussion of haptics, mechatronics will be introduced in this chapter along with additional physical computing prototyping methods. Figure 7-1 shows the parts required for the hands-on projects and experiments.

## Parts List

1 Arduino Duemilanove or equivalent

1 joystick

1 470K resistor

4 10K resistor

1 FlexiForce sensor

1 CdS photocell

1 4-bit DIP switch

1 2 N3904 NPN transistor

1 IFR630A N-channel MOSFET

1 keypad

1 vibration motor

1 small solderless breadboard

22 AWG solid wire

Digital multimeter

Oscilloscope (optional)

Electronic tools

Robotics kits

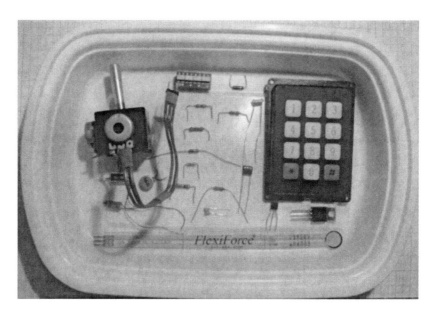

*Figure 7-1. Parts required for the haptics projects and experiments*

## Remixing Physical Computing and Driver Interface Circuits

Continuing with the technique of remix, you will make several physical computing and driver interface circuits using FlexiForce sensors, 4-bit DIP switch, CdS (cadmium sulphide) photocell, speakers, and a keypad to allow human interaction with the haptics controller. The BJT and PMOSFET electronic components drive a vibration motor. The Arduino provides the control signal to switch the BJT and PMOSFET drivers ON and OFF. Figure 7-2 shows the system block diagram for the physical computing/haptics controller. A pictorial diagram of a simple robotic haptics system is illustrated in Figure 7-3.

---

■ **Tip**    The transistor driver sub-circuit block can either be a BJT or a PMOSFET. Flexibility is king!

---

■ **Note**    1 DOF is the abbreviation for degree of freedom. It's just an average ordinary robot!

---

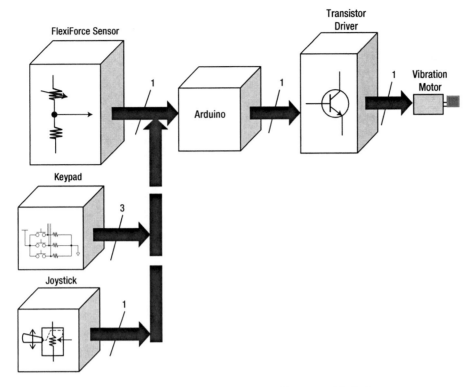

***Figure 7-2.*** *An Arduino-based physical computing/haptics controller system block diagram*

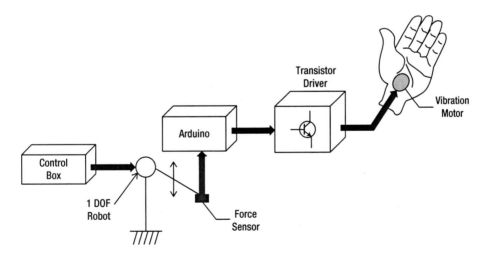

***Figure 7-3.*** *A simple experimental robotics-based haptics system*

In Figure 7-2, there are several input devices connected to the Arduino. All of these devices are not connected at the same time but the diagram illustrates the versatility of the experimental setup for exploring haptics on the lab bench or workshop. The interfacing concepts and techniques discussed in previous chapters will be revisited but with a remix slant.

## How It Works

The system block diagram in Figure 7-2 shows a low-cost setup for exploring this technology using the Arduino computational platform along with off-the-shelf components. By attaching either a digital sensor (tactile switch or keypad) or an analog part (CdS photocell or FlexiForce sensor) to the input of the Arduino, the Atmega328 microcontroller will provide sensory/detection information to the chip's physical layer for processing a decision-making event. Upon the appropriate value being present at the input port, the Atmega328 microcontroller will make the decision to switch its output port ON or OFF based on the device's binary logic or analog signal level. For driving a haptics component, the output signal must be short in duration, providing a one-shot pulse to the target electromechanical part. (A *one-shot pulse* is a quick ON-OFF voltage signal used to trigger electronic circuits). With each triggering of the input sensor/detection component, the Atmega328 will provide a one-shot pulse to the wired output electromechanical part. To start the investigation of haptics, let's try a simple test and experiment on driving a vibration motor.

## Experimenting with a Vibration Motor

A vibration motor is simply a DC motor with a small weight placed off-center on its shaft. With the weight being off-center or *asymmetric*, the motor vibrates. Vibration motors are found in old style pagers, hand video controllers, and today's cellphones. The vibration motor comes in various sizes and shapes, and can easily be placed in small consumer electronics. Figure 7-4 shows a few examples of vibration motors.

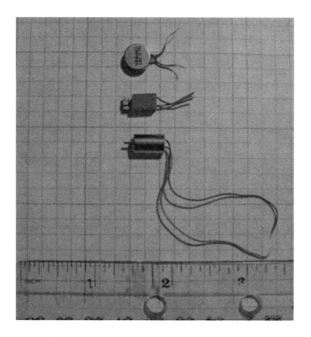

***Figure 7-4.*** *Vibration motor examples*

▨ **Note**  Examples of simple haptic interfaces include computer keyboards, mice, trackballs, and instrumented gloves. Back in the old days of computer technology, these components were known as *input devices*. Times have truly changed!

The top vibration motor in Figure 7-4 is a recycled component from a non-working cellphone. The wires attached to the vibration motor are quite small in diameter, making them useless in solderless breadboard prototyping. Figure 7-5 shows a close-up of the recycled vibration motor and its tiny electrical leads.

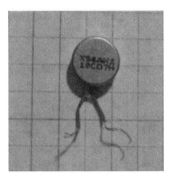

*Figure 7-5. A vibration motor recycled from a non-working cellphone. The leads are quite small, making it difficult to wire to the Arduino and the solderless breadboard.*

To make it easy to attach the vibration motor to the breadboard, additional 22AWG wires are soldered to the tiny leads, as shown in Figure 7-6. Now the vibration motor can easily be wired to the Arduino for experimenting and testing, as shown in Figure 7-7. Circuit analysis for determining the amount of current sourcing thru the motor's Ra (armature resistance) is quite easy to do. The paper analysis steps are shown in the following equation. Figure 7-8 shows Ra being measured using an ohmmeter.

▨ **Tip**  Although mathematically simple, Ohm's Law is a very powerful analytical tool for circuit analysis. Georg Simon Ohm (1787-1854) rocks!

The measured armature resistance is used to build a circuit model using Multisim software to compare the simulation total current (Itotal) with the paper analysis. The paper analysis is based on using Ohm's Law to determine Itotal value of the simple series DC circuit.

The equation for Itotal is Itotal = Vsupply/Ra

where

Vsupply = 5VDC and Ra (measured) = 29.2Ω

Itotal = Vsupply / Ra

Itotal = 5VDC / 29.2Ω

Itotal = 171.2 mA

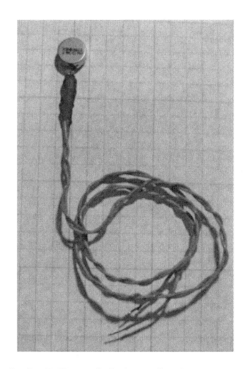

*Figure 7-6. Adding extension leads of 22AWG stranded wire to vibration motor*

*Figure 7-7. The vibration motor wired to the Arduino computational platform*

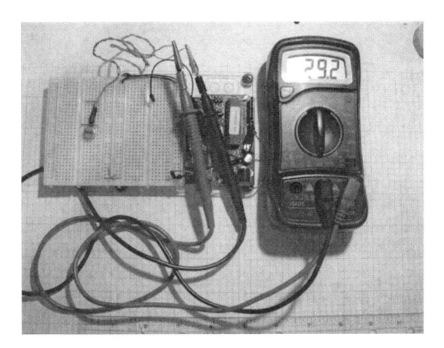

**Figure 7-8.** *Measuring the vibration motor's Ra using a DMM (digital multimeter) ohmmeter*

The results from the Multisim simulation are in Figure 7-9. The equivalent circuit schematic diagram for the vibration motor prototype build along with measuring total current (Itotal) is shown in Figure 7-10.

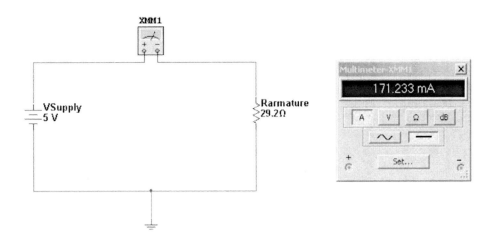

**Figure 7-9.** *Measuring the vibration motor's Ra current (Itotal) using a virtual DMMs ammeter*

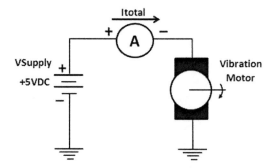

*Figure 7-10. Measuring Itotal of a vibration motor circuit schematic diagram*

With a baseline value of voltage and current captured, the next investigative step is to measure the output voltage of the Arduino driving the vibration motor. The motor current can measured using an ammeter. Figures 7-11 and 7-12 show the measurement setup with results of the output sourcing voltage and current from the Arduino. The circuit schematic diagrams for measuring the Arduino port D5 output voltage and the current flowing thru the vibration motor are shown in Figures 7-13 and 7-14. The sketch for running the vibration motor is shown in Listing 7-1.

*Listing 7-1.* Vibration Motor Test Sketch

```
int motorPin = 5;

void setup()
{

  pinMode(motorPin, OUTPUT);
  digitalWrite(motorPin, HIGH);
}

void loop()
{

    delay(100);

}
```

Compile and execute the sketch in the usual way. For instructions on how to upload the test sketch to the Arduino computational platform, see Chapter 1.

**Figure 7-11.** *Measuring the output voltage of Arduino port D5 with a DMM voltmeter*

**Figure 7-12.** *Measuring the output voltage of Arduino port D5 with a DMM voltmeter*

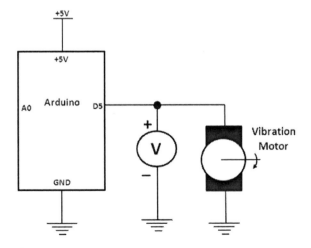

**Figure 7-13.** *The circuit schematic diagram for measuring the output voltage (Vout) at Arduino port D5 with a DMM voltmeter*

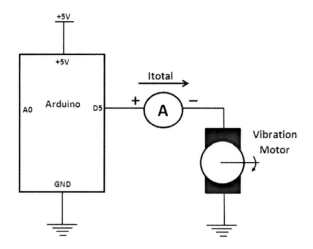

*Figure 7-14. The circuit schematic diagram for measuring the motor current (Ia[armature current] = Itotal) with a DMM ammeter*

With the measured values obtained from the DMM's ammeter and voltmeter for output voltage and the motor current, the Ra can be calculated using Ohm's Law.

---

■ **Tip** Based on the vibration motor used in your lab experiment, the measurement values will vary slightly.

---

The equation for Ra is

Ra = Vout/Imotor

where

Vout (measured) = 2.98VDC and Imotor (measured) = 102.6 mA

Ra = Vout/ Imotor

Ra = 2.98VDC / 102.6 mA

Ra = 29.04Ω

A Multisim circuit model for this analysis is shown in Figure 7-15.

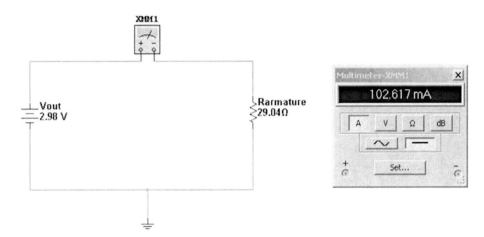

*Figure 7-15. Measuring the vibration motor's Itotal based on the Arduino's port D5 output voltage (Vout) using a virtual DMM ammeter*

The electrical parameters of Ra measured and Ra calculated are pretty close to each other in value. To determine the %difference between the measured Ra and the calculated value, the following equation is used:

%difference = [|Ra(calculated)-Ra(measured)| / Ra(measured)] × 100

Making the appropriate substitutions, the resultant answer is

%difference = [| 29.04Ω − 29.2Ω | /29.2Ω] × 100

%difference = [| −0.16Ω | /29.2Ω] × 100

%difference = | −0.00547 | × 100

%difference = 0.547%

To manage the experimental and analysis data for this lab experiment, create an Excel spreadsheet. The creation of this data management tool is left as a self discovery task for the reader!

# Physical Computing: A Vibration Motor

The system block diagram shown in Figure 7-2 illustrates three physical computing devices to control a vibration motor: a FlexiForce sensor, a keypad, and a joystick. First, let's look at using the joystick to control the vibration motor. The joystick will be used to control the speed of the vibration motor. The new system block diagram is shown in Figure 7-16.

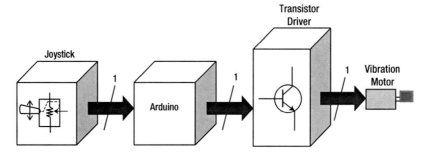

**Figure 7-16.** *A joystick-controlled vibration motor system block diagram*

The circuit schematic diagram for the system block diagram is shown in Figure 7-17. By moving the joystick back and forth, the speed of the vibration motor changes. The frequency change is proportional to the speed. Low frequencies provide a slow rotational speed of the vibration motor. Higher frequencies trigger faster rotational speeds of the vibration motor. Placing a finger on top of the vibration motor causes a buzzing sound quite similar to a pager or cellphone call notification.

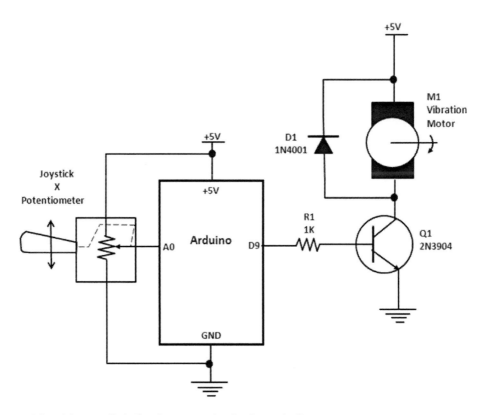

**Figure 7-17.** *A joystick-controlled vibration motor circuit schematic diagram*

The prototype build of the joystick controlled vibration motor is shown in Figure 7-18. The joystick is held in place on the solderless breadboard by bridging a small jumper wire across the attached wires of the potentiometer. The PWM signal generated by the Arduino D9 digital port pin can be monitored using an oscilloscope, which is shown in Figure 7-19. The PWM signal has little in the way of oscillatory peaks or *ripple*, which doesn't impede in the stability in controlling the vibration motor. Figure 7-20 is a screenshot image of the PWM signal generated by the Arduino computational platform.

***Figure 7-18.*** *A joystick-controlled vibration motor prototype*

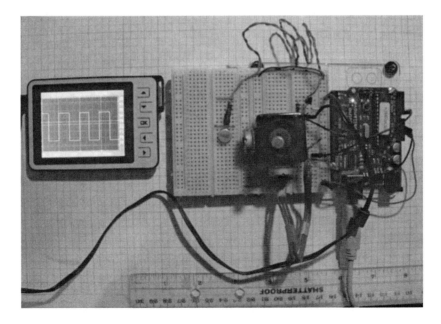

***Figure 7-19.*** *Lab setup for monitoring the output PWM signal of the Arduino computational platform*

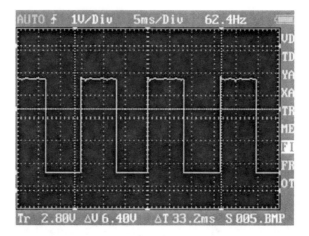

*Figure 7-20. Screen shot of the Arduino-generated output PWM signal*

The output PWM signal parameters measured with a digital oscilloscope are as follows:

- Vmax = 4.27 V

- Vavg = 2.07 V

- DC(Duty Cycle) = 49.7 %

- Frequency = 62.5 Hz

The sketch used to generate the output PWM for speed control is shown in Listing 7-2.

*Listing 7-2.* Stepper Motor Control Sketch

```
/*
Stepper Motor Control - speed control

This program drives a unipolar or bipolar stepper motor.
The motor is attached to digital pins 8 - 11 of the Arduino.
A potentiometer is connected to analog input 0.

The motor will rotate in a clockwise direction. The higher the potentiometer value,
the faster the motor speed. Because setSpeed() sets the delay between steps,
you may notice the motor is less responsive to changes in the sensor value at
low speeds.

Created 30 Nov. 2009
Modified 28 Oct 2010
by Tom Igoe

*/

#include <Stepper.h>

const int stepsPerRevolution = 200; // change this to fit the number of steps per revolution
// for your motor
```

```
// initialize the stepper library on pins 8 through 11:
Stepper myStepper(stepsPerRevolution, 8,9,10,11);

int stepCount = 0;        // number of steps the motor has taken

void setup() {
 // initialize the serial port:
 Serial.begin(9600);
}

void loop() {
 // read the sensor value:
 int sensorReading = analogRead(A0);
 // map it to a range from 0 to 100:
 int motorSpeed = map(sensorReading, 0, 1023, 0, 100);
 // set the motor speed:
 if (motorSpeed > 0) {
  myStepper.setSpeed(motorSpeed);
  // step 1/100 of a revolution:
  myStepper.step(stepsPerRevolution/100);
 }
}
```

■ **Tip**    Although this sketch is written for stepper motor speed control, it works well with a vibration motor. A motor is a motor, of course of course…

# Try It Out

There is a direct relationship between the vibration motor's speed and the output frequency of the PWM signal that controls it. To explore this speed vs. frequency relationship, consider this line of code (it manages the speed of the vibration motor as well as the frequency):

```
const int stepsPerRevolution = 200;
```

By increasing the value of the stepsPerRevolution constant, the output PWM signal's frequency increases as well. With the aid of an oscilloscope, here are two measured examples:

- stepsPerRevolution = 1000, PWM frequency = 280 Hz
- stepsPerRevolution = 3000, PWM frequency = 345 Hz

The example waveform of a 285 Hz using a 1200 stepsPerRevolution value is shown in Figure 7-21.

■ **Note**    PWM frequency results may vary based on size and manufacturer of vibration motor. No fine print here!

***Figure 7-21.*** *A 285 Hz PWM signal based on a 1200 stepsPerRevolution value*

Observed with the decrease in input voltage, the output PWM signal's frequency produces a buzzer sound traditionally associated with cellphones on vibrate mode. Using the test-measurement setup shown in Figure 7-22, the following input voltage/output frequency data was obtained from the prototype:

- Joystick input voltage = 110 mV, output PWM frequency = 1.67 Hz

- Joystick input voltage = 74.6 mV, output PWM frequency = 0.83 Hz

***Figure 7-22.*** *Test and measurement setup for capturing the PWM output frequency with a given joystick input voltage*

The buzzing sound based on the position of the joystick allows you to create an application that sounds a warning when certain objects are detected. The solderless breadboard prototype can be adapted to a robotic system used for simple object detection. Contact with a small part (such as a ball) causes the vibration motor to vibrate, communicating the status of operation.

As a self discovery exercise, create a spreadsheet with column headings of "Joystick input voltage settings," "Measured output PWM frequencies," and "Comments." Populate these columns with the measured data. Based on the buzzing sound emitting from the vibration motor, try characterizing the type of tone in the Comments column.

Next, create a plot or characteristic curve showing the data. On the plot, place notes referencing the characterized tone on it. When a particular warning notification sound is needed for an electronics gadget, the input voltage setting can be used to dial in the target tone with ease. Try it out!

# Keypad Haptics

The Real Calculator app on my Android Droid X smartphone (shown in Figure 7-23) provides feedback after each key-touch on the screen. With each touch of the screen's keypad, a small vibration is felt. The following project is based on keypad haptics of the Real Calculator app.

*Figure 7-23. Real Calculator app vibrates the Android Droid X smartphone with each touch of the keys.*

A typical keypad is made with a plastic blister that makes contact with a matrix of conductors when pressed. The row/column construction allows for each key to be identified upon closing an electrical node and reading the status of the short circuit; no two switches will ever provide the same short circuit electrical node. Software techniques are used to read or scan the short circuits of the keys and provide a quick and efficient method of determining whether a key was pressed or not.

A three-button keypad can easily be built in Multisim to test the basic operation of the part (Figure 7-24). Basically, pressing either one of the target buttons on the keypad will provide a +5VDC output signal displayed on a virtual DMM's digital voltmeter. The basic keypad circuit will be wired to port D2 of the Arduino, allowing it to read a button press. Upon detecting a +5 VDC input signal, the Arduino will provide a short pulse to the transistor driver circuit wired to port D13, allowing it to turn on the vibration motor. Each target button on the keypad will provide the same pulse, allowing the vibration motor response to be equal in a short turn ON duration. This basic simulator behaves like the Real Calculator app installed on the Android phone. Figures 7-25 and 7-26 show the circuit schematic diagram for the keypad haptics demonstrator.

---

■ **Note** The idea behind keypad haptics on a touch screen is to provide sensory-audible feedback of button presses. The wonders of electronics technology never stop amazing me!

---

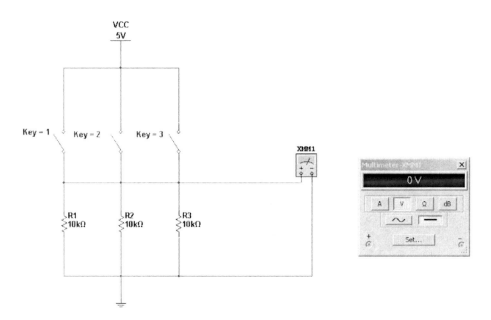

**Figure 7-24.** *A virtual three-button keypad circuit model built using Multisim. If no key is pressed, the output voltage equals 0VDC.*

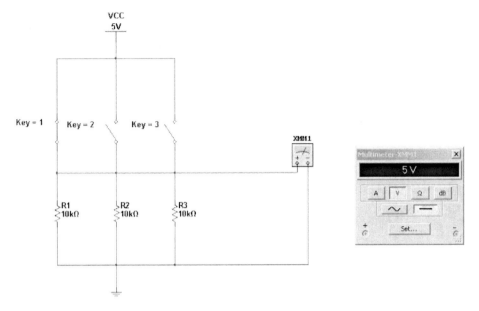

**Figure 7-25.** *With a key pressed, the output voltage equals 5VDC.*

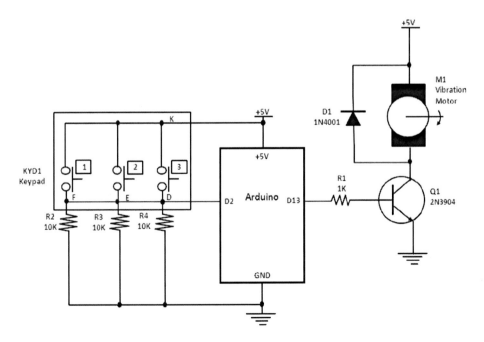

**Figure 7-26.** *Keypad haptics circuit schematic diagram*

When you use the keypad in the project, you identify the target button-switch combination required for activating the vibration motor. As shown in the circuit schematic diagram of Figure 7-25, button-switches 1, 2, and 3 are chosen for actuating the vibration motor. The wiring of the keypad to the Arduino is accomplished by wiring the three pins of components in parallel that connect all button-switch contacts together. As shown in the circuit schematic diagram, pins D, E, and F are wired together. The common pin that connects the other contacts of the button-switches internally is identified with the letter K. To see how to wire the keypad to the Arduino, look at the datasheet. Figure 7-27 shows the wiring matrix or truth table as it relates to the individual button-switches, their terminals or pins, and the common contacts for the keypad. A *truth table* is a tool showing combinations of input signals and their output values. The actual keypad along with the designated pins is illustrated in Figure 7-28.

---

■ **Tip** When using new electronic or electromechanical parts, always consult the datasheet for pinout and technical information regarding operation, theory, and special handling consideration. How's that for immediate tech support?!

---

## Code and Truth Table

Dots in the chart indicate connected terminals when switch is closed. Terminals are identified on the keyboard.

| 3x4 | CODES | | | | | | | | | | | | | | | | | | | |
|---|---|---|---|---|---|---|---|---|---|---|---|---|---|---|---|---|---|---|---|---|
| | Matrix | | | | | | | Single Pole/Common Bus | | | | | | | | | | | | |
| BUTTON LOCATION | F | E | D | K | J | H | G | J | E | A | K | F | B | L | G | C | M | H | D | N |
| 1 | • | | | • | | | | • | | | | | | | | | | | | • |
| 2 | | • | | • | | | | | • | | | | | | | | | | | • |
| 3 | | | • | • | | | | | | • | | | | | | | | | | • |
| 4 | • | | | | • | | | | | | • | | | | | | | | | • |
| 5 | | • | | | • | | | | | | | • | | | | | | | | • |
| 6 | | | • | | • | | | | | | | | • | | | | | | | • |
| 7 | • | | | | | • | | | | | | | | • | | | | | | • |
| 8 | | • | | | | • | | | | | | | | | • | | | | | • |
| 9 | | | • | | | • | | | | | | | | | | • | | | | • |
| 10 | • | | | | | | • | | | | | | | | | | • | | | • |
| 11 | | • | | | | | • | | | | | | | | | | | • | | • |
| 12 | | | • | | | | • | | | | | | | | | | | | • | • |
| | TERMINAL LOCATION | | | | | | | | | | | | | | | | | | | |

*Figure 7-27. A typical keypad switch matrix datasheet courtesy of Grayhill. The keypad is constructed in a row-column structure.*

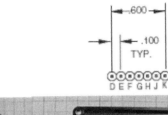

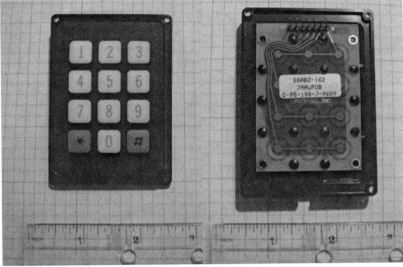

*Figure 7-28. A typical keypad with pin identification*

As shown in the keypad switch matrix diagram of Figure 7-27, the * and # are not listed. To use these button-switches, numbers 11 and 12 respectively will be substituted for the two character symbols. If a 16 button-switch keypad (shown in Figure 7-29) is desired for a haptics application, the matrix diagram on the right is consulted for proper wiring.

*Figure 7-29. A typical Grayhill 16 keypad. The keypad wiring is based on the right hand matrix shown in Figure 7-27.*

The final stage of the project is the prototype build. Figure 7-30 shows the keypad haptics prototype. A test to assure the keypad interface circuit is working properly consists of measuring the button–switch actuations using a DMM digital voltmeter. Pressing button-switches 1, 2, or 3 will allow a +5VDC signal to be displayed on a digital voltmeter's LCD (see Figure 7-31). This signal behavior was illustrated in Figure 7-25 in the Multisim circuit model. The software code to test the keypad haptics electronics hardware is the Button sketch. To gain access to this sketch, go to the Arduino-Processing IDE ➤ Example ➤ Digital ➤ Button. Once displayed in the IDE's text editor, the sketch can then be uploaded to the Arduino.

---

■ **Tip**   In designing I/O (input/output) interfaces for the Arduino, you should build and simulate Multisim circuit models to obtain baseline data on target electrical parameters such as voltage and current. In addition, the electrical behavior can be observed virtually. After building the actual prototype circuit, test measurements and electrical behavior should be similar to the Multisim model. Also, Multisim can be used to troubleshoot errors in a circuit design prior to the prototype build as well. How's that for rapid development of a circuit concept idea? The power of Multisim is truly awesome!

---

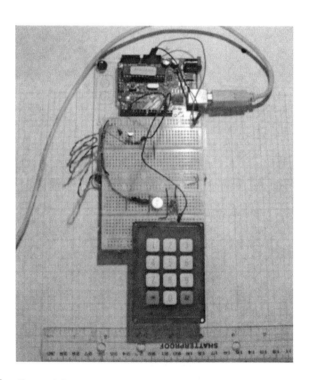

*Figure 7-30. The keypad haptics prototype*

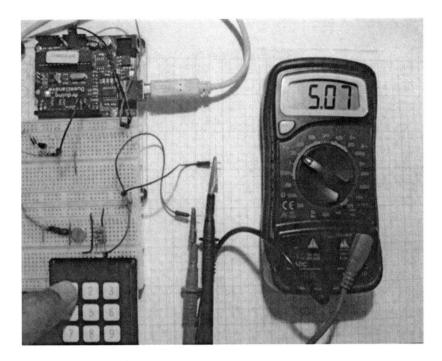

**Figure 7-31.** *Testing the keypad interface circuit using a DMM.*

The Button sketch is shown in Listing 7-3.

**Listing 7-3.** The Button Sketch

```
/*
Button

Turns on and off a light emitting diode(LED) connected to digital
pin 13, when pressing a pushbutton attached to pin 2.

The circuit:
* LED attached from pin 13 to ground
* pushbutton attached to pin 2 from +5V
* 10 K resistor attached to pin 2 from ground

* Note: on most Arduinos there is already an LED on the board
attached to pin 13.

created 2005
by DojoDave <http://www.0j0.org>
modified 30 Aug 2011
by Tom Igoe

This example code is in the public domain.

http://www.arduino.cc/en/Tutorial/Button
*/
```

```
// constants won't change. They're used here to
// set pin numbers:
const int buttonPin = 2;    // the number of the pushbutton pin
const int ledPin = 13;    // the number of the LED pin

// variables will change:
int buttonState = 0;      // variable for reading the pushbutton status

void setup() {
 // initialize the LED pin as an output:
 pinMode(ledPin, OUTPUT);
 // initialize the pushbutton pin as an input:
 pinMode(buttonPin, INPUT);
}

void loop(){
 // read the state of the pushbutton value:
 buttonState = digitalRead(buttonPin);

 // check if the pushbutton is pressed.
 // if it is, the buttonState is HIGH:
 if (buttonState == HIGH) {
  // turn LED on:
  digitalWrite(ledPin, HIGH);
 }
 else {
  // turn LED off:
  digitalWrite(ledPin, LOW);
 }
}
```

Pressing keys 1, 2, and 3 will turn on the vibration motor. Releasing them will stop the vibration motor. The final requirement of the sketch is to allow only a short ON duration of the vibration motor with the target keys. The remixed code to meet this new requirement is shown in Listing 7-4.

***Listing 7-4.*** The Keypad_VibrationMotor_control Sketch for the New Keypad Haptics Requirement

```
/*
Keypad

Turns on and off a vibration motor connected to digital
pin 13, when pressing a 3 specified buttons (1,2,3) on a keypad attached to pin 2.

The circuit:
* transistor driver base resistor attached from pin 13 and emitter to ground
* keypad pushbutton common "K" attached to pin 2 from +5 V
* keypad pins D, E, F attached to 3 - 10 resistors wired to 2
* 3-10 K resistors attached to pin 2 from ground

* Note: on most Arduinos there is already an LED on the board
attached to pin 13.

created 2005
by DojoDave <http://www.0j0.org>
```

```
modified 30 Aug 2011
by Tom Igoe
modified 09 Feb 2012
by Don Wilcher

This example code is in the public domain.

http://www.arduino.cc/en/Tutorial/Button
*/

// constants won't change. They're used here to
// set pin numbers:
const int keypadPin = 2;    // the number of the pushbutton pin
const int vibrationMotorPin = 13;    // the number of the LED pin

// variables will change:
int buttonState = 0;        // variable for reading the pushbutton status

void setup() {
 // initialize the vibrationMotorPin pin as an output:
 pinMode(vibrationmotorPin, OUTPUT);
 // initialize the pushbutton pin as an input:
 pinMode(keypadPin, INPUT);
}

void loop(){
 // read the state of the pushbutton value:
 buttonState = digitalRead(keypadPin);

 // check if the pushbutton is pressed.
 // if it is, the buttonState is HIGH:
 if (buttonState == HIGH) {
  // turn vibration motor on:
  digitalWrite(vibrationmotorPin, HIGH);
  delay(1); //Pulse vibration motor for a 1millisec
 }
 else {
  // turn vibration motor off:
  digitalWrite(vibrationmotorPin, LOW);
 }
}
```

The original Button sketch was modified by changing the constants referencing the LED and button with vibration motor and keypad, thereby making the code more reflective of the target I/O associated with the electronics hardware of the prototype. Also, an additional instruction (shown next) is added to the sketch to allow the vibration motor to be pulsed when the target button-switches on the keypad are pressed.

```
delay(1); //Pulse vibration motor for a 1msec
```

With a quick press/release of the target button-switches, the vibration motor will turn ON for 1 second, then turn OFF. This operation is similar to the Real Calculator app when keys are actuated by the touch screen of the Android phone. If a longer ON delay is required, changing the number parameter within the delay instruction will accomplish this task. If additional button-switches are needed, consult the wiring matrix diagram of Figure 7-27 and make the change to the circuit schematic diagram (Figure 7-26) accordingly.

---

■ **Note**   The creation of software is rarely started from ground zero. To meet customer demand and to be competitive in today's marketplace, software development is based on modifying original code with new feature/function requirements. Can you say remix?!

---

---

■ **Tip**   The delay() is based on 1/1000 (ms). To create a 1 second delay, use 1000 in the parentheses.

---

# Mechatronics and Haptics

Mechatronics is an interdisciplinary field of engineering that integrates design techniques in precision mechanical engineering, control theory, computer science, and electronics into the overall design process, helping to create more functional and adaptable products. The word *mechatronics* has been around for some 30 years; it was coined in Japan, spread throughout Europe, and now is commonly used in the United States. Mechatronic devices are sometimes known as intelligent machines. The terms *intelligent machine* or *smart machine* are used to describe complex devices that use logic, feedback, and computation to simulate human actions or thinking. As mentioned, haptics is a sub-category of mechatronics because of the integration of mechanical, electrical-electronics, and computer science applied to the sensing and manipulation of objects using touch. The system block diagram in Figure 7-3 provides the foundation for discussion in this section of the chapter.

# FlexiForce Sensor Haptics

The FlexiForce sensor was introduced in Chapter 5 for controlling the angular rotation of a servo motor. By pressing the sensing surface of the FlexiForce, the Arduino is able to provide a series of command pulses to drive the servo motor to its correct angular position. Taking the same sketch and uploading it to new electronics hardware (the vibration motor circuit), a new operating device is created. The system block diagram used to manage this haptics controller is shown in Figure 7-32.

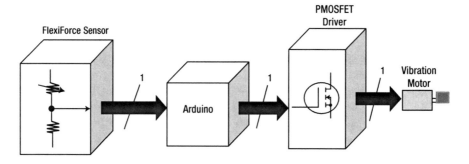

*Figure 7-32. FlexiForce-based haptics controller*

▨ **Note** The word *mechatronics* was invented by Hitachi Mechanical Engineer Takashi Yamaguchi working in a lab designing products that exhibit fast, precise performance. Just dropping some engineering technology history on ya!

The amount of force (touch) to the FlexiForce sensing surface allows the Arduino to command the PMOSFET to switch ON or drive the vibration motor. The more force applied to the FlexiForce sensor, the faster the vibration of the motor. The circuit schematic diagram for the FlexiForce sensor haptics controller is shown in Figure 7-33.

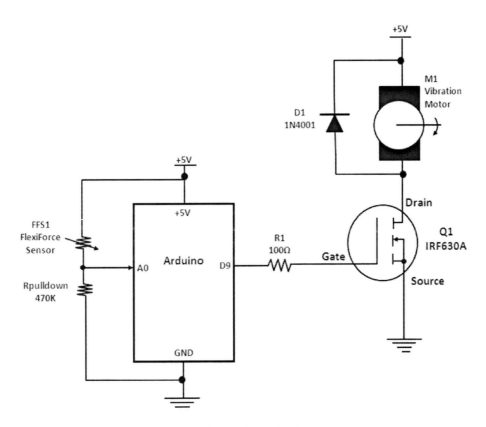

*Figure 7-33. FlexiForce sensor haptics controller circuit schematic diagram*

The prototype build of the FlexiForce sensor haptics controller is shown in Figure 7-34. If a DMM digital voltmeter is available, before uploading the sketch to the Arduino, test the FlexiForce sensor interface circuit. Touch the surface of the sensor and the voltage will swing from 0V to some DC value depending on the force applied. If the FlexiForce sensor is working properly, the stepper_speedControl sketch can be uploaded to the Arduino. The stepper_speedControl sketch is shown in Listing 7-5. The sketch can be obtained from the Arduino-Processing IDE ➤ Examples ➤ stepper ➤ stepper_speedControl.

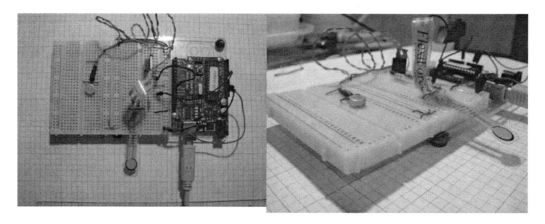

**Figure 7-34.** *FlexiForce sensor haptics prototype*

**Listing 7-5.** The stepper_speedControl Sketch

```
/*
 Stepper Motor Control - speed control

 This program drives a unipolar or bipolar stepper motor.
 The motor is attached to digital pins 8 - 11 of the Arduino.
 A potentiometer is connected to analog input 0.

 The motor will rotate in a clockwise direction. The higher the potentiometer value,
 the faster the motor speed. Because setSpeed() sets the delay between steps,
 you may notice the motor is less responsive to changes in the sensor value at
 low speeds.

 Created 30 Nov. 2009
 Modified 28 Oct 2010
 by Tom Igoe

 */

#include <Stepper.h>

const int stepsPerRevolution = 200; // change this to fit the number of steps per revolution
// for your motor

// initialize the stepper library on pins 8 through 11:
Stepper myStepper(stepsPerRevolution, 8,9,10,11);

int stepCount = 0;      // number of steps the motor has taken

void loop() {
 // read the sensor value:
 int sensorReading = analogRead(A0);
 // map it to a range from 0 to 100:
 int motorSpeed = map(sensorReading, 0, 1023, 0, 100);
 // set the motor speed:
 if (motorSpeed > 0) {
  myStepper.setSpeed(motorSpeed);
```

```
 // step 1/100 of a revolution:
 myStepper.step(stepsPerRevolution/100);
 }
}
```

# A Robot End Effector Test Stand

To illustrate the versatility of the FlexiForce sensor haptics controller, it can be applied in an industrial application for testing a robot's gripping strength. In this final project, a Robotix motorized construction set is used to build a 1 DOF robot. Its end effector can be tested for proper gripping strength using the FlexiForce sensor haptics controller.

The DOF of a robot is based on the number of moving mechanical assemblies. In this robot, the gripper is the only mechanical assembly that moves. The robot's end effector applies pressure to the sensor's sensing surface, which provides feedback through the vibration motor. If the robot's end effector is able to cause the vibration motor to turn ON, the mechanical gripper will be properly adjusted. If the robot's end effector lacks the necessary gripping force, the vibration motor will stay OFF. Varying the amount of gripper force strength will allow the vibration motor to turn at various speeds. Figure 7-35 shows the robot end effector test stand.

---

■ **Note** Although they are no longer being manufactured, the Robotix motorized construction sets can be purchased online at www.e-clec-tech.com/robotix.html. Isn't the Web a wonderful thing!

---

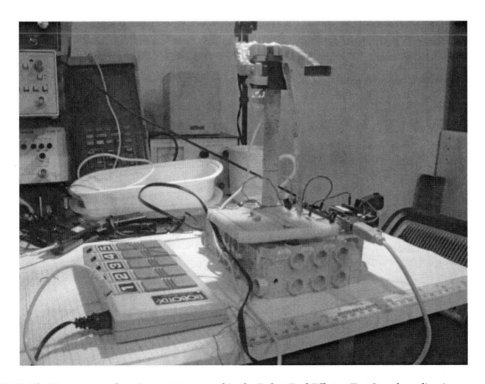

*Figure 7-35. FlexiForce sensor haptics prototype used in the Robot End Effector Test Stand application*

Although the Robotix motorized set is used in this haptics application, other construction kits like the LEGO Mindstorms or a homebrew mechatronics device can be used as well. To obtain profiles of varying gripper strengths detected by the FlexiForce sensor, a digital oscilloscope can be attached to the gate resistor of the PMOSFET. The change in command pulses applied to the solid-state vibration motor driver circuit is correlated to the FlexiForce sensor's varying resistance based on applied force changes. The waveforms can be captured as a .bmp file and analyzed later.

# Final Testing of Haptics Controllers

In this chapter, a series of subsection testing activities have been outlined to capture bugs in building the hardware circuits. Using a DMM and an oscilloscope, the testing techniques described can be validated on the bench. Depending on the vendor of the testing instruments, the results may vary by +/-10 %. Make sure the wiring is correct prior to applying voltage to the Arduino and supporting circuits. Use proper wiring methods as discussed in Chapter 3. The "How It Works" section of this chapter is a great reference to verify that the circuit breadboard is working correctly. Also, review the sketch entered into the Arduino IDE Editor for typos that may cause the hardware device to operate improperly.

# Further Discovery Method Suggestions

For the haptics controllers introduced in this chapter, try experimenting with other kinds of vibration motors. Try adding more button-switches to the project to test your knowledge in electronics hardware upgrade and software code modification. Build the haptics feedback device shown in the system block diagram (Figure 7-3). In the joystick haptics controller, replace the handle-operated potentiometer with a light detection circuit and observe the control operation of the vibration motor to varying light levels. Finally, in the "Try It Out" section, experiment with the sketch constant const int stepsPerRevolution = 200 and observe the PWM signal and frequency on an oscilloscope. As mentioned in the "Physical Computing: A Vibration Motor" section, record the data in a spreadsheet and plot a characteristic curve to capture the relationship between the two electrical parameters and the effects on vibration motor functional behavior. Document designs and sketch modifications in a lab notebook!

# CHAPTER 8

■ ■ ■

# LCDs and the Arduino

Making machines talk to humans is quite easy using light indicators or other illumination devices. The most common way of providing information is through a visible light source. By establishing a protocol (set of rules), a messaging scheme is created based on the application definition.

Incandescent lightbulbs were once the component of choice for visual indicators because of their ability to alert someone of a change in a process or the approaching of a dangerous threshold. LEDs improved on the incandescent lightbulb because of low thermals (heat), small size, and greater longevity.

With the arrangement of seven discrete LEDs into a single package, sophisticated messages can be created because of the optoelectronic device's ability to be wired for displaying numbers and letters. The ability to make alphanumerics (numbers and letters) with multiplexed seven-segment LED displays allows long messages to be displayed easily. Although seven-segment LED displays are better than both discrete LEDs and incandescent lightbulbs for visual information, washout and heat are problems with the optoelectronic part of the seven-segment LED. (*Washout* is the effect of the sun making LEDs hard to see in daylight).

The LCD (liquid crystal display) eliminates both heat and washout, and can be packaged to create characters and sophisticated graphics as well. In this chapter, we'll investigate the LCD using an experimental test jig that allows individual numbers, characters, and letters to be displayed based on an 8-bit binary code. Also, we'll explore physical-computing techniques for using the Arduino to create text messages by interacting with an LCD using a variety of solid-state and electromechanical sensors. Figure 8-1 shows the parts required for the hands-on projects and experiments.

## Parts List

Arduino Duemilanove or equivalent

11 47K resistors

470K resistor

4 10K resistors

CdS photocell

8-bit DIP switch

74LS00 or 7400 NAND Logic IC

SPDT (single-pole, double-throw) switch

SPST (single-pole, single-throw) switch

16×2 LCD

20×4 LCD

470Ω resistor

Solderless breadboard

22AWG solid wire

Digital multimeter

Oscilloscope (optional)

Electronic tools

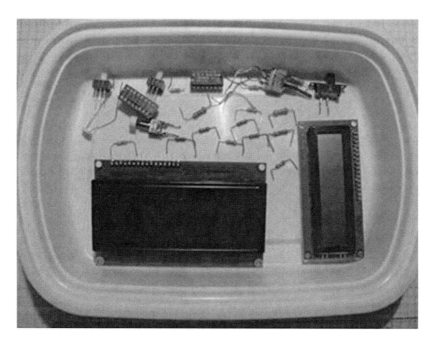

***Figure 8-1.*** *Parts required for the LCD projects and experiments*

# Remixing Physical-Computing Input Interface Circuits

Continuing the remixing technique of physical-computing and driver interface circuits, you'll use a FlexiForce sensor, 8-bit DIP switch, CdS photocell, thermistor, joystick, and potentiometer to allow human interaction with the LCD. The input interface circuits that you will build will allow different sensors to operate with the Arduino and typical LCDs. You will build a prototype test jig for checking different sensors to work with the Arduino and display the electrical operation on an LCD. You will be able to see the sensor's data being displayed and interact with the monitoring devices by means of physical-computing techniques.

The input interfacing circuits introduced in Chapters 4 and Chapters 5 will be remixed so that you can see the electrical data that is produced by them. The Arduino will process the input signals and drive the control lines on a basic LCD. To allow variety in experimentation with sensors, input interface circuits, and the LCD, several physical-computing models will be presented, allowing you the opportunity to explore and learn how electrical data can be displayed on this unique optoelectronic device. Figures 8-2 through 8-6 show systems block diagrams for displaying information using physical-computing techniques.

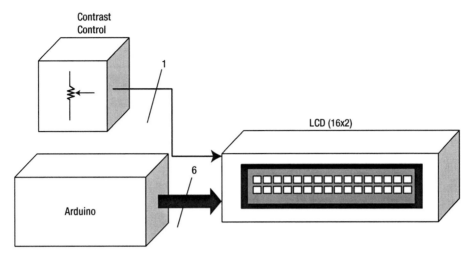

*Figure 8-2.* *Systems block diagram for an Arduino-based LCD controller*

---

■ **Note** In 1936, the Marconi Wireless Telegraph company patented the first practical application of this technology, calling it the Liquid Crystal Light Valve.

---

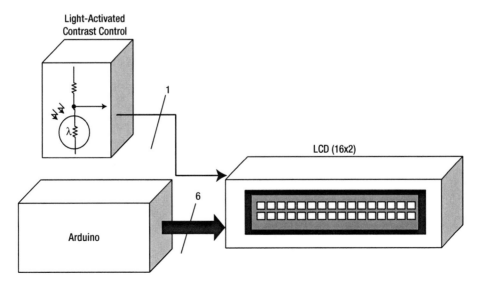

*Figure 8-3.* *Systems block diagram for an Arduino-based LCD controller with auto-adjust contrast control*

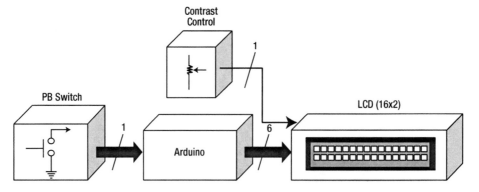

*Figure 8-4. Systems block diagram for an Arduino-based LCD controller with simple event detection*

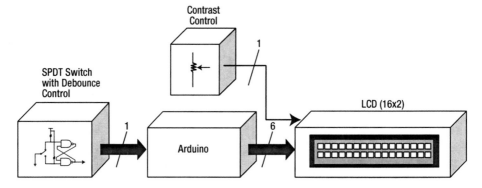

*Figure 8-5. Systems block diagram for an Arduino-based LCD controller with an improved event trigger*

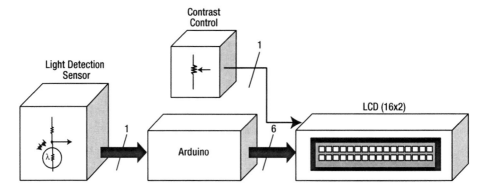

*Figure 8-6. Systems block diagram for an Arduino-based LCD controller with light detection*

■ **Note** By keeping the core Arduino-based LCD controller design and changing the input interface detection circuit, five new devices were created quite easily. Can you say "imagination"?

The five Arduino LCD controllers I've shown are examples of creating new physical-computing designs using different input detection circuits. In the pages to follow, I will show how to develop each one of these input circuit-operated LCD controllers with a few junk-box electronic parts. To build these devices, I will introduce an evaluation-kit approach to wiring the interface circuits to the Arduino-operated LCD controller.

# How It Works: The LCD Test Jig

The approach I'm going to take in explaining the basics of an LCD is to use the test jig systems block diagram shown in Figure 8-7. As shown in the diagram, there are four main subcircuits required to display characters, letters, and numbers on an LCD. The 8-bit binary code circuit provides the necessary data for changing the LCD operation or displaying characters and/or alphanumerics.

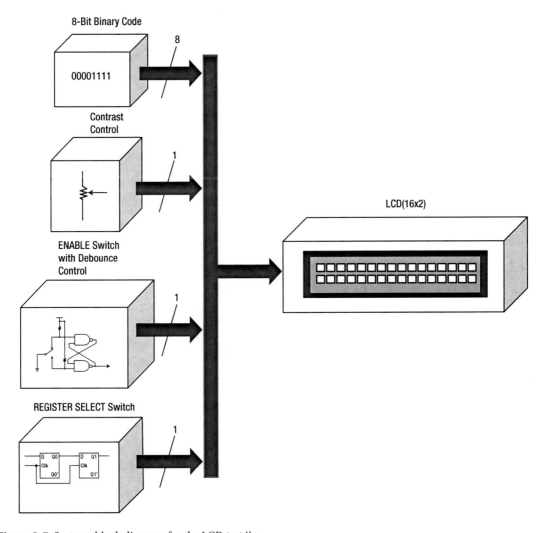

*Figure 8-7. Systems block diagram for the LCD test jig*

The operation of the LCD is based on simple command-control codes. Figure 8-8 shows a table listing the command-control codes for the LCD. As shown in the table, LCD display operations such as Clear Display, Display & Cursor Home, and Display On/Off & Cursor are executed by entering an 8-bit binary code.

| Command | Binary | | | | | | | | Hex |
|---|---|---|---|---|---|---|---|---|---|
| | D7 | D6 | D5 | D4 | D3 | D2 | D1 | D0 | |
| Clear Display | 0 | 0 | 0 | 0 | 0 | 0 | 0 | 1 | 01 |
| Display & Cursor Home | 0 | 0 | 0 | 0 | 0 | 0 | 1 | x | 02 or 03 |
| Character Entry Mode | 0 | 0 | 0 | 0 | 0 | 1 | I/D | S | 04 to 07 |
| Display On/Off & Cursor | 0 | 0 | 0 | 0 | 1 | D | U | B | 08 to 0F |
| Display/Cursor Shift | 0 | 0 | 0 | 1 | D/C | R/L | x | x | 10 to 1F |
| Function Set | 0 | 0 | 1 | 8/4 | 2/1 | 10/7 | x | x | 20 to 3F |
| Set CGRAM Address | 0 | 1 | A | A | A | A | A | A | 40 to 7F |
| Set Display Address | 1 | A | A | A | A | A | A | A | 80 to FF |

I/D: 1=Increment*, 0=Decrement  R/L: 1=Right shift, 0=Left shift

S: 1=Display shift on, 0=Display shift off*  8/4: 1=8 bit interface*, 0=4 bit interface

D: 1=Display On, 0=Display Off*  2/1: 1=2 line mode, 0=1 line mode*

U: 1=Cursor underline on, 0=Underline off*  10/7: 1=5x10 dot format, 0=5x7 dot format*

B: 1=Cursor blink on, 0=Cursor blink off*

D/C: 1=Display shift, 0=Cursor move  x = Don't care    * = Initialisation settings

*Figure 8-8.* Command-control codes (courtesy of Everyday Practical Electronics)

The data entry of the 8-bit code is done by using an 8-bit DIP switch. By setting the individual switches to either Open or Closed, discrete binary bits of 1 or 0 will be fed to the eight data lines (D7–D0) of the LCD.

The contrast control is a potentiometer responsible for adjusting the visibility of the discrete LCD squares.

The Enable switch allows the 8-bit code entered using the DIP switch to be sent to the LCD's data lines. This switch is debounced to prevent sporadic data entry of the 8-bit code from being displayed on the LCD. Figure 8-9 shows the Debounce switch's circuit schematic diagram, and the operation of the debounce circuit is illustrated in Figure 8-10.

If you don't wire this circuit to pin 6 of the LCD and use an ordinary switch, the LCD will show multiple letters after each switch toggle, which is not a cool thing. Figure 8-11 shows the complete circuit schematic diagram for the LCD test jig. The LCD test jig prototype is shown in Figure 8-12.

The Register Select switch is used to put the LCD in either command-control or alphanumeric/character mode. I used this switch to set up the LCD test jig by placing it in command-control mode. After wiring the LCD, I placed the switch in the alphanumeric/character mode position to allow the LCD display to show letters, numbers, and special characters using the correct 8-bit code. Figure 8-13 shows the table of letters, numbers, and characters. Notice the table is divided into upper and lower bits. It's very important that you enter the binary data on the 8-bit DIP switch in proper order. If you don't, strange characters or a blank screen will be displayed on the LCD. The upper four bits relate to DIP switches D7 through D4 and the lower bits use the remaining D3 through D0 data lines.

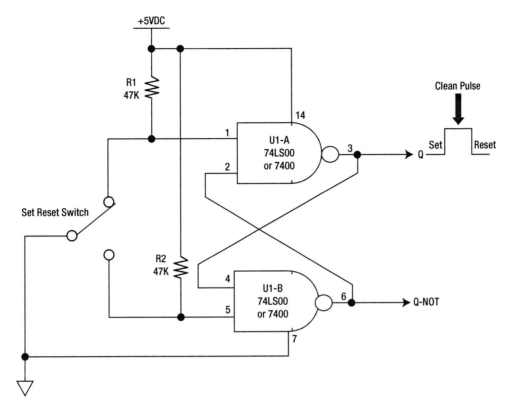

**Figure 8-9.** *A debounce circuit using two NAND logic gates*

---

■ **Tip**    If an 8-bit DIP switch is not available, individual slide switches can be used instead. More than one way to skin a cat!

---

To use the command-control codes to do a specific operation for the LCD, you should have the Register Select switch in a binary 0 position. Place a digital or analog voltmeter across the switch and adjust it so 0 volts is displayed on the meter. Adjust the contrast control (10K potentiometer) so the squares on the LCD are slightly visible.

Next, set the 8-bit DIP switch using the binary code 00001111 and toggle the Enable switch. A small square will flash at the left side of the LCD.

Entering a letter, number, or character is quite easy as well. Toggle the Register Select switch and enter **01000001** on the 8-bit DIP switch. Toggle the Enable switch, and the letter *A* will be displayed on the LCD.

The flashing square moves to the right side on the LCD screen with each binary code entered using the 8-bit DIP switch. For the final exam, enter **00111000** on the 8-bit DIP switch, and the number 8 will be displayed on the LCD. You can make some unique and cool messages by entering the 8-bit binary code on the DIP switch. Try displaying your name on the LCD using a series of 8-bit binary codes. The test jig can be used to check other LCDs you may have sitting in a junk box in your lab or workshop. What a cool way to test your surplus LCDs using this awesome testing device!

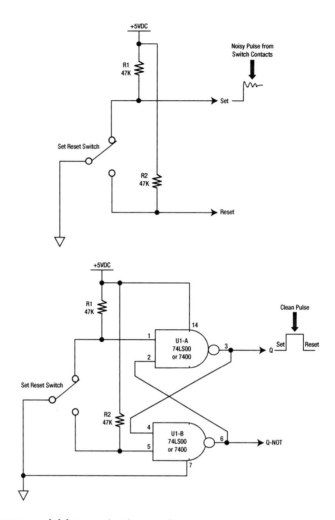

**Figure 8-10.** Contact bounce and debounce circuit operation

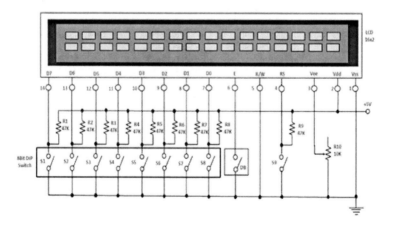

**Figure 8-11.** The LCD test jig

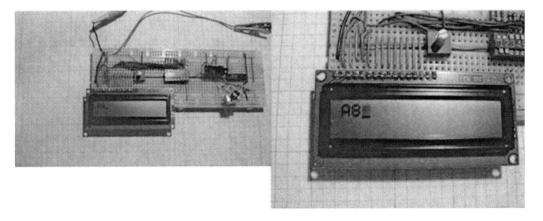

***Figure 8-12.*** *The LCD test jig prototype: Complete build (left) and LCD close-up (right)*

■ **Tip** Remember, with an active-low switch, a binary 1 means "Open contacts" and a binary 0 means "Closed contacts." And always use a Debounce switch when building digital circuits that need a smooth sequential operation. That's how you do the Binary Slide!

# The Real "Hello World": Arduino and the LCD

The test jig provides a cool way to understand the operation of the LCD, but making messages is quite a slow and long task. The Arduino makes it a snap because all you need is six control lines and a basic sketch. You wire the Arduino to the LCD using the circuit schematic shown in Figure 8-14.

In the circuit schematic diagram, I'm using a standard LCD with 20×4 white text on a blue background. Some key features about the LCD are listed here:

- The LCD is 20 characters wide and 4 rows tall.

- It has white text on a blue background.

- Its connection port has a 0.1-inch pitch and is single-row, allowing for easy breadboarding and wiring.

- It includes a single LED backlight that can be dimmed easily with a resistor or PWM, and it uses much less power than an LCD with EL (electroluminescent) backlights.

- It can be fully controlled with only six digital lines.

- It has a built-in character set that supports English and Japanese text (see the HD44780 datasheet for the full character set).

- Up to eight extra characters can be created for custom glyphs (such as special accent marks) for foreign-language support.

**Lower Four Bits**

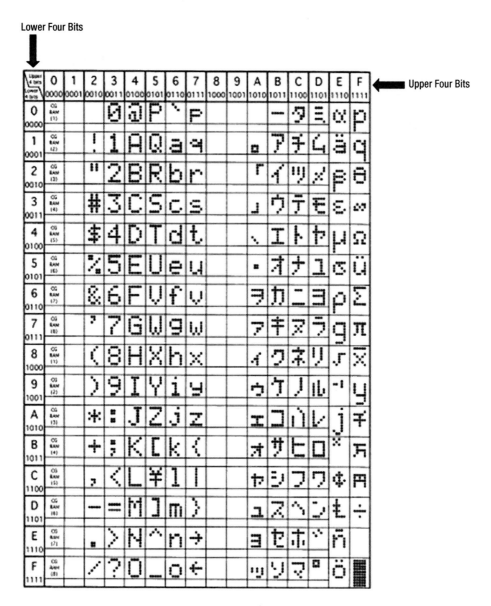

*Figure 8-13. The LCD letters, numbers, and character codes (courtesy of Everyday Practical Electronics)*

Figure 8-15 shows the actual kit I purchased from Adafruit Industries to build the different LCD projects in this chapter.

The basic circuits of this LCD module, as well as other optoelectronic versions, consist of a controller IC, LCD panel, driving IC, and backlight driver. The controller IC is responsible for operating the six control lines, consisting of the Register Select (RS), Enable (E), Contrast Control (V0), Read/Write (R/W), Source Supply Voltage (Vss), and Drain Supply Voltage (Vdd). The controller IC sends the 8-bit binary data available on its data

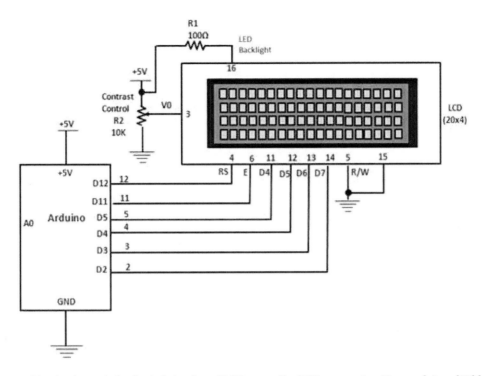

***Figure 8-14.*** *Circuit schematic for the Arduino-based LCD controller. LCD power pins: Vss equals 1 and Vdd equals 2*

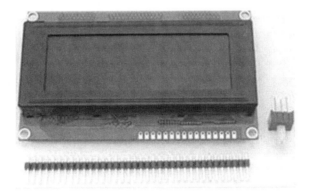

***Figure 8-15.*** *Standard 20×4 LCD with header pins and 10K potentiometer (courtesy of Adafruit Industries)*

lines (DB7–DB0) to the LCD panel for displaying letters, characters, and numbers. The driving IC operates the LCD panel by applying the correct voltage and current levels to it. Last, and optional on some LCD modules, there is a backlight LED used to light up the device for nighttime viewing. The systems block diagram for an LCD module is shown in Figure 8-16.

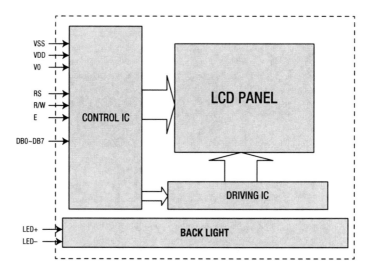

***Figure 8-16.*** *Systems block diagram for an LCD module (courtesy of Tinsharp datasheet)*

The circuit schematic diagram shown in Figure 8-14 will allow you to display the familiar "Hello World" message on the 20×4 LCD module. You can adjust the contrast of the LCD using the 10K potentiometer. The Arduino LCD controller I built from the circuit schematic diagram is shown in Figure 8-17. The wiring technique used in connecting the LCD correctly to the Arduino is to align the 16 pins to their corresponding numbers on the solderless breadboard. Using this layout technique, I had no wiring errors when connecting the LCD to the Arduino and the contrast control (10K potentiometer). After you have completed the wiring of the LCD circuit, turn on the power supply, and the LCD module will display segmented squares for a few seconds, and then light up with a bluish glow. You can adjust the sharpness of the display to your liking using the contrast control.

The next step is to upload the Hello World sketch to the Arduino. The Hello World sketch is shown in Listing 8-1.

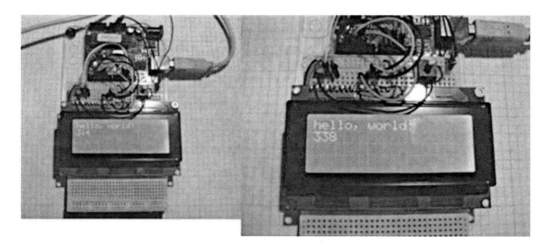

***Figure 8-17.*** *An Arduino-based LCD controller prototype*

■ **Note** In addition to selling Arduinos and accessory kits (shields), Adafruit Industries also stocks electronic parts, toolkits, and electronic tech books. Can you say "one-stop store"?

*Listing 8-1.* Hello World Sketch

```
/*
LiquidCrystal Library - Hello World

Demonstrates the use of a 16x2 LCD display. The LiquidCrystal
library works with all LCD displays that are compatible with the
Hitachi HD44780 driver. There are many of them out there, and you
can usually tell them by the 16-pin interface.

This sketch prints "Hello World!" to the LCD
and shows the time.

The circuit:
* LCD RS pin to digital pin 12
* LCD Enable pin to digital pin 11
* LCD D4 pin to digital pin 5
* LCD D5 pin to digital pin 4
* LCD D6 pin to digital pin 3
* LCD D7 pin to digital pin 2
* LCD R/W pin to ground
* 10K resistor:
* ends to +5 V and ground
* wiper to LCD VO pin (pin 3)

Library originally added 18 Apr 2008
by David A. Mellis
library modified 5 Jul 2009
by Limor Fried (http://www.ladyada.net)
example added 9 Jul 2009
by Tom Igoe
modified 22 Nov 2010
by Tom Igoe

This example code is in the public domain.

http://www.arduino.cc/en/Tutorial/LiquidCrystal
*/

// include the library code:
#include <LiquidCrystal.h>

// initialize the library with the numbers of the interface pins
LiquidCrystal lcd(12, 11, 5, 4, 3, 2);

void setup() {
 // set up the LCD's number of columns and rows:
 lcd.begin(16, 2);
 // Print a message to the LCD.
```

```
 lcd.print("hello, world!");
}

void loop() {
 // set the cursor to column 0, line 1
 // (note: line 1 is the second row, since counting begins with 0):
 lcd.setCursor(0, 1);
 // print the number of seconds since reset:
 lcd.print(millis()/1000);
}
```

# Try It Out!

There are fun and cool things you can play with using this basic circuit and sketch. The most obvious activity is to change the message. Here is the line of code you can modify to change the message:

```
lcd.print("hello, world!");
```

Instead of using lowercase letters for "hello, world," make them all uppercase. Change the message altogether by having the LCD display your name or favorite hobby. I changed the "hello, world!" to "Arduino: Hi," as shown in Figure 8-18. Coding messages is easy to do on an Arduino. Also, notice the seconds counting up on the LCD. The counter is showing the number of seconds since the Arduino has been powered off. To speed up counting, try changing the 1000 in `lcd.print(millis()/1000);` to 100, and then watch the numbers. When you upload the new value to the Arduino's ATmega328 microcontroller, the counter's speed increases.

**Figure 8-18.** *A talking Arduino!*

Another cool feature to try out is sending text to the LCD using the Arduino-Processing serial monitor. The serial monitor is used to display information from sensors or troubleshooting prompts during a software debug session. You can use the serial monitor as a mini-keyboard to send short text messages to the Arduino. The serial monitor sends the text message at a rate of 9600kbps (kilobits per second) to the Arduino using the USB connection. Whatever you type in the serial monitor's text box is displayed on the LCD. Long messages will wrap to show the message on the LCD. The Serial Monitor sketch is shown in Listing 8-2.

***Listing 8-2.*** Serial Monitor Sketch

```
/*
LiquidCrystal Library - Serial Input

Demonstrates the use of a 16x2 LCD display. The LiquidCrystal
library works with all LCD displays that are compatible with the
Hitachi HD44780 driver. There are many of them out there, and you
can usually tell them by the 16-pin interface.

This sketch displays text sent over the serial port
(e.g., from the serial monitor) on an attached LCD.

The circuit:
* LCD RS pin to digital pin 12
* LCD Enable pin to digital pin 11
* LCD D4 pin to digital pin 5
* LCD D5 pin to digital pin 4
* LCD D6 pin to digital pin 3
* LCD D7 pin to digital pin 2
* LCD R/W pin to ground
* 10K resistor:
* ends to +5 V and ground
* wiper to LCD VO pin (pin 3)

Library originally added 18 Apr 2008
by David A. Mellis
library modified 5 Jul 2009
by Limor Fried (http://www.ladyada.net)
example added 9 Jul 2009
by Tom Igoe
modified 22 Nov 2010
by Tom Igoe

This example code is in the public domain.

http://www.arduino.cc/en/Tutorial/LiquidCrystal
*/

// include the library code:
#include <LiquidCrystal.h>

// initialize the library with the numbers of the interface pins
LiquidCrystal lcd(12, 11, 5, 4, 3, 2);

void setup(){
  // set up the LCD's number of columns and rows:
 lcd.begin(16, 2);
 // initialize the serial communications:
 Serial.begin(9600);
}
```

```
void loop()
{
 // when characters arrive over the serial port…
 if (Serial.available()) {
  // wait a bit for the entire message to arrive
  delay(100);
  // clear the screen
  lcd.clear();
  // read all the available characters
  while (Serial.available() > 0) {
   // display each character to the LCD
   lcd.write(Serial.read());
  }
 }
}
```

After uploading to the code to the Arduino, I copied the title of the sketch, pasted it inside of the serial monitor, and clicked the Send button with the mouse. A few seconds later, the title was visible on the LCD. Talk about teleportation! Figure 8-19 shows an experiment of sending a portion of the sketch to be displayed on the LCD . The speed for receiving the text from the serial monitor to the LCD can be explored by changing the delay time. Here is the sketch instruction that's used to manage the speed at which the LCD displays text:

```
delay(100);
```

You can change the number inside the parentheses to tweak how quickly the message reaches the LCD. Making the number small allows quick display of the message on the LCD. A big number allows you time to get a cup of coffee before the message is displayed. Replace the existing number (100) with 10, and upload the new sketch change to the Arduino. You should see the message pop up immediately on the LCD. Now change the number to 800, and the message will be delayed by a few seconds.

You can also program the Arduino to scroll the message using a simple sketch. Messages can be scrolled either left or right using the following code instructions below:

```
scrollDisplayLeft();
scrollDisplayRight();
```

Some really cool physical-computing devices can be built using these code instructions. If you wire a sensor to the Arduino, a message can be made to move right or left on the LCD based on the sensor's signal level. For example, you can use a thermistor (a temperature-activated resistor) and the Arduino to detect body temperature and display the message "You're Healthy" on the LCD, scrolling from left to right. If there is no human contact with the thermistor, the message "You're a Zombie" will scroll on the LCD. The basic Scroll Text sketch is shown in Listing 8-3. Figure 8-20 shows "hello, world!" scrolling in both directions on the LCD.

---

■ **Note**  *Marquee display* denotes an electronic device filled with rows and columns of discrete LEDs. Each row and column is addressable, enabling the software to scroll messages. In industrial environments, assembly-line operations are sent to a marquee display to get the attention of factory personnel. Using the `scrolldisplay()` instruction is a cool way to create miniature marquee displays to allow ordinary household machines to alert occupants of conditions in the home.

---

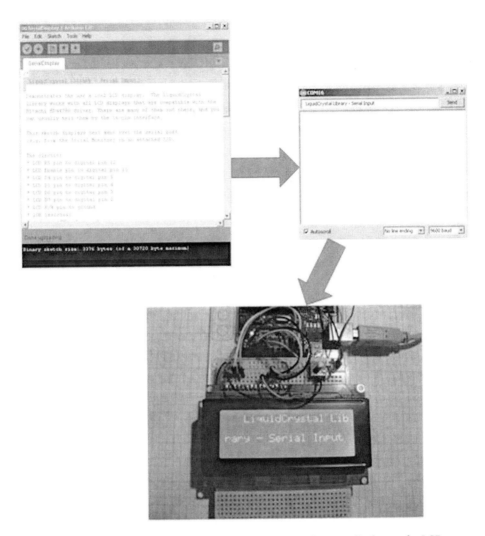

***Figure 8-19.*** *Text from sketch can be pasted into the serial monitor, and sent to display on the LCD*

***Listing 8-3.*** Hello World Sketch

```
/*
LiquidCrystal Library - scrollDisplayLeft() and scrollDisplayRight()

Demonstrates the use of a 16x2 LCD display. The LiquidCrystal
library works with all LCD displays that are compatible with the
Hitachi HD44780 driver. There are many of them out there, and you
can usually tell them by the 16-pin interface.

This sketch prints "Hello World!" to the LCD and uses the
scrollDisplayLeft() and scrollDisplayRight() methods to scroll
the text.
```

```
The circuit:
* LCD RS pin to digital pin 12
* LCD Enable pin to digital pin 11
* LCD D4 pin to digital pin 5
* LCD D5 pin to digital pin 4
* LCD D6 pin to digital pin 3
* LCD D7 pin to digital pin 2
* LCD R/W pin to ground
* 10K resistor:
* ends to +5 V and ground
* wiper to LCD VO pin (pin 3)

Library originally added 18 Apr 2008
by David A. Mellis
library modified 5 Jul 2009
by Limor Fried (http://www.ladyada.net)
example added 9 Jul 2009
by Tom Igoe
modified 22 Nov 2010
by Tom Igoe

This example code is in the public domain.

http://www.arduino.cc/en/Tutorial/LiquidCrystal
*/

// include the library code:
#include <LiquidCrystal.h>

// initialize the library with the numbers of the interface pins
LiquidCrystal lcd(12, 11, 5, 4, 3, 2);

void setup() {
 // set up the LCD's number of columns and rows:
 lcd.begin(16, 2);
 // Print a message to the LCD.
 lcd.print("hello, world!");
 delay(1000);
}

void loop() {
 // scroll 13 positions (string length) to the left
 // to move it offscreen left:
 for (int positionCounter = 0; positionCounter < 13; positionCounter++) {
  // scroll one position left:
  lcd.scrollDisplayLeft();
  // wait a bit:
  delay(150);
 }
```

```
// scroll 29 positions (string length + display length) to the right
// to move it offscreen right:
for (int positionCounter = 0; positionCounter < 29; positionCounter++) {
 // scroll one position right:
 lcd.scrollDisplayRight();
 // wait a bit:
 delay(150);
}

 // scroll 16 positions (display length + string length) to the left
 // to move it back to center:
for (int positionCounter = 0; positionCounter < 16; positionCounter++) {
 // scroll one position left:
 lcd.scrollDisplayLeft();
 // wait a bit:
 delay(150);
}

// delay at the end of the full loop:
delay(1000);

}
```

***Figure 8-20.*** *The "hello, world!" message scrolling left and right on the LCD*

What's really nice about these three sketches is the ability to personalize the Arduino by coding and displaying unique messages. You can do the personalization task by adding the message inside the parentheses of the lcd.print() code instruction. The delay() instruction to change message speed on the LCD is another sketch operation that allows for quick remixing of the electronics device as well. So what are you waiting for? Try it out!

197

# The Vanishing Message

This project is pretty cool and fun because the light detection circuit discussed in Chapter 1 has been remixed to provide interaction with the LCD's contrast without the need to turn a knob. I slightly modified the light detection circuit in Figure 8-2, whereby the CdS cell and the fixed resistor have been swapped to act as a contrast control for the LCD. The potentiometer contrast control provides approximately 0 V at pin 3 of the LCD, allowing full sharpness of the message, number, or character on the LCD. To meet this electrical requirement with an auto-adjust feature, I created the circuit schematic diagram shown in Figure 8-21.

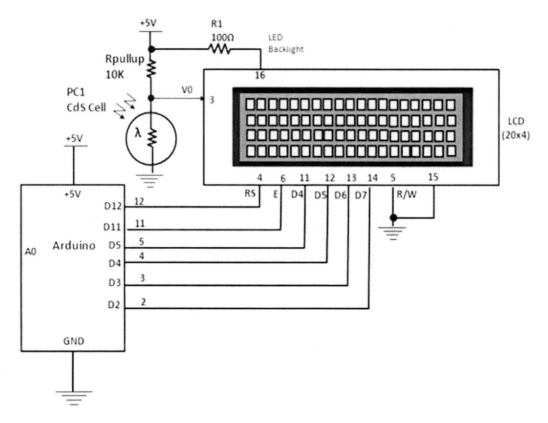

**Figure 8-21.** *The auto-adjust contrast control for the Arduino-based LCD controller. LCD power pins: Vss equals 1 and Vdd equals 2*

I modified the contrast control feature by removing the 10K potentiometer and replacing it with the CdS cell and a 470Ω resistor voltage divider circuit. Next, I measured the voltage across the 470Ω resistor using a DMM's digital voltmeter to ensure the DC voltage at pin 3 (V0) of the LCD was less than 1.0VDC. To measure this DC value, I placed a small piece of electrical tape over the CdS cell. The DC voltage I measured with the digital voltmeter was 0.231 V, or 231 mV. Figure 8-22 illustrates the new contrast control circuit. The DC voltage measured at pin 3 of the LCD is shown in Figure 8-23.

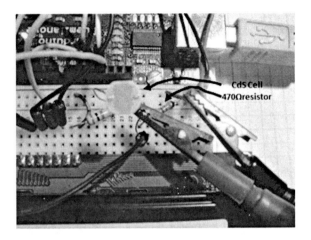

*Figure 8-22. The auto-adjust contrast control circuit built on the solderless breadboard*

---

■ **Tip** Instead of doing the circuit design with paper and a calculator for interface circuits, try building the device on the actual prototype and test for proper operation. That's how the 470Ω resistor was determined. Jump in, the water is fine!

---

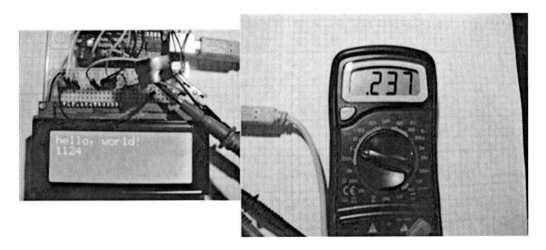

*Figure 8-23. Measuring the DC voltage at pin 3 with a CdS cell covered with electrical tape*

To check the DC voltage at pin 3, I removed the electrical tape from the sensor and measured a value of 1.17VDC on the digital voltmeter. With a high voltage reading, the LCD's message was not visible, as shown in Figure 8-24.

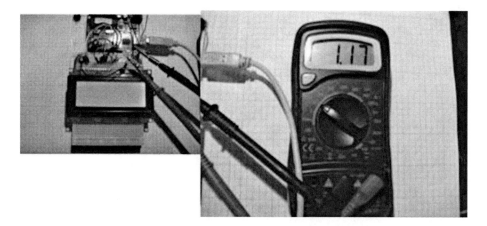

**Figure 8-24.** *Measuring the DC voltage at pin 3 of the LCD with the electrical tape removed from the CdS cell*

Although the Hello World sketch was used to test the light detection sensor, you can use the circuit with the other devices discussed in this chapter to create some cool LCD gadgets that respond to waving hands!

# Building an Evaluation Board

The nice thing about a solderless breadboard is how easy it is to add circuits without the hassle of a soldering iron. To explore some cool sensor-monitoring applications using the Arduino, I combined Figures 8-4 and 8-6 into an *evaluation board*. An evaluation board is a PCB that has target electronic components to test for hardware and software operations. Circuit schematic diagrams for the systems block diagrams are shown in Figures 8-25 and 8-26.

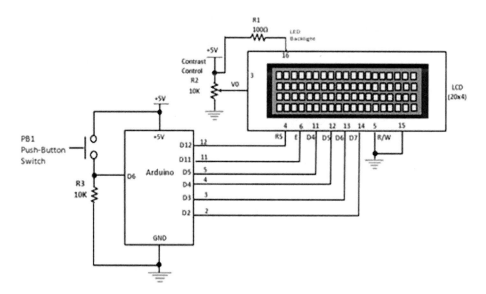

**Figure 8-25.** *Push-button switch for evaluating digital LCD applications. LCD power pins: Vss equals 1 and Vdd equals 2*

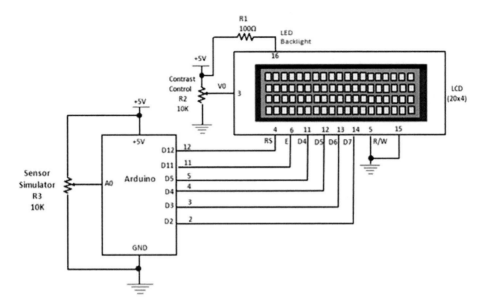

**Figure 8-26.** *Potentiometer for evaluating analog LCD applications. LCD power pins: Vss equals 1 and Vdd equals 2*

Using the schematic diagram in Figure 8-25 and modifying the Hello World sketch, I was able to build an event counter. An *event* is basically an outside triggering device such as a switch, whereby a press or toggle will allow the counter to increment based on the input signal. Every time you press the button, the LCD will show the count value. I've also added an auto-clear feature that makes the LCD go blank if the button switch is not used within a few seconds. You can replace the push-button switch with other digital circuits, such as clocks or logic gate circuits (AND, OR, NAND, NOR) that can provide a 0 to 5VDC input voltage signal to the Arduino. The Manual Counter sketch is shown in Listing 8-4.

___

■ **Note**   The AND, OR, NAND, and NOR logic gates are used to make low-level true/false decisions for computing and embedded-device technology.

___

**Listing 8-4.** Manual Counter Sketch

```
/*
LiquidCrystal Library - Hello World

Demonstrates the use of a 16x2 LCD display. The LiquidCrystal
library works with all LCD displays that are compatible with the
Hitachi HD44780 driver. There are many of them out there, and you
can usually tell them by the 16-pin interface.

This sketch prints "Hello World!" to the LCD
and shows the time.
```

```
The circuit:
* LCD RS pin to digital pin 12
* LCD Enable pin to digital pin 11
* LCD D4 pin to digital pin 5
* LCD D5 pin to digital pin 4
* LCD D6 pin to digital pin 3
* LCD D7 pin to digital pin 2
* LCD R/W pin to ground
* 10K resistor:
* ends to +5 V and ground
* wiper to LCD VO pin (pin 3)

Library originally added 18 Apr 2008
by David A. Mellis
library modified 5 Jul 2009
by Limor Fried (http://www.ladyada.net)
example added 9 Jul 2009
by Tom Igoe
modified 22 Nov 2010
by Tom Igoe
added counter feature 20 Feb 2012
by Don Wilcher

This example code is in the public domain.

http://www.arduino.cc/en/Tutorial/LiquidCrystal
 */

// include the library code:
#include <LiquidCrystal.h>

// initialize the library with the numbers of the interface pins
LiquidCrystal lcd(12, 11, 5, 4, 3, 2);
int inputPin = 6;
int val = 0;
int count = 0;

void setup() {
 // set up the LCD's number of columns and rows:
 lcd.begin(16, 4);
 pinMode(inputPin, INPUT);
}

void loop() {
  val = digitalRead(inputPin);
 if(val==HIGH) {
// Print a message to the LCD.
  count = count + 1;
  lcd.setCursor(0,3);
  lcd.print(count);
  delay(500);
 } else{
```

```
   lcd.setCursor(0,3);
   //lcd.print(count);
   delay(1000);
   //lcd.setCursor(0,3)
   count = 0;
   lcd.clear();
  }
}
```

The circuit schematic diagram in Figure 8-26 allows you to test analog sensors such as photocells (CdS cells), FlexiForce resistors, microphones, joysticks, and thermistors. The sketch allows the raw analog data to be displayed on the LCD. I used the potentiometer to test the sketch with success. As I adjusted the potentiometer, the ATmega328 microcontroller's ADC (analog-to-digital converter) processed the voltage data and displayed the digital values on the LCD. You can easily replace the potentiometer with a light detection circuit to create a cool electronic light-level meter. The Read Sensor sketch is shown in Listing 8-5.

*Listing 8-5.* Read Sensor Sketch

```
int sensorPin = A0;
int sensorValue = 0;
/*
 LiquidCrystal Library - Read Sensor
 by Don Wilcher
 20 Feb 2012

 Demonstrates the use of a 20x4 LCD display. Analog values are displayed on the Liquid Crystal
Display based on a change in sensor value.*/

//include the library code:
#include <LiquidCrystal.h>

// initialize the library with the numbers of the interface pins
LiquidCrystal lcd(12, 11, 5, 4, 3, 2);

void setup() {
 pinMode(sensorPin, INPUT);
 digitalWrite(sensorPin, HIGH); // turns on the internal pull-up resistor
 lcd.begin(20,4);

}

void loop() {
 sensorValue = analogRead(sensorPin);
 lcd.setCursor(0,0);
 lcd.print("Sensor value = ");
 lcd.setCursor(0,1);
 lcd.print(sensorValue);
 delay(100);
 sensorValue = 0;
 lcd.clear();
}
```

One last item to explain about the sketch is that the internal pull-up resistor is used instead of an external part. The ATmega328 microcontroller provides this neat feature to save PCB space and cost when designing with the device. Here is the code instruction used for the internal pull-up resistor:

```
digitalWrite(sensorPin, HIGH); // turns on the internal pull-up resistor
```

The sketch operates quite nicely. As you change the sensor signal, the LCD updates quickly (in real time). The prototype build of the miniature evaluation board is shown in Figure 8-27.

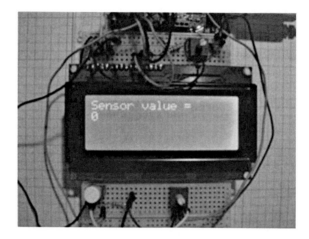

*Figure 8-27.* *Low-cost proto-evaluation breadboard. The push-button switch and potentiometer allow quick evaluation of the Manual Counter and Read Sensor sketches.*

## Further Discovery Methods

For the LCD controllers introduced in this chapter, try experimenting with other kinds of digital and analog sensor circuits. Try replacing the potentiometer for the analog sensor with a joystick or FlexiForce sensor. Modify the Read Sensor sketch to make the message display the Arduino conversion data related to the actual application. Build a temperature controller using a thermistor to measure heat and a small DC motor to cool it when the temperature threshold value is reached. Remember to document your designs in a lab notebook along with any modifications you made to the sketches for the new controllers you've created.

■ ■ ■

# CHAPTER 9

# A Logic Checker

In this chapter I'm going to explain how to build simple-to-intermediate logic checkers using an Arduino together with common electronics parts that you may have in your junk box. Also, I'll show how the Arduino can drive a seven-segment LED display directly using a basic circuit and a sketch. I will use the design of my open source logic probe as a case study to illustrate the design process you can use to create your own electronic gadgets. In the process I'll show you how to create truth tables to design and troubleshoot digital circuits.

A *truth table* is a graphical analysis tool used to explain the operation of digital circuits such as logic gates, counters, and shift registers. The table provides a list of circuit inputs and corresponding outputs. By setting the proper inputs from the truth table, you can check the outputs using a special tester such as a logic probe or logic analyzer.

Figure 9-1 shows the parts required for the hands-on projects and experiments.

## Parts List

Arduino Duemilanove or equivalent

AND logic gate IC (74LS08 or 7408)

OR logic gate IC (74LS32 or 7432)

NAND logic gate IC (74LS00 or 7400)

Hex inverter IC (74LS04 or 7404)

4-bit DIP switch

16×2 LCD

20×4 LCD

2×8 330Ω DIP resistor pack

MAN72 common anode seven-segment LED display

2 (two) 10KΩ resistors

Solderless breadboard

22AWG solid wire

Digital multimeter

Oscilloscope (optional)

Electronic tools

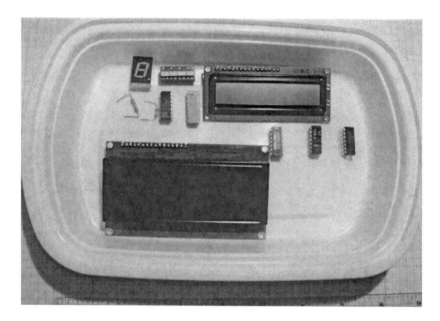

*Figure 9-1. Parts required for the logic checker projects and experiments*

## Input Interface Circuits

The logic checker projects and lab experiments in this chapter will require basic input circuits to operate the digital device under test (DDUT). Active-high and active-low logic switches, discussed in Chapter 4, can be used to provide input binary codes for the DDUT, and its output signal is wired to the Arduino for displaying the test results. I'll provide a brief discussion about logic gates in this chapter. As I explain digital electronics, you'll learn by building and testing circuits using the logic checkers.

## How It Works

Logic checkers are testing circuits used to check out the operation of a digital device. The operation of logic checkers is based on setting binary switches to the input data from a truth table and having the Arduino capture and display the output signal of the DDUT. The testing results of the DDUT can be shown on an LCD or a seven-segment LED display. Figure 9-2 shows the system block diagram of a logic checker.

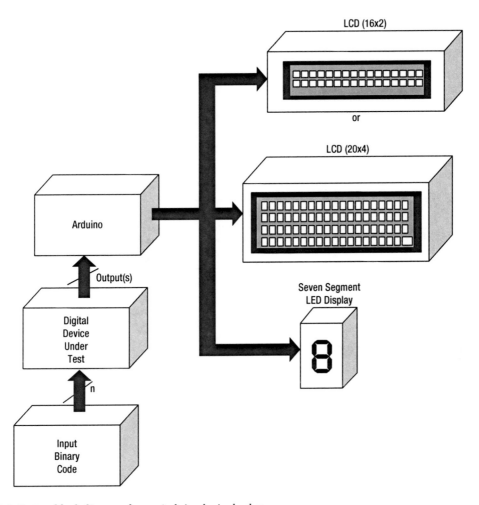

*Figure 9-2. System block diagram for an Arduino logic checker*

---

■ **Tip**  If two lines of text are required for your logic checker, use a 16×2 LCD; otherwise, use a 20×4 screen.

---

Figure 9-3 shows a system block diagram for a basic logic checker. As you can see, the logic probe circuit is used to test the DDUT.

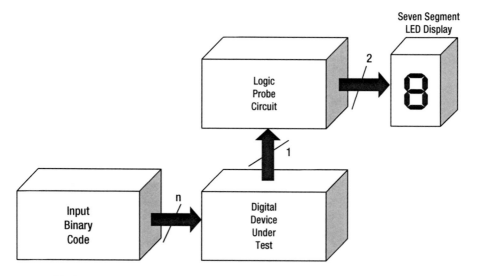

**Figure 9-3.** *System block diagram for a basic logic checker*

## Testing a NAND Gate

The circuit schematic diagram for the logic probe is shown in Figure 9-4. To test this logic checker I used a 74LS00 NAND gate as the DDUT. The NAND (Not AND) gate requires at least one input pin to be +5VDC for its output to turn on. If both input pins are +5VDC, the logic gate's output will be 0VDC. To explain the logic gate operation, a math equation called the Boolean expression is used. The NAND gate Boolean expression, shown following, is *C equals not (A and B)*.

$$C = Not(AB) \text{ or } C = (AB)'$$

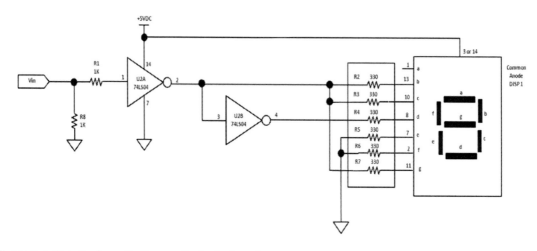

**Figure 9-4.** *Circuit schematic diagram for the logic probe*

The symbol and truth table of a NAND gate is shown in Figure 9-5. To test the circuit, I built a Multisim model using the schematic diagram of Figure 9-6. I used the binary codes from the truth table to operate the NAND gate.

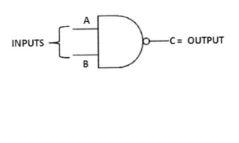

| INPUTS | | OUTPUT |
|---|---|---|
| A | B | C |
| 0 | 0 | 1 |
| 0 | 1 | 0 |
| 1 | 0 | 0 |
| 1 | 1 | 0 |

**Figure 9-5.** *The NAND gate with its corresponding truth table*

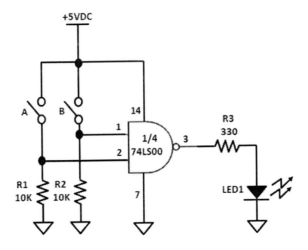

**Figure 9-6.** *NAND gate circuit schematic diagram*

---

■ **Note** In 1854, George Boole published a paper titled *An Investigations of the Laws of Thought on Which Are Founded the Mathematical Theories of Logic and Probabilities.* This paper established Boolean algebra, a branch of math used (among other things) to express the operation of logic circuits. In 1938, Claude Shannon of MIT was the first to apply Boole's work to the analysis and design of logic circuits. Boole and Shannon were rock stars of the digital electronics movement. Rock on, Boole and Shannon!

---

Opening a binary switch (A or B) turns on the LED. If you close both of the binary switches, the LED turns off. Figure 9-7 shows the Multisim NAND gate being operated by the binary switches. You can build a NAND gate circuit (Figure 9-6) on a breadboard and test it using the truth table of Figure 9-5.

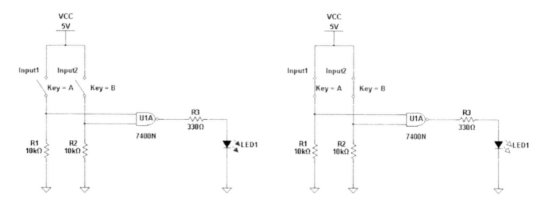

***Figure 9-7.*** *Operating a NAND gate using Multisim*

I was so happy with the operation of the logic probe on the solderless breadboard that I went on to create an open source version. Figure 9-8 shows the Smart Logic Probe kit assembled and ready for digital circuit testing. I used a free PCB software package called ExpressPCB (see `www.expresspcb.com`) to create the logic probe board. The components shown in Figure 9-4 are soldered onto the PCB, making a permanent digital testing tool for my lab bench. You can purchase the kit at my web site, at `www.family-science.net/store.htm`.

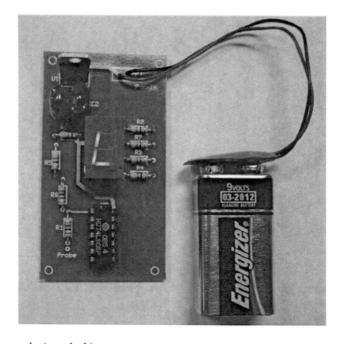

***Figure 9-8.*** *An open source logic probe kit*

---

■ **Tip** Instead of using individual resistors (R2–R7), use a 330Ω DIP pack. That will make wiring easy and save breadboard space!

---

The NAND gate circuit can be tested thoroughly using the truth table. You can wire the NAND gate to the logic probe using the circuit schematic diagram of Figure 9-9. Set the binary switches to the off (open) position, and the seven-segment LED display will show the letter *H* (for *logic high*). If you place either binary switch in the on (closed) position, the letter *L* (for *logic low*) will be displayed. Complete the logic testing of the NAND gate using the truth table. The 74LS00 has four logic gates packaged into one IC. You can check the remaining logic gates using the same testing technique. If you have any other logic gates in your junk box, you can check that they are working with this handy testing tool.

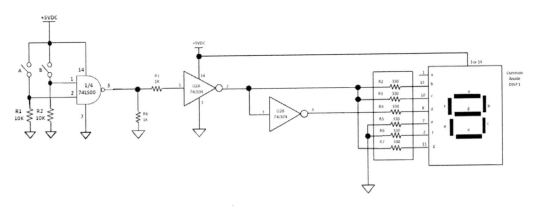

**Figure 9-9.** *Circuit schematic diagram for a logic checker with a seven-segment LED display*

# The Seven-Segment LED Display and the Arduino

In Chapter 2, I introduced the seven-segment LED display through a series of lab projects and experiments. In that chapter, I explained how the 7447 BCD Decade Decoder Driver IC is used to operate the seven-segment LED display. In this section, I'll show how the Arduino is capable of directly operating the seven-segment LED display. Each segment is controlled by the Arduino using a basic driver sketch. The sketch operates the LED display by turning on the individual LEDs inside of it. The table shown in Figure 9-10 illustrates how the digits 0 through 9 are made to appear on the display by turning on designated segments.

The binary 1 in the table equals an electrical +5VDC, and the binary 0 equals 0VDC. The seven-segment LED display uses the electrical voltages of +5VDC and 0VDC for operating properly. By looking at the placement of the 1s and 0s in the table, we can see that this display is a *common cathode* type. Common cathode seven-segment LEDs have one ground connection, and the other pins require a positive voltage for proper operation. In the table in Figure 9-10, the segments are set to binary 1 (+5VDC) to display numbers 0 through 9. The *common anode* seven-segment LED display (discussed in Chapter 2) works in exactly the opposite way from the cathode device. You can create a table like the one in 9-10, but all of the 1s and 0s will be opposite in bit value. I built a test circuit in which the Arduino operates the common anode seven-segment LED display shown in Figure 9-11.

| Digit | Illuminated Segment (1 = illumination) | | | | | | |
|-------|---|---|---|---|---|---|---|
| Shown | a | b | c | d | e | f | g |
| 0 | 1 | 1 | 1 | 1 | 1 | 1 | 0 |
| 1 | 0 | 1 | 0 | 0 | 0 | 0 | 0 |
| 2 | 1 | 1 | 0 | 1 | 1 | 0 | 1 |
| 3 | 1 | 1 | 1 | 1 | 0 | 0 | 1 |
| 4 | 0 | 1 | 1 | 0 | 0 | 1 | 1 |
| 5 | 1 | 0 | 1 | 1 | 0 | 1 | 1 |
| 6 | 1 | 0 | 1 | 1 | 1 | 1 | 1 |
| 7 | 1 | 1 | 1 | 0 | 0 | 0 | 0 |
| 8 | 1 | 1 | 1 | 1 | 1 | 1 | 1 |
| 9 | 1 | 1 | 1 | 1 | 0 | 1 | 1 |

*Figure 9-10. Creating numbers on a seven-segment LED display (courtesy of the Learning Pit)*

■ **Tip**    Letters and characters can be created on a seven-segment LED display by building a table like that in Figure 9-10. Bow down to the coolness of the seven-segment LED display!

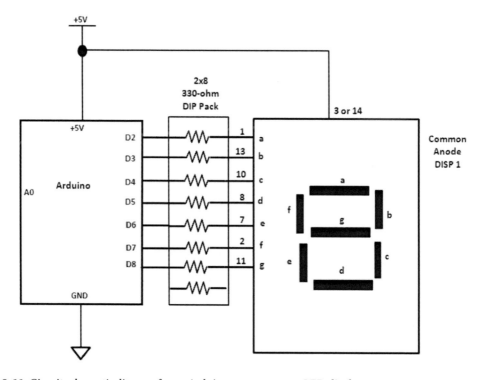

*Figure 9-11. Circuit schematic diagram for an Arduino seven-segment LED display test*

The prototype I built is shown in Figure 9-12. You can use the Fritzing software to lay out your prototype to ensure correct placement of parts and wiring connections between component pins on the solderless breadboard. The seven-segment LED display sketch is shown in Listing 9-1.

***Listing 9-1.*** Sketch for the Seven-Segment LED Display

```
/*
Make Projects: How to Drive a seven-segment LED
URL:
By: Riley Porter
Modified by: Don Wilcher 3/07/12

This is an introduction on how to drive a seven-segment LED using only a Arduino. This is
not the best way to do this; it is a simplified learning exercise. In later tutorials
I will show you how to use an dedicated IC using SPI or a shift register. Enjoy.
digitalWrite(A, HIGH) = turn off the "A" segment in the LED display
digitalWrite(B, LOW) = turn on the "B" segment in the LED display
*/

int A=2;
int B=3;
int C=4;
int D=5;
int E=6;
int F=7;
int G=8;

void clr()
{
 //Clears the LED
 digitalWrite(A, HIGH);
 digitalWrite(B, HIGH);
 digitalWrite(C, HIGH);
 digitalWrite(D, HIGH);
 digitalWrite(E, HIGH);
 digitalWrite(F, HIGH);
 digitalWrite(G, HIGH);
}

void char_A()
{
digitalWrite(D, HIGH);
digitalWrite(E, LOW);
digitalWrite(F, LOW);
digitalWrite(G, LOW);
digitalWrite(A, LOW);
digitalWrite(B, LOW);
digitalWrite(C, LOW);
}
```

```
void char_B()
{
//Displays B
digitalWrite(D, LOW);
digitalWrite(E, LOW);
digitalWrite(F, LOW);
digitalWrite(G, LOW);
digitalWrite(A, HIGH);
digitalWrite(B, HIGH);
digitalWrite(C, LOW);
}

void char_C()
{
//Displays C
digitalWrite(D, LOW);
digitalWrite(E, LOW);
digitalWrite(F, LOW);
digitalWrite(G, HIGH);
digitalWrite(A, LOW);
digitalWrite(B, HIGH);
digitalWrite(C, HIGH);
}

void char_D()
{
//Displays D
digitalWrite(D, LOW);
digitalWrite(E, LOW);
digitalWrite(F, HIGH);
digitalWrite(G, LOW);
digitalWrite(A, HIGH);
digitalWrite(B, LOW);
digitalWrite(C, LOW);
}

void char_E()
{
//Displays E
digitalWrite(D, LOW);
digitalWrite(E, LOW);
digitalWrite(F, LOW);
digitalWrite(G, LOW);
digitalWrite(A, LOW);
digitalWrite(B, HIGH);
digitalWrite(C, HIGH);
}
```

```
void char_F()
{
//Displays F
digitalWrite(D, HIGH);
digitalWrite(E, LOW);
digitalWrite(F, LOW);
digitalWrite(G, LOW);
digitalWrite(A, LOW);
digitalWrite(B, HIGH);
digitalWrite(C, HIGH);
}

void char_H()
{
// Displays H
digitalWrite(D, HIGH);
digitalWrite(E, LOW);
digitalWrite(F, LOW);
digitalWrite(G, LOW);
digitalWrite(A, HIGH);
digitalWrite(B, LOW);
digitalWrite(C, LOW);
}

void char_L()
{
// Displays L
digitalWrite(D, LOW);
digitalWrite(E, LOW);
digitalWrite(F, LOW);
digitalWrite(G, HIGH);
digitalWrite(A, HIGH);
digitalWrite(B, HIGH);
digitalWrite(C, HIGH);
}

void one()
{
//Displays 1
digitalWrite(D, HIGH);
digitalWrite(E, HIGH);
digitalWrite(F, HIGH);
digitalWrite(G, HIGH);
digitalWrite(A, HIGH);
digitalWrite(B, LOW);
digitalWrite(C, LOW);
}
```

```
void two()
{
//Displays 2
digitalWrite(D, LOW);
digitalWrite(E, LOW);
digitalWrite(F, HIGH);
digitalWrite(G, LOW);
digitalWrite(A, LOW);
digitalWrite(B, LOW);
digitalWrite(C, HIGH);
}

void three()
{
//Displays 3
digitalWrite(D, LOW);
digitalWrite(E, HIGH);
digitalWrite(F, HIGH);
digitalWrite(G, LOW);
digitalWrite(A, LOW);
digitalWrite(B, LOW);
digitalWrite(C, LOW);
}

void four()
{
//Displays 4
digitalWrite(D, HIGH);
digitalWrite(E, HIGH);
digitalWrite(F, LOW);
digitalWrite(G, LOW);
digitalWrite(A, HIGH);
digitalWrite(B, LOW);
digitalWrite(C, LOW);
}

void five()
{
//Displays 5
digitalWrite(D, LOW);
digitalWrite(E, HIGH);
digitalWrite(F, LOW);
digitalWrite(G, LOW);
digitalWrite(A, LOW);
digitalWrite(B, HIGH);
digitalWrite(C, LOW);
}
```

```
void six()
{
//Displays 6
digitalWrite(D, LOW);
digitalWrite(E, LOW);
digitalWrite(F, LOW);
digitalWrite(G, LOW);
digitalWrite(A, LOW);
digitalWrite(B, HIGH);
digitalWrite(C, LOW);
}

void seven()
{
//Displays 7
digitalWrite(D, HIGH);
digitalWrite(E, HIGH);
digitalWrite(F, HIGH);
digitalWrite(G, HIGH);
digitalWrite(A, LOW);
digitalWrite(B, LOW);
digitalWrite(C, LOW);
}

void eight()
{
//Displays 8
digitalWrite(D, LOW);
digitalWrite(E, LOW);
digitalWrite(F, LOW);
digitalWrite(G, LOW);
digitalWrite(A, LOW);
digitalWrite(B, LOW);
digitalWrite(C, LOW);
}

void nine()
{
//Displays 9
digitalWrite(D, LOW);
digitalWrite(E, HIGH);
digitalWrite(F, LOW);
digitalWrite(G, LOW);
digitalWrite(A, LOW);
digitalWrite(B, LOW);
digitalWrite(C, LOW);
}

void zero()
{
//Displays 0
digitalWrite(D, LOW);
```

```
digitalWrite(E, LOW);
digitalWrite(F, LOW);
digitalWrite(G, HIGH);
digitalWrite(A, LOW);
digitalWrite(B, LOW);
digitalWrite(C, LOW);
}
void LoopDisplay()
{
//Loop through all Chars and Numbers
char_A();
delay(1000);
char_B();
delay(1000);
char_C();
delay(1000);
char_D();
delay(1000);
char_E();
delay(1000);
char_F();
delay(1000);
char_H();
delay(1000);
char_L();
delay(1000);
one();
delay(1000);
two();
delay(1000);
three();
delay(1000);
four();
delay(1000);
five();
delay(1000);
six();
delay(1000);
seven();
delay(1000);
eight();
delay(1000);
nine();
delay(1000);
zero();
delay(1000);
}
```

```
void setup()
{
//Set up our pins
pinMode(A, OUTPUT);
pinMode(B, OUTPUT);
pinMode(C, OUTPUT);
pinMode(D, OUTPUT);
pinMode(E, OUTPUT);
pinMode(F, OUTPUT);
pinMode(G, OUTPUT);
Serial.begin(9600); //Begin serial communcation
}

void loop()
{
Serial.println("Starting\n");
LoopDisplay();
}
```

*Figure 9-12. The Arduino seven-segment LED display prototype*

A couple of cool things about this sketch make it fun to use and easy to remix:

- Numbers 0 through 9 code are included.

- Letters *A* through *F* are included.

- I also added the letters *H* and *L* for the logic checker project (sneaky, aren't I?).

- The serial monitor will display "Starting" at the beginning of the letters-numbers sequence cycle (see Figure 9-13).

- Based on the code structure, you'll be able to display your own cool characters on the seven-segment LED device.

■ **Note** Although the sketch is quite long, it's worth doing, since learning about seven-segment LED displays provides a huge benefit in electronics technology education.

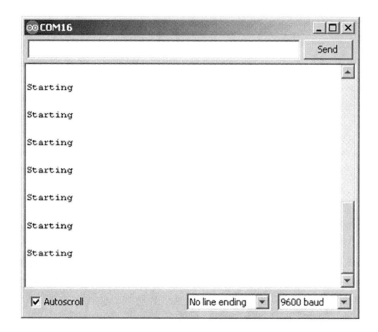

*Figure 9-13. The serial monitor displaying "Starting" at the beginning of the letters-numbers sequence cycle*

Once you've uploaded the sketch to the Arduino, a sequence of letters and numbers will be shown on the display. You can change the order by moving the char_letter() code, creating a new display pattern.

■ **Tip** You can create diagnostics in your Arduino sketches using the Serial.println() instruction and have them display error messages on the serial monitor.

# Building a Smart Logic Probe

To make a logic checker (Smart Logic Probe), I wrote a new sketch by adding the char_H() and char_L() code to the Button sketch. Listing 9-2 shows the Smart Logic Probe sketch. I also remixed the circuit schematic diagram in Figure 9-11 with two changes:

- A digital port (D12) is used to check high and low voltages from the DDUT.

- A 10K resistor is attached from digital port D12 to ground.

The Smart Logic Probe circuit schematic diagram is shown in Figure 9-14. The prototype I built is shown in Figure 9-15.

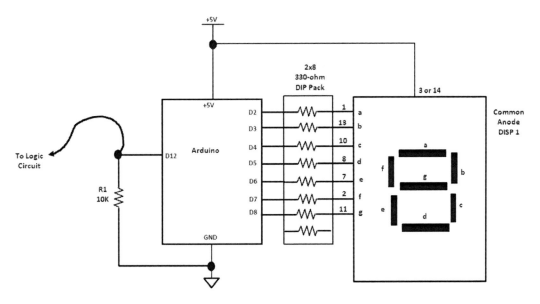

*Figure 9-14. Smart Logic Probe circuit schematic diagram*

---

▒ **Tip** If you're looking for new electronics projects to build, take a discrete digital circuit and remix it with an Arduino and a sketch. Who said you can't teach an old dog new tricks! Ruff!

---

*Listing 9-2.* Smart Logic Probe Circuit Sketch

```
/*
Smart Logic Probe

Don Wilcher 3/07/12

Displays the letters "H" and "L" when detecting a Hi or Low voltage level.
Turns on and off a light emitting diode (LED) connected to digital pin 13.
Input signal is received at pin 12.

The circuit:
* LED attached from pin 13 to ground
* push-button attached to pin 2 from +5V
* 10K resistor attached to pin 12 from ground

* Note: on most Arduinos there is already an LED on the board
attached to pin 13.

Based off of orginal Button Sketch created 2005
by DojoDave <http://www.0j0.org>
modified 30 Aug 2011
by Tom Igoe

This example code is in the public domain.
```

221

```
    http://www.arduino.cc/en/Tutorial/Button
    */

    // constants won't change. They're used here to
    // set pin numbers:
    const int buttonPin=12; // the number of the push-button pin
    const int ledPin=13; // the number of the LED pin

    // variables will change:
    int buttonState=0; // variable for reading the push-button status
    int A=2;
    int B=3;
    int C=4;
    int D=5;
    int E=6;
    int F=7;
    int G=8;

    void setup() {
     // initialize the LED pin as an output:
     pinMode(ledPin, OUTPUT);
     // initialize the push-button pin as an input:
     pinMode(buttonPin, INPUT);
     //Set up our pins
     pinMode(A, OUTPUT);
     pinMode(B, OUTPUT);
     pinMode(C, OUTPUT);
     pinMode(D, OUTPUT);
     pinMode(E, OUTPUT);
     pinMode(F, OUTPUT);
     pinMode(G, OUTPUT);
    }

    void char_H(){
     digitalWrite(D, HIGH);
     digitalWrite(E, LOW);
     digitalWrite(F, LOW);
     digitalWrite(G, LOW);
     digitalWrite(A, HIGH);
     digitalWrite(B, LOW);
     digitalWrite(C, LOW);
    }

    void char_L(){
     digitalWrite(D, LOW);
     digitalWrite(E, LOW);
     digitalWrite(F, LOW);
     digitalWrite(G, HIGH);
     digitalWrite(A, HIGH);
     digitalWrite(B, HIGH);
     digitalWrite(C, HIGH);
    }
```

```
void loop(){
 // read the state of the push-button value:
 buttonState=digitalRead(buttonPin);

 // check if the push-button is pressed.
 // if it is, the buttonState is HIGH:
 if (buttonState == HIGH) {
  // turn LED on:
  digitalWrite(ledPin, HIGH);
  // Displays H
  char_H();
 }
  else {
  // turn LED off:
  digitalWrite(ledPin, LOW);
  // Displays L
  char_L();
 }
}
```

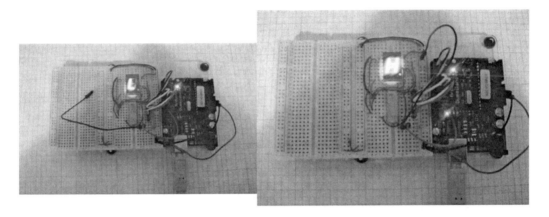

***Figure 9-15.*** *Smart Logic Probe prototype*

Before testing an OR gate IC (7408) that I found in my junk box, I used the +5VDC and GND rails on the solderless breadboard to check out the operation of the Smart Logic Probe. As shown in Figure 9-15, when I applied a 0V source to the Smart Logic Probe, it displayed an *L*. When I connected the probe wire to +5VDC, an *H* was displayed on the optoelectronic device. Truly amazing and smart!

---

■ **Tip**  If you want to add an Easter egg to your Arduino project, use the Serial.println() instruction to print a message on the serial monitor during normal operation Here comes Peter Cottontail...

---

# Building an Improved Smart Logic Probe

What's really cool about the Arduino is the ability to remix a sketch to create a new tech gadget. The improvement I made to the original Smart Logic Probe is to have the seven-segment LED display "HI" and "Lo" based on the digital circuit's binary output. I left the circuit input, but remixed the sketch shown in Listing 9-2 to toggle the two words on the seven-segment LED display. The new sketch for the improved logic probe is shown in Listing 9-3.

***Listing 9-3.*** Sketch for the Improved Smart Logic Probe

```
/*
Smart Logic Probe

Don Wilcher 3/07/12

Displays the words "HI" and "Lo" when detecting a high or low voltage level.
Turns on and off a light emitting diode (LED) connected to digital pin 13.
Input signal is received at pin 12.

The circuit:
* LED attached from pin 13 to ground
* push-button attached to pin 2 from +5V
* 10K resistor attached to pin 12 from ground

* Note: on most Arduinos there is already an LED on the board
attached to pin 13.

Based off of orginal Button Sketch created 2005
by DojoDave <http://www.0j0.org>
modified 30 Aug 2011
by Tom Igoe

This example code is in the public domain.

http://www.arduino.cc/en/Tutorial/Button
*/

// constants won't change. They're used here to
// set pin numbers:
const int buttonPin=12;    // the number of the push-button pin
const int ledPin=13;       // the number of the LED pin

// variables will change:
int buttonState=0; // variable for reading the push-button status
int A=2;
int B=3;
int C=4;
int D=5;
int E=6;
int F=7;
int G=8;

void setup() {
 // initialize the LED pin as an output:
 pinMode(ledPin, OUTPUT);
 // initialize the push-button pin as an input:
```

```
  pinMode(buttonPin, INPUT);
  //Set up our pins
  pinMode(A, OUTPUT);
  pinMode(B, OUTPUT);
  pinMode(C, OUTPUT);
  pinMode(D, OUTPUT);
  pinMode(E, OUTPUT);
  pinMode(F, OUTPUT);
  pinMode(G, OUTPUT);
}

void char_H(){
 digitalWrite(D, HIGH);
 digitalWrite(E, LOW);
 digitalWrite(F, LOW);
 digitalWrite(G, LOW);
 digitalWrite(A, HIGH);
 digitalWrite(B, LOW);
 digitalWrite(C, LOW);
}

void char_L(){
 digitalWrite(D, LOW);
 digitalWrite(E, LOW);
 digitalWrite(F, LOW);
 digitalWrite(G, HIGH);
 digitalWrite(A, HIGH);
 digitalWrite(B, HIGH);
 digitalWrite(C, HIGH);
}

void char_I(){
//Displays I
digitalWrite(D, HIGH);
digitalWrite(E, HIGH);
digitalWrite(F, HIGH);
digitalWrite(G, HIGH);
digitalWrite(A, HIGH);
digitalWrite(B, LOW);
digitalWrite(C, LOW);
}

void char_o(){
//Displays I
digitalWrite(D, LOW);
digitalWrite(E, LOW);
digitalWrite(F, HIGH);
digitalWrite(G, LOW);
digitalWrite(A, HIGH);
digitalWrite(B, HIGH);
digitalWrite(C, LOW);
}
```

```
void loop(){
  // read the state of the push-button value:
  buttonState=digitalRead(buttonPin);

  // check if the push-button is pressed.
  // if it is, the buttonState is HIGH:
  if (buttonState == HIGH) {
   // turn LED on:
   digitalWrite(ledPin, HIGH);
   // Displays H and I
   char_H();
   delay(1000);
   char_I();
   delay(1000);
  }
  else {
   // turn LED off:
   digitalWrite(ledPin, LOW);
   // Displays L and o
   char_L();
   delay(1000);
   char_o();
   delay(1000);
  }
}
```

# Further Discovery Methods

The discovery method challenge for this chapter is to design, build, and test an LCD-based logic checker for the OR gate (7408) shown in Figure 9-16. You will write the code for the sketch to display "Binary –Hi" and "Binary –Lo" on the LCD. Wire active-high digital switches to feed the binary data of the truth table shown in Figure 9-16 to the OR gate inputs. Refer to the gate's datasheet for pinout information. When the logic checker is operating properly, you can record the final design in your lab notebook along with the sketch.

An additional discovery method challenge is to add a piezo buzzer to make two tones in sync with binary messages being displayed on the LCD. Have fun!

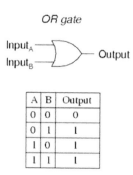

*Figure 9-16. An OR gate with truth table (courtesy of All About Circuits [www.allaboutcircuits.com])*

# CHAPTER 10

∎ ∎ ∎

# Man, It's Hot: Temperature Measurement and Control

Besides controlling motors, LCDs, and LEDs, the Arduino can also be used to measure temperature. An analog temperature sensor can be wired to the Arduino, turning it to an electronic thermometer. This chapter will show you how to wire and test the precision centigrade temperature sensor. You will also learn how to build an electronic thermometer using the sensor and off-the-shelf electronic parts. In addition, you will learn how to display the data using a serial monitor and an LCD. Finally, you will learn how to wire a DC motor for temperature control of electromechanics. Figure 10-1 shows the parts required for these hands-on projects and experiments.

## Parts List

1 Arduino Duemilanove or equivalent

1 LM35 precision centigrade temperature sensor

1 10K potentiometer

1 2N3904 NPN transistor

1 small DC motor

1 1N4001 diode

1 1K resistor

1 100Ω resistor

1 16x2 LCD

1 SPST switch

1 LED

Solderless breadboard

22 AWG solid wire

Digital multimeter

Oscilloscope (optional)

Electronic tools

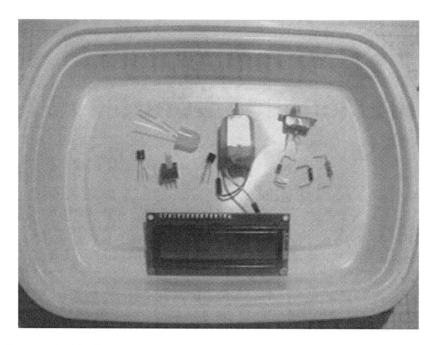

***Figure 10-1.*** *Parts required for the temperature measurement projects and experiments*

# What Is a Precision Centigrade Temperature Sensor?

A precision centigrade temperature sensor is an IC whose output voltage is directly proportional to the Celsius temperature scale. It doesn't require any external components to calibrate for temperature accuracies because they're added at the wafer level of the IC. If you want to add external readout devices like LEDs or LCDs to the sensor, it's no problem because the IC has low output impedance (AC resistance), a proportional output driver circuit, and precision external calibration components that help in operating these optoelectronic displays properly.

Another cool feature of the precision centigrade temperature sensor is that you can operate it using a single DC power supply or bipolar (positive/negative) voltage source, so it's convenient for the hobbyist! To use a temperature IC, you just have to add three wires to the device and provide a DC power supply.

# How It Works

The temperature sensor IC delivers an output voltage based on the temperature (Celsius scale). The LM35 temperature sensor's output is approximately 0.23 V in room air. When you apply heat to the IC, the sensor's output voltage increases. To see the changing output voltage of the sensor, you can attach a voltmeter to the IC's output pin. The system block diagram for monitoring the temperature sensor's output voltage is shown in Figure 10-2.

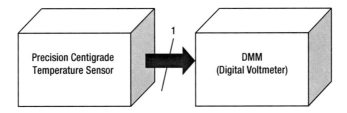

**Figure 10-2.** *Measuring a temperature sensor's output voltage with a digital voltmeter system block diagram*

Using the system block diagram as a design guide, you can build a simple electronic thermometer. I used the block diagram in Figure 10-2 to create the simple electronic thermometer circuit schematic diagram shown in Figure 10-3.

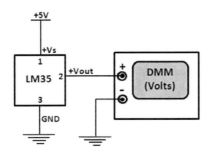

**Figure 10-3.** *A simple electronic thermometer circuit schematic diagram*

# Building an Electronic Thermometer

In building the electronic thermometer, I used a recycled computer ribbon cable to allow the sensor to move freely instead of soldering it to a prototype board. The ribbon cable provides flexibility in attaching the sensor to the Arduino because you can insert the three pins of the IC into the cavities (holes) of the connector. The other end of the ribbon cable connector can be extended by inserting wires into it. I can change the ribbon cable length by using longer wires to the connector. If you have a different way of allowing the sensor to move freely for remote temperature measurements, go for it! Figure 10-4 shows the temperature sensor attached to the computer ribbon cable.

---

■ **Tip**　When recycling electronics, remember to save screws, nuts, and mini jumper wires for future Arduino projects!

---

I used an ohmmeter to match up the temperature sensor pins inserted into one connector with the wires attached to the other end of the computer ribbon cable. I placed the ohmmeter in continuity mode while matching the sensor pins to the jumper wires during this assembly step. Figure 10-5 shows a close-up of the ribbon cable end connectors.

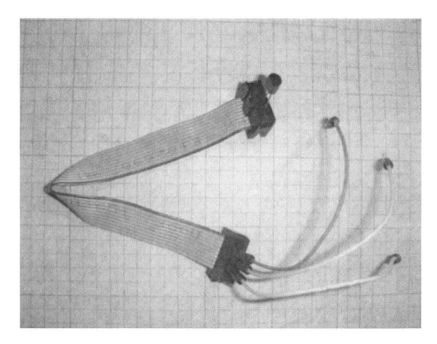

**Figure 10-4.** *Extending the temperature sensor pins by using a recycled computer ribbon cable and additional wires*

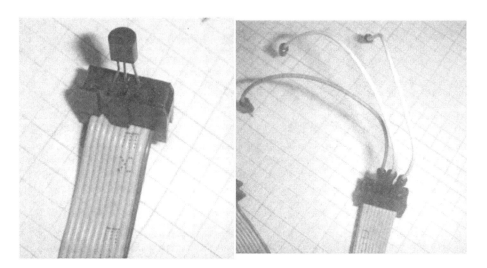

**Figure 10-5.** *Close-up of ribbon end connectors with attached temperature sensor and jumper wires*

I used the LM35 datasheet's pinout for assembly of the sensor IC to the ribbon cable end connector. Figure 10-6 shows the LM35 pinout. After assembling the ribbon cable, I completed the final wiring of the simple electronic thermometer on the solderless breadboard. Figure 10-7 shows the completed electronic thermometer.

TO-92
Plastic Package

+Vs  Vout  GND

BOTTOM VIEW

*Figure 10-6.* *LM35 precision centigrade temperature sensor IC T0-92 package. Pinout courtesy of Texas Instrument datasheet.*

■ **Note**   Building cool temperature sensing gadgets is easy with the Arduino because no additional amplifier circuits are needed. We love you, Arduino!!

*Figure 10-7.* *A LM35-based electronic thermometer*

231

# A Computer Thermometer

You can build a computer thermometer by replacing the DMM digital voltmeter with the Arduino-Processing Serial Monitor. By opening a serial connection with the computer, you can view the voltage values from the temperature sensor. Figure 10-8 shows the system block diagram for a computer thermometer. I found information on how to read temperature sensor data and display it on the Serial Monitor at www.ladyada.net/learn/sensors/tmp36.html.

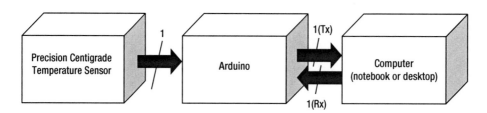

*Figure 10-8. A computer-based thermometer*

To convert the temperature sensor data, the following equation is used:

Voltage at pin (Vpin) = (readings from ADC) × (5000 / 1024)

Listing 10-1 shows the sketch for programming the Arduino to convert the temperature sensor data to volts and display it on the Serial Monitor.

*Listing 10-1.* LM35 Sensor Sketch

```
/* Converting LM35 Sensor data to Volts
Sketch will take sensor data and convert it to volts.
Volts value will be displayed on serial monitor

Remixed sketch of ladyada's TM36 sensor tutorial
http://www.ladyada.net/learn/sensors/tmp36.html

Don Wilcher 03/16/12

*/

//LM35 Pin Variables

int sensorPin = 0;// The analog pin the LM35's Vout is connected to.

/*
 Initialize serial connection with the computer*/
void setup()
{
  Serial.begin(9600); // Begin serial connection with the computer
  pinMode(sensorPin, INPUT);

}
```

```
void loop()
{
 int reading = analogRead(sensorPin);// read data from LM35 using Arduino (A0) pin
 float voltage = reading *5.0;// Convert sensor data to voltage
 voltage /= 1024.0;
 Serial.print(voltage); Serial.println("volts");// Print voltage on serial monitor

 delay(1000);// print data every second
}
```

You can use the analog pin (A0) of the Arduino to read the LM35's output voltage. The circuit schematic diagram is shown in Figure 10-9.

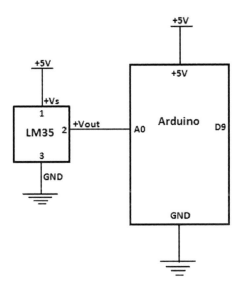

*Figure 10-9. The computer thermometer circuit schematic diagram*

After building the circuit schematic diagram, upload the sketch and open the Serial Monitor. You will see voltage data scrolling on the screen, as shown in Figure 10-10.

---

■ **Tip**   Removing the check from the Autoscroll box will show one line of data.

---

To manage the computer ribbon cable on the solderless breadboard, I placed a jumper wire across it, as shown in Figure 10-11.

By placing an SPST (single pole single throw) switch between pin 1 of the IC and +5VDC, you can stop the sensor from supplying data to the Arduino. Figure 10-12 shows the circuit schematic diagram of the modified computer thermometer. To test the prototype, I used my bench light as a heat source. As I moved the bench light to the sensor, the output voltage increased (see Figure 10-13).

*Figure 10-10. Serial Monitor displaying sensor data*

*Figure 10-11. Temperature sensor prototype with ribbon cable management via a jumper wire*

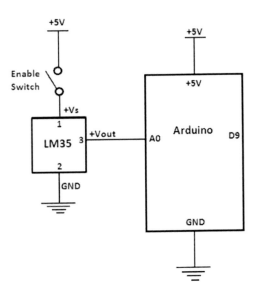

**Figure 10-12.** *Data start switchd (enable) added to temperature sensor*

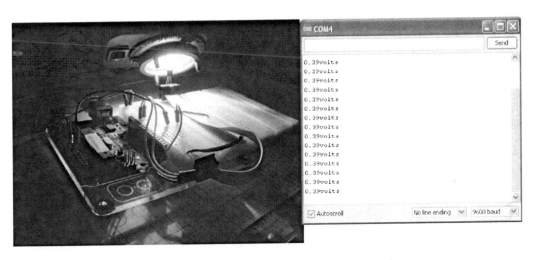

**Figure 10-13.** *Testing temperature sensor with bench light and Serial Monitor results*

# Final Completion of Computer Thermometer

With the LM35 sensor circuit working correctly, you can remix the sketch to show actual temperature readings. Add the following lines of code to the LM35 sketch so temperature data will display on the Serial Monitor:

```
Serial.print(voltage); Serial.println("volts"); // Print voltage on serial monitor

float temperatureC=(0.5-voltage)*100; //Convert voltage to temperature

Serial.print(temperatureC); Serial.println(" degrees C");// Print Temperature in C
```

Upload the remixed sketch to the Arduino to see voltage and temperature (Celsius) values scrolling on the Serial Monitor, as shown in Figure 10-14.

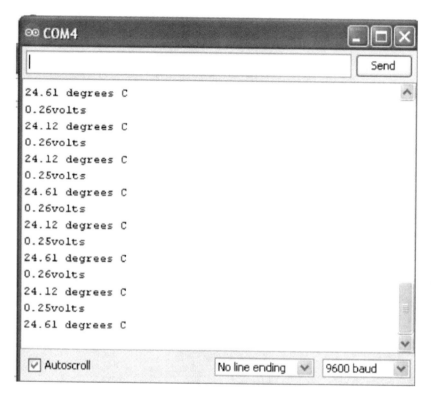

*Figure 10-14. LM35 sensor IC output voltage and equivalent temperature value*

---

■ **Note**    Room temperature (ambient) is 25 °C (78 °F). The serial monitor is displaying 24.61 °C. The Arduino is the ultimate in personal environmental measurement gear for amateur scientists and professional meteorologists. Man, it rocks!

---

To show Fahrenheit temperature, you can use the following lines of code:

```
float temperatureF=(temperatureC*9.0/5.0)+32; //Convert voltage to temperature
Serial.print(temperatureF); Serial.println("degrees F");// Print Temperature in C
```

The results of the remixed sketch on the Serial Monitor are shown in Figure 10-15.

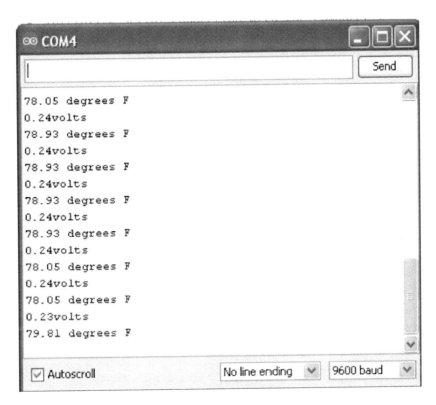

*Figure 10-15. Farenheit temperature readings scrolling on the Serial Monitor*

Listing 10-2 is the sketch for the displaying Celsius temperature and Listing 10-3 displays Fahrenheit.

*Listing 10-2.* LM35 Celsius Temperature Sketch

```
/* Converting LM35 Sensor data to Volts
Sketch will take sensor data and convert it to volts.
Volts value will be displayed on serial monitor

Remixed sketch of ladyada's TM36 sensor tutorial
http://www.ladyada.net/learn/sensors/tmp36.html

Don Wilcher 03/16/12

*/

//LM35 Pin Variables

int sensorPin = 0;// The analog pin the LM35's Vout is connected to.
```

```
/*
 Initialize serial connection with the computer*/
void setup()
{
 Serial.begin(9600); // Begin serial connection with the computer
pinMode(sensorPin, INPUT);

}

void loop()
{
 int reading = analogRead(sensorPin); // read data from LM35 using Arduino (A0) pin
 float voltage = reading *5.0; // Convert sensor data to voltage
 voltage /= 1024.0;
 Serial.print(voltage); Serial.println("volts"); // Print voltage on serial monitor

 float temperatureC=(0.5-voltage)*100; //Convert voltage to temperature

 Serial.print(temperatureC); Serial.println("degrees C");// Print Temperature in C

 delay(1000);// print data every second
}
```

**Listing 10-3.** *LM35 Farenheit Temperature Sketch*

```
/* Converting LM35 Sensor data to Volts
Sketch will take sensor data and convert it to volts.
Volts value will be displayed on serial monitor
```

```
Remixed sketch of ladyada's TM36 sensor tutorial
http://www.ladyada.net/learn/sensors/tmp36.html
```

```
Don Wilcher 03/16/12
```

```
*/
```

```
//LM35 Pin Variables
```

```
int sensorPin = 0;// The analog pin the LM35's Vout is connected to.
```

```
/*
 Initialize serial connection with the computer*/
void setup()
{
 Serial.begin(9600); // Begin serial connection with the computer
 pinMode(sensorPin, INPUT);

}

void loop()
{
 int reading = analogRead(sensorPin); // read data from LM35 using Arduino (A0) pin
 float voltage = reading *5.0; // Convert sensor data to voltage
 voltage /= 1024.0;
 Serial.print(voltage); Serial.println("volts"); // Print voltage on serial monitor
```

```
float temperatureC=(0.5-voltage)*100;

float temperatureF=(temperatureC*9.0/5.0)+32; //Convert voltage to temperature

Serial.print(temperatureF); Serial.println(" degrees F");// Print Temperature in C

delay(1000);// print data every second
}
```

---

**Tip** If you want your Arduino interactive art piece to respond to touch, wire a temperature sensor IC to it. Man, it's hot!

---

## Try It Out!

The LM35 sensor is an awesome IC for temperature-measuring applications, as demonstrated in the computer thermometer project. You can take the basic sensor circuit, the Fahrenheit sketch, and remix them into a temperature monitor. Figure 10-16 shows a system block diagram of a temperature monitor.

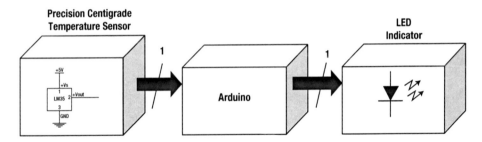

***Figure 10-16.** Temperature monitor system block diagram*

The concept behind the monitoring device is to turn off the flashing LED when the temperature is greater than a threshold value hard-coded into the sketch. The threshold value I used is 78 °F, which is above normal room temperature. The circuit schematic diagram you can use to build the prototype temperature monitor is shown in Figure 10-17.

The prototype I built using the circuit schematic diagram is shown in Figure 10-18. After the sketch in Listing 10-4 is uploaded to the Arduino, the LED will flash at a rate of 2 seconds. Blowing on the temperature sensor will stop the flashing LED. As you experiment with different hot and cold levels, watch the temperature measurements scroll on the Serial Monitor. Remix the flash rate and the threshold values in the sketch, and watch changes on the LED and the serial monitor. Also, see how fast the sensor responds between hot and cold. Record your observations in a lab notebook.

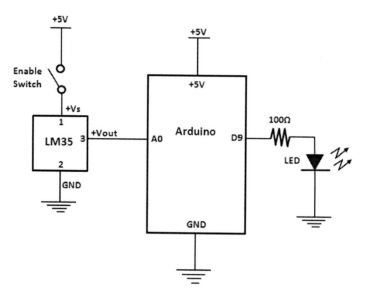

**Figure 10-17.** *Temperature monitor circuit schematic diagram*

**Listing 10-4.** LM35 Farenheit Temperature with Flashing LED Sketch

```
/* Converting LM35 Sensor data to Volts
Sketch will take sensor data and convert it to volts.
Volts value will be displayed on serial monitor

Remixed sketch of ladyada's TM36 sensor tutorial
http://www.ladyada.net/learn/sensors/tmp36.html

Don Wilcher 03/16/12

*/

//LM35 Pin Variables

const int sensorPin = 0;// The analog pin the LM35's Vout is connected to.
const int ledPin = 9; //the number of the LED Pin
/*
 Initialize serial connection with the computer*/
void setup()
{
 Serial.begin(9600); // Begin serial connection with the computer
 pinMode(ledPin, OUTPUT);
 pinMode(sensorPin, INPUT);

}
```

```
void loop()
{
 int reading = analogRead(sensorPin); // read data from LM35 using Arduino (A0) pin
 float voltage = reading *5.0; // Convert sensor data to voltage
 voltage /= 1024.0;
 Serial.print(voltage); Serial.println("volts"); // Print voltage on serial monitor

 float temperatureC=(0.5-voltage)*100;

 float temperatureF=(temperatureC*9.0/5.0)+32; //Convert voltage to temperature

 Serial.print(temperatureF); Serial.println(" degrees F");// Print Temperature in C

 if(temperatureF >78){
   digitalWrite(ledPin, HIGH);
   delay(1000);
   digitalWrite(ledPin, LOW);
   delay(1000);
 }
 else{
   digitalWrite(ledPin, LOW);
 }

 delay(1000);// print data every second
}
```

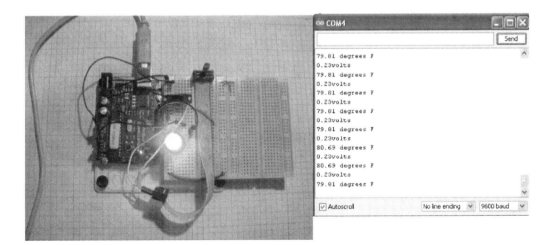

***Figure 10-18.*** *Responding to room temperature*

Another cool sketch remix is to have different flash rates for normal and high temperatures. I took the flashing LED code, duplicated it, and made the flash rate faster under high temperatures. The LED flashes slowly under normal room temperatures. The remix sketch for this temperature monitor effect is shown in Listing 10-5.

***Listing 10-5.*** LM35 Farenheit Temperature with Dual LED Flash Rates Sketch

```
/* Converting LM35 Sensor data to Volts
Sketch will take sensor data and convert it to volts.
Volts value will be displayed on serial monitor

Remixed sketch of ladyada's TM36 sensor tutorial
http://www.ladyada.net/learn/sensors/tmp36.html

Don Wilcher 03/16/12

*/

//LM35 Pin Variables

const int sensorPin = 0;// The analog pin the LM35's Vout is connected to.
const int ledPin = 9; //the number of the LED Pin
/*
 Initialize serial connection with the computer*/
void setup()
{
 Serial.begin(9600); // Begin serial connection with the computer
 pinMode(ledPin, OUTPUT);
 pinMode(sensorPin, INPUT);

}

void loop()
{
 int reading = analogRead(sensorPin); // read data from LM35 using Arduino (A0) pin
 float voltage = reading *5.0; // Convert sensor data to voltage
 voltage /= 1024.0;
 Serial.print(voltage); Serial.println("volts"); // Print voltage on serial monitor

 float temperatureC=(0.5-voltage)*100;

 float temperatureF=(temperatureC*9.0/5.0)+32; //Convert voltage to temperature

 Serial.print(temperatureF); Serial.println("degrees F");// Print Temperature in C

 if(temperatureF >78){
   digitalWrite(ledPin, HIGH);
   delay(1000);
   digitalWrite(ledPin, LOW);
   delay(1000);
 }
  else{
   digitalWrite(ledPin, HIGH);
   delay(100);
   digitalWrite(ledPin, LOW);
   delay(100);
  }

  delay(1000);// print data every second
}
```

You can add a second LED and have it flash separately from the first one. Also, change the monitor threshold value to detect a window of temperatures. Try it out!

# An LCD Electronic Thermometer

Using the base circuit schematic shown in Figure 10-12 as the core measuring device, you can build a cool LCD electronic thermometer. The parts needed for this project are the LCD and two resistors. Figure 10-19 shows the system block diagram for the LCD electronic thermometer. In designing the circuit, I added the LCD to make the electronic instrument portable for field temperature measurements. If you want temperature readings to be displayed on a computer, connect a USB cable between the Arduino and the desktop PC or notebook. In wiring the LCD to the Arduino, the power (Vdd) and ground (Vss) pins are connected with the 10 K potentiometer adjusted so the pixel-squares are not shown on the display. The LCD's LED backlight is wired to a 100ohm resistor. This preliminary step will ensure proper operation of the LCD before final wiring of the part to the Arduino. The LCD electronic thermometer circuit schematic diagram is shown in Figure 10-20.

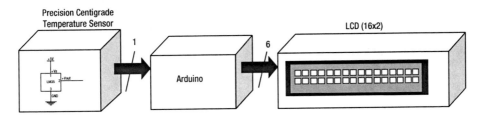

*Figure 10-19. The LCD electronic thermometer system block diagram*

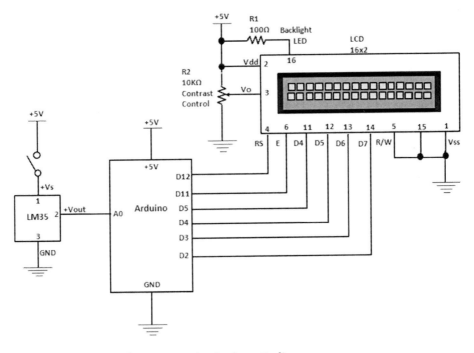

*Figure 10-20. The LCD electronic thermometer circuit schematic diagram*

You can mount the LCD where pin 1 matches the same row location on the solderless breadboard to ease Arduino wiring. Figure 10-21 shows the final LCD electronic thermometer prototype.

**Figure 10-21.** *The LCD electronic thermometer prototype*

After you upload the LCD electronic thermometer sketch to the Arduino, a temperature reading will be on the screen. You can increase the temperature by placing the sensor between your fingers. The temperature data updates every 10milliseconds (ms) and can easily be changed in the sketch with the delay(10) instruction. The complete sketch for the LCD electronic thermometer is shown in Listing 10-6.

*Listing 10-6.* Sensor Data to Temperature Sketch

```
/* Converting LM35 Sensor data to Temperature
Sketch will take sensor data and convert it to volts then to temperature.
Volts and Temperature values will be displayed on serial monitor and LCD.

Remixed sketch of ladyada's TM36 sensor tutorial
http://www.ladyada.net/learn/sensors/tmp36.html

Don Wilcher 03/17/12

*/

//LM35 Pin Variables

int sensorPin = 0;// The analog pin the LM35's Vout is connected to.

#include <LiquidCrystal.h>
LiquidCrystal lcd(12, 11, 5, 4, 3, 2);
/*
 Initialize serial connection with the computer*/
void setup()
```

```
{
 Serial.begin(9600); // Begin serial connection with the computer
 lcd.begin(16,2);
 analogReference(INTERNAL);
 pinMode(sensorPin, INPUT);

}

void loop()
{
 int reading = analogRead(sensorPin); // read data from LM35 using Arduino (A0) pin
 float voltage = reading *5.0; // Convert sensor data to voltage
 voltage /=1024.0;

 Serial.print(voltage); Serial.println("volts"); // Print voltage on serial monitor

 float temperatureC=((100*1.1*voltage)/1024)*100;

 float temperatureF=(temperatureC*(9.0/5.0))+32; //Convert voltage to temperature

 Serial.print(temperatureF); Serial.println(" degrees F");// Print Temperature in C

 // display Temperature on LCD
 lcd.setCursor(0,0);
 lcd.print("Temperature=");
 lcd.setCursor(0,1);
 lcd.print(temperatureF); lcd.println(" degrees F ");

 delay(10);// print data every 10milliseconds
}
```

# A Temperature Controller

You can change the LCD electronic thermometer into a temperature controller using a few electronic parts. A temperature controller is a device used to operate an external component such as a light bulb or a motor when the sensor's electrical signal exceeds some trigger value. Here, the Arduino will turn on a transistor DC motor driver circuit when the temperature is greater than the sketch preset value.

A trigger (threshold) value is built in the sketch using if-else statements. You program the sketch condition using the "greater- than" sign to monitor the sensor's temperature. The Arduino stops the motor when the temperature is below the threshold and turns the motor on when the temperature is above the threshold. The temperature controller circuit schematic diagram is shown in Figure 10-22.

I used a separate DC supply for the transistor motor driver circuit to prevent electrical interference with the LCD. Setting the transistor motor driver circuit to 1.5VDC reduces electrical interference to the LCD. The prototype for the controller is shown in Figure 10-23.

Check for wiring mistakes before powering the transistor motor circuit and uploading the sketch to the Arduino. With the temperature sensor held between your fingers, the rising value should show on the LCD. When the temperature reaches 58 °F, the motor turns on until the reading drops below this value. The temperature controller sketch is shown in Listing 10-7.

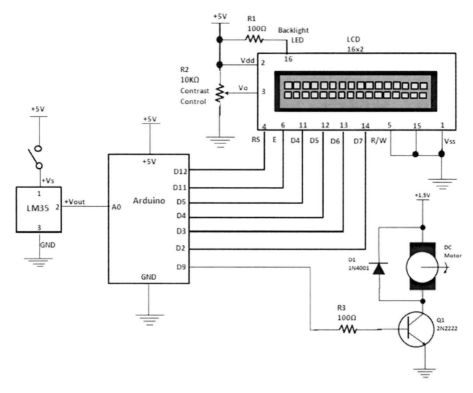

**Figure 10-22.** *The temperature controller circuit schematic diagram*

**Listing 10-7.** Temperature Controller Sketch

```
/* Converting LM35 Sensor data to Temperature
Sketch will take sensor data and convert it to volts then to temperature.
Volts and Temperature values will be displayed on serial monitor and LCD.
It turns ON a small dc motor when sensor temperature is greater than the threshold value.

Remixed sketch of ladyada's TM36 sensor tutorial
http://www.ladyada.net/learn/sensors/tmp36.html

Don Wilcher 03/17/12

*/

//LM35 Pin Variables

int sensorPin = 0;// The analog pin the LM35's Vout is connected to.
const int motorPin = 9; // the number of the motor pin
```

```
#include <LiquidCrystal.h>
LiquidCrystal lcd(12, 11, 5, 4, 3, 2);

/*
 Initialize serial connection with the computer*/
void setup()
{
 Serial.begin(9600); // Begin serial connection with the computer
 lcd.begin(16,2);
 analogReference(INTERNAL);
    /* for Arduino Mega please use analogReference(INTERNAL1v1); */
 pinMode(motorPin, OUTPUT);

}

void loop()
{
 int reading = analogRead(sensorPin); // read data from LM35 using Arduino (A0) pin
 float voltage = reading *5.0; // Convert sensor data to voltage
 voltage /=1024.0;

 Serial.print(voltage); Serial.println("volts"); // Print voltage on serial monitor

 float temperatureC=((100*1.1*voltage)/1024)*100;

 float temperatureF=(temperatureC*(9.0/5.0))+32; //Convert voltage to temperature

 Serial.print(temperatureF); Serial.println(" degrees F");// Print Temperature in C

 // display Temperature on LCD
 lcd.setCursor(0,0);
 lcd.print("Temperature=");
 lcd.setCursor(0,1);
 lcd.print(temperatureF); lcd.println(" degrees F ");

 //DC Motor control
 if(temperatureF >58){
   digitalWrite(motorPin, HIGH);
  }
  else{
   digitalWrite(motorPin, LOW);
  }

  delay(10);// print data every 10milliseconds
}
```

*Figure 10-23. The temperature controller prototype*

# Further Discovery Method

The activity challenge for this chapter is to design a system block diagram for the temperature controller. Additional activities include the following:

- Add an LED to turn on and off with the small DC motor when detecting temperature limits.

- Replace the motor and the LED with a piezo-buzzer for audible temperature alerts.

- Replace the 16x2 display with a 20x4 LCD.

- Replace the DC motor with a vibration unit and observe the electrical operation.

- Add a speed control feature as the temperature increases to operate a small DC motor.

As always, record the final designs in your lab notebook along with the sketches. Enjoy!

# Final Thoughts and Suggestions

The intent of this book was to explain basic electronics concepts using the Arduino and common parts. I hope you found the lab experiments and projects to be entertaining and educational. I had fun building the Arduino electronic circuits and writing the sketches to make cool gadgets. Here's a list of additional project ideas that use the Arduino electronic circuits discussed in this book.

- Build a temperature-activated robot using the TM35 temperature sensor discussed in this chapter.

- Operate a LEGO NXT machine using an Arduino and FlexiForce sensor.

- Build an LCD-based logic checker using the Arduino.

- Build an electronic dice game using an LCD and the Arduino.

- Build an Arduino AM transmitter using a PWM signal.

- Build an electronic lock using an Arduino and a keypad.

Have fun with these project suggestions as you continue to learn electronics with Arduino!

# Index

CPSIA information can be obtained at www.ICGtesting.com
Printed in the USA
LVOW112055080712

289209LV00002BA/4/P